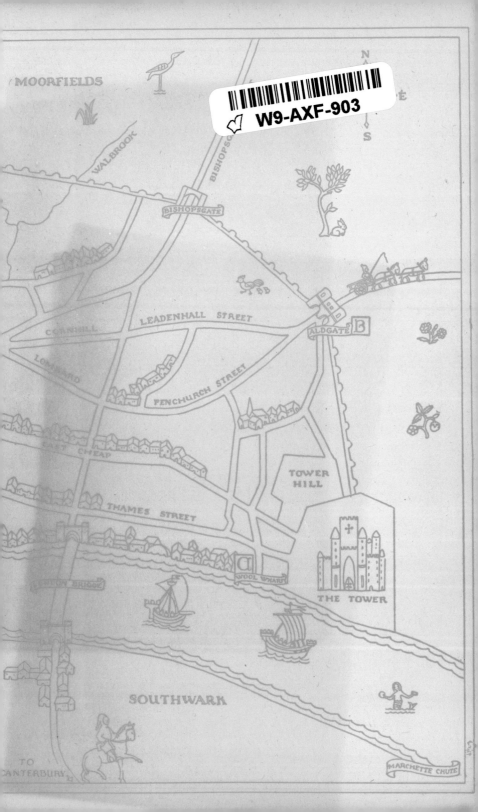

MOORFIELDS

WALBROOK

BISHOPSGATE

BISHOPSGATE

CORNHILL

LEADENHALL STREET

LOMBARD

ALDGATE

FENCHURCH STREET

EAST CHEAP

TOWER HILL

THAMES STREET

WOOL WHARF

THE TOWER

LONDON BRIDGE

SOUTHWARK

TO CANTERBURY

MARCHETTE CHUTE

GEOFFREY CHAUCER OF ENGLAND

GEOFFREY CHAUCER OF ENGLAND

written and
decorated by

MARCHETTE CHUTE

E. P. DUTTON AND CO., INC.
NEW YORK 1947

First printing, March 1946
Second printing, May 1946
Third printing, August 1947

To E. M. C. *who likes writers*

FOREWORD

A REALLY GOOD WRITER is always a modern writer, whatever his century. That is to say, he is able to establish himself promptly and intimately in the minds of his readers and behave there as though he were a contemporary. People do not change as much as they might, or perhaps as much as they should, and a good poet or a good dramatist can usually make himself comfortably at home with his subsequent generations of readers.

Geoffrey Chaucer is a modern writer in a more specific way than that. The fourteenth century had a great deal in common with the twentieth century—much more, for instance, than either of them had with the eighteenth. It was a thrusting, excitable, anxious century, racked by wars and labor disputes and high taxes and dangerous new ideas. It was also a cheerful, civilized, tough-minded century, with a lively sense of the ridiculous and blessed by the presence of a writer who knew a good joke when he saw one.

Chaucer is the most readable of men, and it is unfortunate that the shifting of the English language has made him a stranger to many people who would normally be his close friends. This book has tried to make him a little less of a stranger; and I am hoping that any reader who enjoys meeting Chaucer in this book will go on and extend the acquaintance. There are few writers who are so well worth knowing.

I have modernized the spelling somewhat in quoting from his poems. There is no fourteenth-century version of Chaucer's work extant, and there is no reason why the spelling of fifteenth-century scribes should be treated with exaggerated respect as long as no harm is done to the rhythm of the lines.

The buying power of money in Chaucer's day is difficult to estimate since prices, of course, varied from year to year as they do now. The matter is further complicated by the disproportionate cost of some items (like books), the fact that labor costs skyrocketed after the Black Death while land costs did not, and the further fact that an English coin did not have absolutely stable value. But in general it seems safe to say that a medieval penny could buy about fifteen times as much as a modern one.

Acknowledgments are due J. M. Dent & Co. for permission to quote from the Ellis translation of *The Romance of the Rose*, and to the University of Pennsylvania Press for quotations from the Griffin and Myrick translation of Boccaccio's *The Filostrato*. Acknowledgments are also due my sister Joy, without whom the index would probably never have been finished.

The decorations are all based on fourteenth-century illuminations. The expression of affable imbecility is characteristic of the beasts and birds of the period.

M. C.

GEOFFREY CHAUCER OF ENGLAND

CHAPTER I

WHEN GEOFFREY'S FATHER, John Chaucer, was not yet fourteen he was kidnaped by his Aunt Agnes. She was assisted in this enterprise by force of arms, "viz. swords, bows and arrows" and by three men.

The event took place on a winter Monday, December the third, 1324. John was living in London in a house in Cordwainer Street ward with his mother and his stepfather. His own father, Robert Chaucer, had died some years earlier, and his mother Mary had married a first cousin of his father's named Richard Chaucer.

The Chaucer family had come to London from Ipswich, and Robert Chaucer had owned property in Ipswich which young John was to inherit as soon as he came of age. But the Ipswich branch of the family, as represented by Robert's sister, Agnes, had no intention of letting good rental properties pass to Londoners. The matter had already been fought out at least twice in the Ipswich law courts (the fourteenth century was a highly litigious age) but as far as the courts were concerned the two shops and the homestead were still John's legal inheritance.

Agnes was a woman of resource and she also had two daughters. It occurred to her that if a marriage could be arranged between her daughter Joan and her nephew John, the Ipswich rentals would be automatically under her jurisdiction. All that she lacked to fulfill this program was the actual person of John, and to obtain it she enlisted the help of two Ipswich men, Geoffrey and Thomas Stace, and of Geoffrey's servant Lawrence.

Geoffrey Stace later married Agnes, and it may be that he had a more than neighborly interest in the property. He and his brothers had a record of appearances in the long-suffering Ipswich courts for offenses that ranged from robbery to beating a bailiff; although it must be admitted that in the matter of the Ipswich court records the Malyns (Agnes was a Malyn) were not much better. Nearly all the documents that are extant concerning the Malyns are notices of various trespasses against the public peace, or pardons for the same.[1]

The Chaucers of Cordwainer Street ward, London, were a much more sober and respectable group of people than the Malyns of Ipswich, but they did not endure the kidnaping of the young heir with any meekness. His stepfather Richard rode at once to Ipswich, taking with him a young man named Thomas Heyroun who was Mary Chaucer's son by an earlier marriage; and according to Agnes' outraged claim the two men carried off forty pounds' worth of goods from her home.

The youthful John was retrieved, still safely unmarried, and the Chaucer family ended by filing suit against the four unhappy abductors. They asked damages of three hundred pounds, which would be over twenty thousand dollars in modern money.

The trial was an extended affair. It began before the King in Hilary term, was adjourned, was adjourned again, kept on being adjourned in the familiar legal way, and finally went before a jury three years after the actual kidnaping.

The Chaucers won, the jury awarding damages at only fifty pounds less than Richard and Mary were asking. Geoffrey Stace, who in the meantime had married his fellow-defendant, appealed. He pointed out that young John was still unmarried and that in any case the Ipswich property was worth only twenty shillings a year. He lost the appeal, tried again on a technical point, and lost again. He and his new wife Agnes were committed to Marshalsea prison, where they remained until John gave them letters of acquittance two years later. Then, single-minded to the end, they

---

[1] The Malyns and the Chaucers were the same family; Robert Chaucer was known interchangeably as Robert Malyn, Robert de Dennington, Robert le Saddler and Robert Chaucer. He probably got his new London name from his place of residence, for he settled in Cordwainer Street ward and both Cordwainer and Chaucer (from the French *chaussier*) mean shoemaker.

Examples could be multiplied of men who acquired surnames from their place of residence. Geoffrey Chaucer's own stepfather, for instance, was named Bartholomew atte Chapel.

bought the Ipswich property from him, and a family argument that had lasted for nearly a decade was finally ended.

John Chaucer was still in his teens when he released his uncle and his aunt, but by medieval standards he was a man full grown. He had already twice borne arms, first as a campaigner in the Scottish wars and then under the banner of the Earl of Lancaster, having been outlawed on the second occasion for his activities.

John's first experience as a soldier took place in the summer of 1327. The newly crowned king of England, fifteen-year-old Edward the Third, led a campaign against the Scots. It was King Edward's first campaign, as it was John Chaucer's, and he returned from it in tears; for the whole affair had degenerated into a tragicomedy of which it was difficult for any Englishman to see the humor.

The Scottish campaign of 1327 has little place in history. But it was so similar in many ways to the military campaign in which John's son, Geoffrey Chaucer, first bore arms that it is perhaps worth describing in detail.

John Chaucer rode north in a London contingent of two hundred men, among whom was his stepbrother, Thomas Heyroun. They were mounted and equipped by the city, with a daily wage of twelvepence, and as ordinary London citizens they were not obliged to burden themselves with the complicated arrangement of chain mail and armor plate that a knight was expected to wear. Thomas and John probably wore no more armor than a steel breastplate, helmet and gauntlets and each man carried a small circular shield about the size of a large pot-lid.

The London company met the rest of the army, and found itself accompanied by the flower of English chivalry as it rode on to Scotland. There was a holiday mood abroad, for there was a general impression in that period that war was only a kind of extended tournament; it was the misfortune of the gallant English army that the Scots were not sufficiently civilized to be aware of the correct attitude towards warfare.

The English rode out in splendor, armor glittering and banners displayed, making their way among the startled Scotch deer whom they frequently mistook for the foe. Their first achievement was to become separated from their baggage train, the little carts that followed the warriors with food and kitchen utensils and tents and all the various impedimenta without which a civilized army could not be expected to operate.

The unwieldy, baggageless array finally found itself huddled on the wrong side of the Tyne, having crossed it only with the greatest difficulty. It was the middle of the night, and the soldiers had no lights. They also had nothing to eat, except the small loaf that was kept tied to the saddle and was now soaked with the sweat of the tired horses. They also had no hatchets, and were obliged to sit up all night holding their horses by the bridles because they had no way of making stakes.

The next morning it began to rain, and it was a thorough Scotch rain which continued without ceasing. The men finally used their swords for hatchets and succeeded in cutting down enough brushwood to build little huts for themselves, inside which they huddled in their cold jerkins and even colder armor.

The country people heard the glad news and flocked to the scene from miles around to sell the marooned soldiers loaves of bread at the profiteering price of sixpence a loaf.[2] Tempers grew steadily worse, a condition which may have had something to do with the fact that there was nothing but river water to drink, except for the few lords who had forehandedly carried bottles of wine for themselves on sumpter horses. Meanwhile it went on raining. The green wood on the bonfires smouldered and went out, and even the leather of the girths and saddles began to rot.

After a week of this, with the rain coming down without ceasing, the English army struggled into motion again and finally located the elusive foe on the far side of the Were.

At last the soldiers knew what to do. They at once formed their lines in the correct battle positions and the excited young King Edward rode in front of the ranks to encourage his men to be

[2] This would be nearly two dollars in modern money. The amount of goods a given coin could buy varied of course from year to year in the fourteenth century, as it does today, but on the average the medieval English penny had about fifteen times the buying power of the modern English one.

brave. Then the whole array moved forward in slow time, banners flying and lines perfectly kept.

Then they stopped. They were obliged to stop, for the River Were was in between and the Scots, having been insufficiently educated in the rules of chivalry, had no intention of leaving the hill upon which they had established themselves.

The unlucky English had no choice but to spend the night where they were. The ground was hard and full of rocks, and again there was no way to make fires or picket the horses. The Scots, meanwhile, retired comfortably to their little huts, whence they emerged the next morning to look down placidly upon the foe.

After three days of this, varied only by a little inconclusive skirmishing, the Scots shifted one night to another hill along the same river. The patient English followed them and again took up battle stations, sending heralds over at frequent intervals to offer the Scots any piece of level ground they might prefer if only they would come down and fight.

Food ran short and, as the chronicler reports with undoubted truth, everyone was very uncomfortable. The Scots finally put an end to the impasse, which was now in its eighteenth day, by leaving suddenly in the night. The English had no alternative but to return to their base at Durham, where the lords were somewhat comforted to find all the missing baggage neatly arranged in barns by the thoughtful citizenry, each cart with a little flag on top to indicate its owner.

King Edward was probably not the only one to return from the Scottish campaign in tears. Even more insulting to English pride was the ignominious peace that followed it, for which everyone blamed the government. The government was not at this time in the hands of the fifteen-year-old King. It was controlled by the Queen Mother and her favorite, Mortimer, who were mismanaging the kingdom between them in a way to which the English people had not been accustomed.

Among those who were especially displeased by the situation was the King's cousin, the Earl of Lancaster. He was an elder statesman, the foremost noble in the kingdom and the King's chief guardian in his minority. But he had no actual authority as long as

Mortimer was in power and finally attempted to overthrow him by force.

John Chaucer took up arms a second time to become a member of the army that marched behind the Earl of Lancaster to Winchester. The association is of interest because his son, Geoffrey Chaucer, was on intimate terms with two generations of the House of Lancaster and was especially well acquainted with the two granddaughters of the Earl. It is pleasant to know that the association was an honorable one from the first, for John was no rebel. He bore arms for a distinguished and gallant old gentleman who was attempting to put a forcible end to a state of affairs that was an insult both to England and to the King.

The rising failed and was therefore labeled a disorderly conspiracy. The Queen Mother did not dare have the Earl of Lancaster executed, but she had him heavily fined. John Chaucer was indicted, and when he very wisely failed to appear in the Court of Hustings to answer the indictment he was declared to be an outlaw.

Mortimer was overthrown and executed in 1330, and everyone concerned in the rising against him received full pardon. The old Earl of Lancaster, lately grown blind, retired from politics to a life of religious meditation and John Chaucer returned to London. He arranged for the release of his aunt and newly acquired uncle from Marshalsea prison and then settled down to a very successful career as a London man of business.

John Chaucer entered the wine business, a step which his family connections made almost inevitable. His father had been associated with the wine business in London both as a purchasing agent and as a customs official. His stepfather, Richard Chaucer, was a vintner, and his stepbrother, Thomas Heyroun, was a vintner also. It was almost to be expected that John Chaucer in his turn should become a vintner.

A vintner was not a taverner. The point needs to be stressed, since the two are sometimes confused and Geoffrey Chaucer is therefore pictured as playing among the wine cups in his father's tavern. In the early days in Ipswich the family had owned and operated taverns (one of their surnames, in fact, was le Taverner) but shortly after their arrival in London the men of the family moved into the dignified ranks of the wine importers.

The taverner was the retailer, keeping the wine stored in his cellar to be dispensed to his customers upstairs. The vintner was the wholesaler, supplying the taverner with his stocks. The two trades were rigidly separated by law and a vintner never retailed wine. But he could, and often did, finance a number of taverns in order to secure for himself an adequate outlet for his merchandise.

Unlike the tavern-keeper, the vintner ranked high in the social scale and more than one Mayor of London had been elected from among the ranks of the importers of wine. The mayor had to be a wealthy man to maintain his position, but it was not hard to grow rich in the wine trade. Wine was the national drink of all classes, since beer had not yet been introduced; and because England was not warm enough to grow grapes commercially all the wine had to be imported from the Continent. Most of it came from France and went through the hands of the vintners.

It was a profitable business but a rigidly restricted one. Even when the government was not interfering with the wine trade by incessant and frequently contradictory legislation, the importer was hampered by the multitude of regulations that had to be obeyed. There was a fee for everything: a fee to the royal gauger, a fee for unloading the wine, a fee for hoisting it to the docks, a fee to the broker, a fee for getting it off the docks again, and even an original fee levied against the wine-ships for the privilege of passing under London Bridge.

Even the laborers that a vintner employed operated under a series of fixed rules that had to be respected. No one could unload the wine on the docks, for instance, unless he belonged to the association of wine-drawers. This was composed of forty-six men who worked at a fixed rate—twopence as far as the wharf, twopence halfpenny to carry the wine to the shore, threepence to take it up the hill to Thames Street; and no wine-drawer could handle a cargo of wine unless twelve of his associates were present.

These rules were devised by the guilds, and like all the guild rules they were designed to prevent competition. Competition was an evil thing from the medieval point of view, and the ideal arrangement was believed to be a series of associations, each with a monopoly in its own particular field. Under the guild system no one was allowed to undersell his associates, and there was no competition because there was nothing to compete against. A high standard of workmanship, which would normally have deteriorated under such a system, was maintained by a rigid police system in each of the separate guilds, and every aspect of medieval manufacture and trade was fully organized, rigidly controlled and minutely subdivided.[3]

An arbitrary fixing of prices worked well enough for the manufacturing guilds, but it worked very badly for the trading guilds, who had not been in existence when the system was conceived. In the wine business, for instance, the cash value of a tun of wine as it was finally delivered into a taverner's basement had a great deal to do with such uncertain factors as storms and shipwrecks and pirates and the vintage weather of a given year in Gascony, and since the vintner could not control his initial costs he should have been allowed some latitude in the matter of final prices. Thomas Heyroun and several other vintners were obliged to go on strike in the thirties after the price of Gascon wine had been set at fourpence a gallon, and the sheriffs went through all the principal streets of London writing down the names of the tavern owners who refused to open their doors to the public. An alternative to losing money would have been to adulterate the wine with cheaper varieties before selling it, but this of course was forbidden by law also.

Fortunately the medieval man was accustomed to rules. They were with him from the moment of his birth and it seemed natural to him to operate as a member of a group instead of as an individual. He was by instinct a joiner. He did not wish to be alone. He wished to be an obedient part of a corporate whole, and individualism was as alien to the medieval business world as it was to the Church or to any other aspect of medieval society.

Moreover, the guild gave its individual members a great deal in

[3] This subdividing went to impressive lengths. It took four guilds to make a knife: the Cutlers, the Bladesmiths, the Hafters and the Sheathers. And it took five guilds to make a saddle.

18

exchange for their entrance fees. It gave them security, an efficient police system, an annual dinner, financial help in case of sickness and a fine funeral at the end with all one's fellow members in attendance. There were not only business guilds but all kinds of religious and social guilds, fulfilling about the same function as modern service clubs and fraternities.

As a member of the vintners' guild John Chaucer found it convenient to live in Vintry ward, facing the River Thames. Vintry was one of the wealthiest of the London wards, with its stone and timber houses inhabited mostly by importers whose business was concerned with the docks and shipping just below. Its principal street was Thames Street, a broad thoroughfare which ran parallel with the river the whole length of the city, and it was on Thames Street that John Chaucer made his home.

His property fronted the thoroughfare and ran from the open stream called Walbrook on one side of it to a street called La Riole on the other. It seems safe to assume that this was the homestead property in which John Chaucer brought up his family, although he owned real estate all over town, because it was the one piece of property that stayed in the family and descended to Geoffrey as his heir.

London was a good city in which to live, and all Londoners were very proud of it. It was not as large as the great cities of the Continent, like Paris and Ghent and Florence, but it had a population of about forty thousand and this made it as large as the next four towns in England combined. Its political prestige was enormous, and whatever king occupied the throne in near-by Westminster, the opinions of the very vocal Londoners had to be considered.

Its ancestry was distinguished, for it was the settled conviction of the Londoners that their city had been founded by the grandson of Aeneas; and its architecture was distinguished also. There was no bridge in Europe, not even the Ponte Vecchio in Florence or the Pont-au-Change in Paris, to match the glory of London Bridge, with its twenty arches, its two-story chapel, and the tremendous weight of houses and shops whose rentals kept it in repair. Nor was any European structure as high as St. Paul's Cathedral, which dominated all London from its hill on the west side of town and raised its wooden spire a full five hundred feet above the ground. The cross on the top of the spire was protected from lightning by the fact that it contained some of the bones of the eleven thousand virgins of Cologne, wrapped in red sendal, and it was gilded to shine like gold in the sun.

The city was growing rapidly and it could no longer be fitted inside the wall that surrounded it. Already the city fathers had been obliged to split Faringdon ward in two, calling one Faringdon Within and the other Faringdon Without, and an almost continuous line of buildings had sprung up between the west gate of the city and the king's palace at Westminster. To the north and east there were still green fields outside the walls, where the citizens could play ball, or keep their hunting dogs, or take their wives to walk in the long summer evenings; but the city itself was becoming steadily more crowded, especially along the waterfront.

In so busy a city, the problems of adequate water supply and sewage disposal and city cleaning were necessarily complicated, but London in the fourteenth century was a much cleaner place than it is usually given credit for being. Each of the twenty-five city wards had the services of at least one full-time street cleaner, and sometimes of several. There were city dumps and city garbage boats, and untidy trades like those of the butchers and tanners were kept as far as possible to the suburbs. Each citizen was required to have the road paved in front of his own house, and the middle of the road was paved out of the city tax on carts entering the gates.

It was a help to have so much running water in the city and in the suburbs, for the Fleet and Walbrook were still open and had to be crossed by bridges. London, in fact, was entirely surrounded by water, for the Thames extended along one side of it and there was a broad city ditch around the whole of the wall. Water was also supplied by that masterpiece of medieval plumbing, the Great Conduit, which brought fresh water all the way from Paddington to West Cheap. It is true that the arrangement was not perfect; the steep descent at Fleet Street often generated enough water pressure to burst the pipes and flood the adjoining cellars, and there was also trouble from frost. But the citizens of London were not backward in registering their complaints, and the number of these complaints has given rise to a darker picture of medieval life in London than is really justified.

The city was democratically and intelligently run, and mostly by men who received no pay for their services. The mayor received a large grant for entertainment purposes, and the town-sergeant and town-clerk were given salaries because theirs were full-time posts. But the citizens who did the real governing of London, serving both as aldermen and as members of the common council, worked for nothing. They watched over the welfare of the city because they were its citizens, seeing that the building ordinances were obeyed, that curfew was enforced, that no empty boxes were left littering the streets, that hooks and ladders and reservoirs of water were provided in every ward in dry weather, that false faces were not worn on the streets at Christmas, and that the shouts of the fruit and vegetable sellers were not permitted to disturb the priests singing matins in St. Paul's.

The police system was handled through the coroner and the sheriffs, supplementing the rigid control each guild exerted over the behavior of its own members, and London seems to have been a remarkably law-abiding city for a period in which a dagger was an indispensable part of the costume of every adult male. When Simon Chaucer, Richard's brother, "lay dead of a death other than his rightful death" in Cordwainer Street ward the coroner and the sheriffs arrived at once and in their careful taking of testimony from witnesses discovered that Simon had been quarreling with a skinner after dinner in High Street and the skinner's son had hit him over the head with a wooden staff. The sheriffs could do nothing in this particular case, however; the murderer had taken refuge in St. Mary's and claimed right of sanctuary, and whomever the Church protected the civil authorities could not touch.

John Chaucer was a true Londoner and most of his life revolved about the city, but he went abroad at least once. This was in the train of King Edward in 1338, when all the royal household and most of the government went to Flanders.

England was on the brink of the conflict with France that later earned for itself the melancholy title of the Hundred Years' War, and King Edward planned a protracted visit to Flanders to round up allies and negotiate for financial backing. Edward's wife was a Flemish woman, the daughter of the Count of Holland and Hainault, and she accompanied her husband abroad. In Antwerp she bore him a son who was named Lionel in honor of the lion on the arms of Brabant, and fifteen months later, in Ghent, she bore him another son who was named John. John was always called John of Gaunt after the English way of pronouncing the city of his birth, and both he and Lionel were later influential in the career of John Chaucer's son Geoffrey.

It is not known precisely why John Chaucer went on the Flanders expedition. His letter of protection states merely that he went in the King's service and by the King's command. An enormous number of men and women accompanied the expedition, and the royal household stayed abroad so long that even the royal mint was established in Flanders. It took the services of a great many professional experts to keep the household functioning; and for lack of any information to the contrary it seems safe to assume that John Chaucer went abroad as an experienced vintner, a man with a thorough knowledge of wines appointed, with others, to assist in the wine department.

John Chaucer had another link with the Court, for his wife was related to the Baron of the Exchequer and Keeper of the King's Wardrobe by her first marriage. She was also an heiress, for she was the niece and sole heir of a wealthy London moneyer named Hamo de Copton who had invested his money in income properties all over London and the suburbs and left his niece a considerable volume of real estate which brought in an excellent annual income. Agnes de Copton was Agnes de Northwell by her first marriage, then Agnes Chaucer, and then after John Chaucer's death the wife of another vintner named Bartholomew atte Chapel. But there is no record that John Chaucer ever had another wife, and it seems reasonably certain that she was Geoffrey Chaucer's mother.

Both the poet's mother and his grandmother were married three times each, a phenomenon that was not at all uncommon in medieval London. Women of their position were almost as independent as men, and possessed a series of civic and personal rights that would have seemed incredible to a woman living in Victorian London. Under common law a woman was her husband's adjunct, but under merchant law she was as free as any man. She could operate any business she chose, even one entirely different to her husband's, and take on her own apprentices. She was free to join the trade guild of her chosen profession and to wear its livery, and in the law courts she could plead as a *femme sole*, independent of her husband. Robert Chaucer, for instance, was once sued by a woman with whom he had professional dealings, over a matter of wine storage, and her husband had no part in the suit.

A married woman had equal freedom when she became a widow, with the further advantage of the property she had inherited from her husband. If she married again it was because she wished to, and not because she was obliged to seek the shelter of a masculine pair of arms. Hers was exactly the contrary position of any medieval woman who was unlucky enough to be an aristocrat instead of a member of the middle class. Under the feudal system a woman was almost useless outside the home and had no choice but to marry or to enter a convent.[4] If she were an heiress she could be sold as though she were real estate, and medieval knights trafficked in the wardships of county heiresses as their modern counterparts would deal in stocks and bonds. But the townsman fitted into no part of this feudal system, and his sturdy middle-class world operated wholly outside its rigidly narrow and increasingly artificial boundaries.

It is not known when John Chaucer married Agnes de Copton, except that it was before 1343. They had been married for some time when John Chaucer went to Southampton as deputy for the King's Butler in 1347.

The King's Butler was the purchasing agent for all the wine used by the Crown and he was also the collector of the wine customs. As his deputy, John Chaucer was responsible for collecting the import duties on each shipment of wine received in the Southampton area, which included Cicestre, Seford, Shorham and Ports-

[4] The only exception to this rule was the King's eldest daughter, Isabelle. Isabelle was allowed to do anything she liked by her indulgent father. She did not marry until she was thirty-three, and then she married for love; her husband was of lower rank than herself, and much younger.

mouth. John Chaucer was not the first member of his family to serve as deputy to the King's Butler, for both his father and his stepfather had held similar posts in the London area.

The same year John Chaucer also became collector of the customs on woolen goods made in England for export. In this he forecast the career of his son Geoffrey, who spent eleven years of his life intimately associated with wool in an important position in the London customhouse.

The Chaucers were in Southampton for two years, and they must still have been there when the plague came down upon England that has since been called the Black Death. It came to England in the cold wet summer of 1348, after almost incredible ravages on the Continent. Rumors had reached the English of whole cities made desolate and ships drifting about on the sea with their cargoes intact but only dead men on board. In August the plague reached England through a port in Dorsetshire and crept to Bristol in spite of the prayers that had been going on publicly in every Bristol parish to avert it. From there it worked to Gloucester, although the men of Gloucester tried to cut off all intercourse between themselves and the stricken city of Bristol. By September it had reached Oxford, and before the first of November it was in London.

By March the death rate in London was still mounting (it can be traced by the increase in the number of wills probated). Parliament was to have met in January but had been postponed to March, and in March it was again postponed. Two large areas of ground were hurriedly fenced in and consecrated for burial places, and for a time it must have seemed to its inhabitants that London was becoming a city of the dead. Then, towards the end of the summer, the plague wore itself out; although it was to appear again and again in that pestilence-ridden century until it became, in the vivid words of a contemporary poet, like rain dripping through a leaky roof.

Among the many Londoners for whom the summer never came were John Chaucer's stepbrother and his stepfather. Thomas Heyroun died in May and Richard Chaucer a short time after. Richard was buried next to his wife in the parish church of St. Mary Aldermany, next to the altar of St. Mary and St. Anne, and his will provided that masses should be said daily for the souls of himself and of his wife Mary and of her son, Thomas Heyroun.

It was very common for London merchants in the fourteenth century to make such bequests, and the Church grew rich upon them. In return for the services of a permanent chaplain to say masses daily, Richard Chaucer bequeathed to St. Mary's a tenement in Vintry ward and to St. Michael Paternoster a tenement in Southwark, and it is easy to see how the Church was able to acquire so many income properties in and about London.

In financing a chantry, Richard Chaucer was probably motivated in part by the sense that he was doing the correct and usual thing for a man of his standing, but it is not wise to underestimate the real terror of hell that prompted it. A sense of sin weighed down the average man of the Middle Ages to a degree that it is now difficult to credit, and while it did not always influence him while he lived it frightened him exceedingly when he was dying.

It did not take London long to right itself after the plague, for its economic structure was much less intricate than that of the great cities of the Continent. John Chaucer took up the course of normal living with the rest, and when his name appears on a London document it is always as a good, solid, law-abiding citizen.

He was evidently of a conservative nature, for he seems to have taken no part in the financial speculations that occupied his colleagues in the first two decades of the war. There were war loans to be made and army contracts to be had, and many London merchants invested their life savings in financial syndicates that sometimes ballooned into huge fortunes and sometimes as quickly collapsed. Henry Picard, a fellow vintner who had accompanied John Chaucer on the trip to Flanders, became the medieval equivalent of a millionaire. The story that he entertained four kings simultaneously in his house in Vintry ward is not correct, but only because those particular kings did not happen to be in London at the same time; it could have happened easily enough to a man of Picard's wealth and social position.

Picard was Mayor of London when John Chaucer was called to a special meeting at the Guildhall in March of 1356. The subject was the old one of assessments for the war with France. For nine years the vintners had been paying an extra tax of two shillings a tun to provide armed protection for the wine fleet, but the money had vanished in other directions and the enemy raids on merchant shipping continued. Now King Edward wanted further levies, since no war can be waged without money, and in particular he wanted the Londoners to supply two light boats for his navy, to be ready to join the fleet by June. Each citizen at the Guildhall made his contribution and collectors were appointed for each ward to raise the remainder. John Chaucer was one of the two collectors appointed for Vintry ward.

The Londoners' investment paid handsome dividends. Their boats helped transport to France the army that in September won the Battle of Poitiers. This was an even greater victory for the English than the earlier Battle of Crécy, for in the course of it the Prince of Wales captured the King of France to the shocked surprise of all Europe.[5]

All London turned out to see the show the day that King John was paraded through the streets on his way to a highly luxurious captivity at the Duke of Lancaster's palace. The French prisoner was astride a glittering palfrey while his captor, the Prince of Wales, rode beside him on a little black hackney, as "lowly" as the very well-bred young squire who later rode among the Canterbury Pilgrims.

If John Chaucer or any of his family were in London that day they were certainly among the cheering crowds that had lined the decorated streets since three in the morning. For it was a great day for London, the kind one describes to one's grandchildren, and John Chaucer would have wanted his family to see it.

It is unfortunately not known how large a family John Chaucer had. There was at least one daughter, whose name was Catherine and who later married into a distinguished Kentish family named Manning. There may have been other children, but it was Geoffrey who inherited the family house on Thames Street.

Nor is it known, unfortunately, when Geoffrey himself was born.

[5] The Prince of Wales became known to history as the Black Prince, but he was not called by that title in the fourteenth century.

The date has been variously conjectured but never on sufficient evidence. At one time it was given as 1326, until the discovery of the documents on the kidnaping trial proved that John Chaucer was unmarried at the time. It is known for certain only that Geoffrey Chaucer first bore arms in 1359, and that in 1386 he testified in court to being "forty years old and more," one of those vague statements that make life so dark for subsequent biographers.

A date somewhere between 1340 and 1344 is the one usually agreed upon, but it is equally possible that Geoffrey Chaucer was born as late as 1345. This would make him fourteen when he first bore arms—an age not far from his father's upon a similar occasion—and forty-one when he testified in court.

At any rate he was born, which after all is the most important consideration.

CHAPTER II

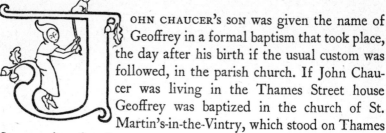

OHN CHAUCER'S SON was given the name of Geoffrey in a formal baptism that took place, the day after his birth if the usual custom was followed, in the parish church. If John Chaucer was living in the Thames Street house Geoffrey was baptized in the church of St. Martin's-in-the-Vintry, which stood on Thames Street only a few feet away.

St. Martin's was not a large church. London was composed of over a hundred small parishes and each of them served a relatively small congregation. But St. Martin's was in a wealthy district and more than one London citizen of importance was buried within its walls.

Geoffrey was probably confirmed here when he was three years old, beginning the religious pattern that held a medieval Englishman from his birth to his death and was as natural and unquestioned as breathing. The bells of St. Martin's would be the first thing he heard when he awoke in the morning, with a hundred and fifty church and chapel bells from all over the city joining in.

The parish church was also the social center of the neighborhood, the place for christenings and marriages and burials and for showing off new clothes on Sunday. Its interior would become thoroughly familiar to a small boy: the rushes on the floor in summer and the straw in winter, the scuffle for seats because there never seemed to be enough benches to go around, and the occasional convivial chatting of the parishioners during services. The sermons were more entertaining on the whole than they became in later centuries, for the preachers used realistic anecdotes and comic stories to enliven the moral lessons they were attempting to inculcate; and there is a strong possibility that young Geoffrey Chaucer was more impressed by some of these than he was by the sermon itself.

His own home, close by St. Martin's, was probably very much like any other home of the period belonging to a merchant of the same social position and income as his father. Englishmen had not yet learned the art of being as comfortable as their contemporaries in France or Flanders or Italy but they did well enough.

The main room in the house was the hall, which was the equivalent of the modern living room. There would be chairs for Geoffrey's father and mother and benches for the rest of the family, upholstered to match the hangings in some clear, bright shade that would satisfy the medieval passion for color. The tables and cupboards were painted and there were probably no decorations on the walls except the hangings and the weapons his father had used in the Scottish campaign.

The solar, or bedroom, was a single upstairs room usually used by the whole family. It might be divided into partitions for convenience, but privacy was not considered needful in the Middle Ages. The beds were the most valuable articles of furniture in the whole house, with expensive mattresses, sheets and pillowcases and the coverlets gay with embroideries. The average family could not support more than one or two beds, and the children usually slept on boards placed over trestles. The clothes were hung on racks or kept in chests, with other chests for the family linen and silver and perhaps a small one for the master's caps.

John Chaucer would conduct his business in a counting-room, or office, with a table for his pen box and inkhorn and an iron-bound chest for his money and for his valuable papers. The kitchen and pantry were well-equipped and the servants were well-paid, for domestic help came high in the Middle Ages after the Great Plague. And lastly there was a storehouse which served, like an attic today, for the accumulation of odds and ends that were too good to throw away.

As far as minor details of living went, each member of the family would be expected to wash his hands and brush his hair before he sat down to meals, for the medieval mind was thoroughly convinced of the value of good manners. If the family slept without clothes, as fourteenth-century citizens are frequently assumed to have done, it is difficult to see what use could have been made of the nightgowns and nightcaps which appear so often in the inventories. On the other hand, there were no forks and it is not likely the family possessed many books. Books were scarce and rather expensive, and it was several centuries before the middle classes formed the habit of reading for pleasure. If there was a book in the house it was probably a Psalter or a history book or a copy of the *Statutes of England.*

The house on Thames Street was somewhat dark, especially when the wooden shutters had to be closed; for while glass was by no means unknown it was expensive and of poor quality. Most of the London houses were built tightly against each other, with each story projecting over the last one and the top floors sometimes leaning out so far they actually met in the middle of the street. On the other hand, a house on a broad thoroughfare like Thames Street would have much more light and air than came to the homes of minor tradesmen huddled in the back streets, sometimes many families to a tenement, or to the tangle of narrow alleys along the river front where the foreign sailors lived.

If Geoffrey Chaucer the boy was anything like Geoffrey Chaucer the man, he must have had a delightful time in the streets around his home. His curiosity, his quick eye for detail, and his warm, uncritical love for all sorts and conditions of people should have made him an ideal child to grow up in a city as varied, as lively and as sociable as medieval London.

The Thames, for instance, was almost at his front door and the Thames was the main street of the city. The shortest and quickest route through London was by boat, and the river was never empty of the private barges of the nobility and the public boats of the watermen, who traveled back and forth as the fourteenth-century equivalent of a taxi system. There was also a constant movement of freight, with local boats bringing rushes from Greenwich and building stone from Yorkshire and the huge daily quantities of fish upon which the city depended.

The nearest anchorage for foreign ships was Queenhithe, slightly to the west of Geoffrey Chaucer's home. The streets down to the waterfront were built straight here so that the porters could take the hill at a run, and there was a steady stream of men carrying up raisins and cotton and pepper and sugar and canvas and soap and various other commodities that had been shipped in from foreign cities. The boats came from France and Norway and Portugal and Spain and Italy and even as far away as Greece, and once a year a great Venetian galley came to unload its cargo of spices at the port of London. Around Christmas time and again at Easter the wine fleet returned to England, heavily convoyed and full of familiar faces, and if Geoffrey Chaucer was not underfoot on the docks during this period he was a most unusual small boy.

For all its weight of traffic the Thames was an unhurried sort of river. There were still swans around London Bridge, and salmon could be caught in midstream. It was a cool place for the boys to swim on summer evenings and a meeting place for the women who brought their washing down to the public stairs between the wharfs. Once a year there were water games, mock tournaments played on the river with an audience lining the shore and the bridge to laugh when anyone fell in.

When the boys wanted skating they went north of the city to Moorfields, where the great shallow marshes froze early. Some of them slid on chunks of ice and some had real skates made of bone. All of them had sticks and they evolved a variety of rough games that must have made their mothers tremble.

In summer there were all kinds of sports, of which one of the most popular was football. Once it had been played in the fields outside the city, by teams composed of boys from the schools and boys from the trades with their proud fathers riding out on horseback. But the practice had been banned about forty years before Chaucer was a boy because too much excitement had been generated.

Games were played everywhere and with great enthusiasm, and there was even an ordinance to keep youngsters from playing prisoner's base within the halls of Westminster when Parliament was in session. There was also a rule against playing ball in St. Paul's Cathedral, but on the whole the city permitted games to be played anywhere, provided that the area was not too crowded or the occupation did not start a fight.

A great deal of life in London went on out-of-doors because the tradesmen's shops were small and crowded and there was little incentive to stay inside them in the summer.[1] Everyone stayed in the streets when he could. This was no drawback to the average Londoner, who delighted in the companionship of his fellow man, and there were celebrations and processions whenever the thinnest excuse could be found. Apart from Christmas, May Day was the gayest single festival of the year, when the blackthorn and the wild roses bloomed and several parishes joined together to bring home the Maypole. Twice during June there was the great procession of the Marching Watch, which had been inaugurated to prevent fires and had become the noisiest festival of the year, with processions and bonfires and dancing in the streets in fancy dress. Every man hung his door with flowers and with little glass lamps that must have made the city look like a convention of fireflies after dark.

As though to compensate for the crooked dark streets and the small dark houses, there was color everywhere that color could be put. Even the hearse cloths were crimson and blue and gold. The outsides of the houses were painted and carved, priests walked abroad in red and green boots, and an inventory of church vestments is a riot of velvet and samite and cloth of gold, with flowers and leopards and ostrich feathers woven of jewels and metallic thread. London may have had its faults in the fourteenth century, but no one could have called it dull.

The language that young Geoffrey Chaucer heard upon the streets was English. It was not, of course, modern English. It was the South East Midland dialect, which later became the basis of modern English because London was the business and political center of the realm.

The authority of the French language was still very strong, however, even on the streets of London. When the common people hummed at their work it was not necessarily an English song that they sang. It was more likely to be a French one, like *Dieu Vous Sauve, Dame Emma* or *J'ai Perdu Mon Temps et Mon Honneur*.

In his own home Geoffrey Chaucer probably heard French at

[1] There were fifteen shops in a space of 150 feet between Old Jewry and Ironmonger Lane, and there were a hundred and thirty-eight shops on the length of London Bridge, which was only twenty feet wide.

least as often as English. French was the language spoken at court, as it had been ever since the Norman Conquest, and the children of gentlefolk were taught to speak French when they were rocked in their cradles. The same fashion was followed with the children of townsmen since their parents wished them to have all the advantages belonging to the gentry. John Chaucer would have been obliged to know French in any case. Not only were his dealings in the wine trade mostly with Gascony, but French was the international business language of the Middle Ages.

When Geoffrey Chaucer went to school it was in French, not English, that he would learn his lessons. This changed, as so much else changed, in Chaucer's lifetime, and the schoolboys of subsequent generations had the much easier task of learning their lessons in English.[2] But when young Geoffrey Chaucer set himself to translate a Latin line in the schoolroom it was into French that he was expected to translate it, and the system at least had the advantage of giving him a thorough knowledge of the most influential modern language of his day.

He probably went to grammar school when he was seven years old, the usual time for a boy to begin his formal education. Before this, however, he would have learned his letters, possibly at home or conceivably in a song school of the kind his Prioress describes in *The Canterbury Tales*. It is much more probable, however, that he was taught to read by the parish priest. In the towns, as in the villages, the rector usually served as the schoolmaster in his little district and gave lessons in the vestry of the church, in a room over it, or in his own home.

Geoffrey Chaucer learned to read from a small primer. The first line was called "criss cross row" because it began with a large cross to remind the small scholar of his devotions. Then came the alphabet, both large letters and small, followed by the exorcism and the Lord's Prayer. Once Chaucer had spelled his way this far he had the key in his hand that led into the great world of books, a world in which Chaucer moved all his life with the same thorough

[2] This reform was the work of a single Oxford schoolmaster, John Cornwall, but he had behind him the rise in English nationalism that had been generated by the long war with France.

enjoyment in which he moved in the world of people. From the first he was the kind of person who sat up half the night to read a book and would have begun again the next morning if he could.

By the time he was seven Geoffrey Chaucer had learned his letters and was ready to go to grammar school. It is frequently assumed that there were only three schools in London in the fourteenth century and that Chaucer must have been sent either to St. Martin's-le-Grand, St. Mary-le-bow, or St. Paul's Cathedral to get his education. This list comes from a twelfth-century description of London by William Fitzstephen, who states that "the three principal churches . . . have famous schools by privilege and by virtue of their ancient dignity." But Fitzstephen adds that "there are other schools licensed by special grace and permission," and there is no reason to suppose that these other schools had vanished by the fourteenth century. It is much more likely that they had multiplied.

The medieval interest in education has been much underestimated. In proportion to the population there were more schools at the beginning of the fourteenth century in England than there were at the end of the eighteenth. One of the grievances, in fact, of a popular social critic of the period, the author of *Piers Plowman*, was that any "beggar's brat" could get an education. The Church honored education and gave it freely, without regard to class distinctions, and the fourteenth century was by no means as illiterate as it is sometimes supposed to have been.

The whole educational system was based squarely upon the time-honored proposition: "This is so because I tell you it is so." Any kind of individual initiative or curiosity was as firmly discouraged in the classroom as in any other part of the medieval system, and a good memory was the mark of a good student.

Most of the classwork was oral, for books were scarce and the students worked from dictation with slates or wooden tablets. This method might have its disadvantages but it gave Chaucer a well-trained memory that served him usefully throughout his life.

If it is not safe to guess where Chaucer went to school, it is fairly safe to say what he was taught there. The Middle Ages did not believe in radical changes within a short space of time, and what

34

was good enough for the fourth century was considered quite good enough for the fourteenth.

Chaucer learned the elements of grammar from the *Eight Parts of Speech* of Aelius Donatus, a Roman grammarian who had taught Saint Jerome. It was given to small boys in a simplified form which they called, probably not at all affectionately, their Donat. The Donat ran to what would now be about ten printed pages, and consisted of questions and answers on the basic principles of Latin grammar. Geoffrey Chaucer may have owned his own copy, since a cheap manuscript copy of so small a book could be bought for threepence (the equivalent of about ninety cents in modern money). Whether he owned a copy or not, the long unbroken paragraphs of the Donat would have been his constant companion throughout his early schooldays. A twelfth-century schoolmaster attempted to make things easier for small boys by turning the grammar into rhyme for the nephews of the Bishop of Dol, and in this new form it became very popular in the fourteenth century; but the original version was not shaken from its schoolroom eminence, and Gutenberg printed a Donat before he printed the Bible.

By the time he had inched his way through his Donat young Geoffrey Chaucer would be ready for some elementary Latin reading. The average medieval textbook was as sternly moral as *McGuffey's Reader*—art for art's sake would have been an unthinkable maxim in the Middle Ages—and every young scholar had his moral nature and his Latin simultaneously benefited by what he called his Cato. This was a collection of adages and proverbs arranged in alphabetical order and supposed to have been written by one Dionysius Cato. Chaucer mentions Cato several times in his poetry, but in any case no medieval schoolboy could have escaped him.

For advanced grammar Chaucer would be subjected to Priscian, who had taught Latin grammar in Constantinople in the sixth century. He would begin with Priscian's shorter work, which consisted of a thorough dissection of the first twelve lines of the *Aeneid*, each word being analyzed as to gender, case, number and so on. Then he graduated to Priscian's larger book on grammar.

The great educator believed in example as well as precept, and his book includes ten thousand lines of quotation from the Roman classics. Chaucer had a good memory and it is likely that some of his later quotations from classical authors come from no closer an acquaintance than through the standard textbooks of his youth.

The case was far otherwise with the first Latin classic he encountered at school. This was Ovid, to whom Chaucer refers in his work more often than to any other single writer and who became his friend for life. The real attraction was that both men were fundamentally alike in temperament. They both had a detached, uncritical view of their fellow man and a strong sense of fun that drew them to each other at once when they met across the centuries. Moreover, Ovid's way of writing had a clearness and facility that may have helped Chaucer somewhat in attaining his own lucid style.

Ovid was above all a storyteller, and it was as a teller of tales that Chaucer first met him in the schoolroom. There he read Ovid's *Metamorphoses,* which was a kind of biographical dictionary of the gods and proved to be a mine of stories for the story-hungry Middle Ages. Ovid had the gift of making his mythological characters come alive, the women especially, and Chaucer says that after he had read the tragic story of Ceyx and Alcyone he was upset all the following day. His friendship with Ovid was not as passionate as Boccaccio's, who almost overdid his youthful devotion, but it lasted much longer. It lasted throughout the whole of Chaucer's life and was one of his rewards for undergoing long hours of Latin grammar in the schoolroom.[3]

All education in the Middle Ages was divided into two parts. (It was a tidy period.) What Chaucer learned in grammar school was called the *trivium* and consisted of grammar, rhetoric and logic. He did not continue with the higher education taught by the

[3] It seems safe to assume that Chaucer was no enthusiast over grammar. He lacked the careful mind of a scholar and in his later translations from Latin he did not always ponder the exact value of tenses and cases. Through a confusion over the ablative, for instance, he failed to give Vergil's goddess rapid wings and instead gave her the wings of a partridge.

universities, which consisted of arithmetic, geometry, astronomy and music and was called the *quadrivium*. This arbitrary division had been mapped out by a ninth-century German educator and was not very well suited to an expanding, commercially minded century like the fourteenth.

In spite of not entering upon the *quadrivium* Chaucer certainly learned some arithmetic. He probably did not attempt to penetrate into the mysteries of division, which was reserved only for advanced students, but he must have learned to do addition and subtraction since in his later career as a civil servant he had a great deal to do with the keeping of accounts. Addition and subtraction were done by means of a counting board, or abacus, for Roman numerals were still in general use and it was impractical to attempt to subtract XIX from XLIV on paper. As for geometry, it is evident from Chaucer's poetry that he had at least a bowing acquaintance with Euclid.

Whatever his formal education in music may have been, Chaucer knew music and loved it, as did everyone in England from the King's son to the most slovenly apprentice. It formed an essential part of daily living and played a large part in the life of the average man until the end of the Renaissance. If Chaucer did not learn to play at least one musical instrument he was very unlike most of his contemporaries.

There is a fourteenth-century treatise on education, now in the Vatican, which states that a boy should begin the study of grammar when he is seven, in the springtime of his youth, and that he should continue it, with some instruction in music and arithmetic, until he is fourteen; and judging by the evidence which is available this is almost exactly what Geoffrey Chaucer must have done.

If the anonymous schoolmaster who wrote the treatise was in any way characteristic of the teachers of the period, Chaucer and his fellow scholars were very fortunate. The intelligent humanity of the essay is in almost incredible contrast to the regimented brutality that was the ideal of most schoolmasters in the eighteenth century. The author reminds his readers that small boys should do their studying in a comfortable temperature, neither too hot nor too cold, and that they should always be allowed a recess or play period to stir their blood and elevate their spirits. He also reminds his readers that each small boy has a different temperament (the Middle Ages called them "humours") and had to be treated accordingly and he makes a further point which an eighteenth-century schoolmaster would have considered preposterous. Each boy learns his lessons at a different rate of speed, and it is the business of the schoolmaster to discover each boy's relative capacity for learning.

Just how many fourteenth-century schoolmasters agreed with these enlightened precepts it would be difficult to say, but it seems clear that Chaucer himself agreed with them. He once had occasion to write a short textbook for a ten-year-old boy, called *A Treatise on the Astrolabe,* and he shows the same sort of courteous consideration for a small boy's mind that was advocated by the anonymous schoolmaster. He is patiently prepared to tell his little Lewis everything twice so that Lewis can remember it once, and he carefully avoids long words because they are "full heavy . . . for . . . a child to lerne." The astrolabe is a complex astronomical instrument and the subject might seem rather advanced for a ten-year-old, but Lewis had asked for the instruction himself and had already shown a definite talent for mathematics. Chaucer was giving full consideration to the child's capacity for learning, and it is a not impossible conjecture that he may have learned this in part from some schoolmaster he himself had in his own youth.

As to the kind of schoolboy young Geoffrey Chaucer may have been, the testimony of some of his contemporary fellow poets concerning their own boyhoods shows that youngsters do not change much from century to century. Both Jean Froissart and John Lydgate wrote engaging accounts of their youth which could pass for that of any small boy today.

Froissart was the more gentlemanly little boy of the two. He took a great interest in the little girls who sat on the benches beside him and offered gifts of apples and pears and small glass rings to ingratiate himself with them. In his spare time he built dams in the gutter and blew soap bubbles and made mud pies, and he liked anyone who loved birds and dogs. Jean had an especial passion for games and he has left a list of fifty-two that he and his

38

companions played, each one lovingly named. As soon as he went to school to learn Latin he also learned how to fight and came home with his clothes torn, but on the whole he was a much better behaved child than John Lydgate. Lydgate penitently records that in his youth he was invariably late to school and that he used to climb the neighbors' walls to steal apples and that he chiefly enjoyed practical jokes and making faces like a young monkey. He hated to get up in the morning but still more to go to bed, and he did his best to avoid washing his hands before he came to dinner. Lydgate, in fact, was in all respects a normal English small boy and it seems probable that Geoffrey Chaucer was not unlike him.

When the time came for him to choose a career, John Chaucer evidently made no attempt to force his son into the wine business. There was none of the family strife that had made Boccaccio's youth so unhappy some thirty years earlier, with young Giovanni passionately resisting every effort his father made to turn him into a business man. Perhaps the English vintner was a wiser man than the Florentine banker, or perhaps there was something about Geoffrey Chaucer which convinced his father that he was destined for greater things than the wine trade.

It is clear that John Chaucer must have had connections with the Court, through his journey with the King to Flanders, his association with the King's Butler, or his connection by marriage with the Northwells. For the first document that exists in connection with Geoffrey Chaucer is dated 1357 and shows him as a page in the household of Elizabeth de Burgh, Countess of Ulster and daughter-in-law of the King.

CHAPTER III

LIZABETH DE BURGH was a granddaughter of the Earl of Lancaster, under whose leadership Geoffrey Chaucer's father had fought in the rising against Mortimer. Elizabeth's mother, Maud of Lancaster, had married the great Irish Earl of Ulster, and when he was murdered a short time later she took ship for England with the one small daughter who was heir to all his vast estates. Maud married again, and her daughter Elizabeth had the good fortune to be brought up by that even-tempered, pleasant-faced, hard-working Flemish woman, Philippa of Hainault, Queen of England.

Queen Philippa had a large family of her own, five sons and four daughters apart from those who died in infancy. Elizabeth was two years younger than Edward, Prince of Wales, and about the same age as the next child, Isabelle, a self-willed pair of young Plantagenets who were allowed to do as they pleased. The next in line was Lionel, six years Elizabeth's junior, and it was to Lionel that Elizabeth was betrothed when she was ten years old, marrying him a short time later.[1]

The marriage was the first example of Edward's sensible policy of marrying off his numerous sons to landed heiresses. In this way he strengthened the royal economic and political position, since land was wealth and power both under the feudal system. Elizabeth was the most valuable matrimonial article in England at the time since she inherited from her murdered father the great estates of Ulster and Connaught, constituting nearly a third of all Ireland. In addition she inherited in 1360 the great lordship of Clare with the death of her father's mother, the delightful Countess of Clare after whom she was named.[2]

[1] This was a comparatively late age for a medieval heiress to marry under the feudal system. Elizabeth's half-sister was married twice before she was twelve.

[2] Elizabeth's grandmother was a very great lady, thrice widowed before she was twenty-nine and after that something of a recluse. She was a famous patron of education and the

Young Prince Lionel, who first became Earl of Ulster and then Duke of Clarence through his wife's inheritances, was not the most intelligent of King Edward's children. But he was a boy of great charm of manner, strong, very tall, and noticeably handsome even for a Plantagenet.

Lionel was the only one of the King's sons to be married at this time, and he and Elizabeth kept a miniature court of their own. The Countess of Ulster had her private income and kept her private accounts separately from her husband in the same way that the Queen of England did, and the Earl and the Countess rotated their residences in the way that was universally characteristic of medieval royalty. They moved about from manor to manor with all their household following and a string of baggage carts creaking patiently in the rear. These carts would be piled high with beds, hangings, floor coverings, silver, money, jewels, and even furniture and kitchen utensils, for when a medieval noble moved he moved everything.

Elizabeth's household accounts reflect this constant moving about that was a commonplace of great houses, and the year of 1356 is characteristic. In April she was in London. Then she went to Southampton. Then she went to Reading. By September she was in Stratford-le-bow, and her household account includes the charges for having her baby's bed and its furniture freighted from Stratford to Campsey. Elizabeth's mother was a nun at Campsey and Elizabeth was evidently sending the baby to stay with its grandmother while she and her husband went up to Court.

Elizabeth was still in the London area in the spring of 1357, outfitting herself and her household for the Easter festivities and for the great social event of the season, the Feast of St. George at Windsor Castle. It was at this time that she ordered a complete new suit of clothes for her young page.

Geoffrey Chaucer received from the Countess an entire outfit, even down to new shoes and to drink-money for the tailors. His

founder of Clare College at Cambridge. Perhaps her most endearing moment occurred when she petitioned the King to be exempted from a pilgrimage vow because she was forty years old, when she was actually forty-nine.

breeches were parti-colored and consisted of the fashionable combination of black and red. His short jerkin, called a "paltok," was probably made of silk since this was in the spring, and it cost the Countess four shillings, which would be about fifteen dollars in modern money.

The jerkin undoubtedly fitted him very tightly, for the age of buttons had dawned and the court tailors were using the new device to the full. His hose were also supposed to fit very tightly, and if Geoffrey Chaucer was a normal teen-age youngster he would have been gratified to find that he could bend over in his new clothes only with the greatest difficulty. Even the serious-minded Francis Petrarch affected tight shoes in his teens, worried greatly if a breath of wind ruffled the neat set of his locks, and wrapped his hair in curlers at night so that he might be beautiful the following morning.

In May the Countess was obliged to outfit herself and her household for the Feast of Pentecost that was being celebrated at Woodstock, and she bought another article of clothing for her young page. And Chaucer's name appears again in her accounts the following December when he was given two shillings and sixpence "for necessaries at Christmas."

Christmas was a season which all pre-Reformation England approached with the greatest earnestness and excitement. King Edward's expenditure list of masks for Christmas, ranging from lions to elephants and from satyrs to bat-eared men, indicates the youthful nature of the festivities at a period when nearly all children's games were still being played by adults. As in London, everything would be hung with holly and ivy and bay, with a Lord of Misrule to keep the proceedings sufficiently cheerful and foolish; but the feasts and dances and entertainments would have the high glitter and expensive pace of a Plantagenet court and must have seemed a long way from the middle-class London house on Thames Street.

The Earl and Countess spent that particular Christmas at Hatfield, and the Earl's younger brother, John, spent it with them. John was seventeen that year but he traveled with his own retinue, and Elizabeth's accounts include the New Year's gifts she gave his cook and the clerk of his kitchen.

John was at the time Earl of Richmond but he is better known as John of Gaunt. He later grew to be on very friendly terms with Geoffrey Chaucer (in fact, he married the poet's sister-in-law) and it has been suggested that it was in Hatfield at this Christmas season that the two young men first met. Whether this supposition is correct would depend upon how noticeable a boy Geoffrey was and how intimate were his family connections with Court.

Seventeen months later John of Gaunt married Blanche of Lancaster, who was also a granddaughter of the Earl of Lancaster under whose banner Geoffrey Chaucer's father had fought. Like her cousin Elizabeth, Blanche had been brought up by Queen Philippa with whom she always remained on terms of especial intimacy; and if the evidence of two poets can be trusted, Blanche was a lovely lady. *"Gaie, douce . . . simple,"* Jean Froissart calls her, and Geoffrey Chaucer describes her as a bright torch who gave everyone a little of her light and never had less for herself.

John of Gaunt's marriage, like that of his brother Lionel, was based on sound economic principles. Blanche's father, the Duke of Lancaster, was the greatest noble in the kingdom. (He and the Prince of Wales were the only two men to hold dukedoms since the Norman Conquest.) He had no sons, and the whole of his vast Lancastrian estates would eventually pass to his daughters.

John and Lionel were men of not more than average capacity, and the enormous grants of land they ultimately received through their wives gave them more political power than they knew how to handle intelligently. It was because he was Earl of Ulster and Connaught that Lionel spent five years of helpless struggle as Lord Lieutenant of Ireland; and John of Gaunt succeeded in becoming one of the most hated men in England partly because he lacked the mental equipment to support the political responsibility that descended upon him when he finally became Duke of Lancaster.

John of Gaunt married Blanche of Lancaster in the month of May at Reading. The following week the wedding was celebrated in London with a tournament in which the King and his four oldest sons took part disguised as the mayor and aldermen. King Edward was passionately fond of games and he considered fighting the most absorbing game of all.

The King was shortly to have more of it, for the two-year truce that had followed the capture of the French King at the Battle of Poitiers was drawing to an uneasy close. The well-intentioned but not very bright King John had signed a treaty in London in March whose terms had been promptly repudiated by his son, the intelligent young Dauphin, in Paris.

Everyone knew that it was only a matter of time before King Edward would again invade the Continent, still in pursuit of his golden dream of becoming King of France. The royal officials had in fact been collecting ships since the previous December, and in February carpenters and miners were mobilized from the Forest of Dean. In July preparations were so far advanced that all Frenchmen were ordered out of the kingdom, and King Edward went on a round of visits to all the holy places in the kingdom as he had done before the Poitiers campaign, ending with an especially solemn visit to Westminster Abbey.

By the autumn of 1359 the English army was assembled in the walled town of Dover, constituting the greatest single array of fighting power that England had ever seen. Everyone between the ages of twenty and thirty-three had been drafted, although many younger men had enlisted also. In Lionel's division, for instance, there was young Geoffrey Chaucer, ready to follow the excited King Edward into battle as his father before him had done.

It took over a thousand ships to transport the English army to France and they made a gay procession with the banners of the different lords glittering in the sun. The sails were dyed in bright colors, the sides of the ships were carved and painted, and there were minstrels gathered in the forecastle with pipes and trumpets and clarions to take the King's mind off the rough waters of the English Channel. His flagship, the *Philip of Dartmouth*, flew the royal lions of England, rather prematurely quartered with the lilies of France, and every ship bore the cross of St. George who was the patron saint of England.

The King's ship arrived in Calais before sunset and all the rest of the round, brightly colored, heavily laden little boats followed it into the harbor. Calais had been in English hands ever since its capture in the summer of 1347, and without it even a confirmed optimist like King Edward could not have attempted an invasion of the Continent.

It took eight days for the army stores to be unloaded, and five thousand baggage carts to hold them all. There were barrels and sacks and chests filled with everything from meat and flour and spices to bandages and candles and horseshoe nails. There were special additions such as hand mills for grinding corn, portable ovens for baking bread, and boats of boiled leather for the lords to go fishing in when they otherwise lacked entertainment. Never had an army attempted to travel with so many provisions. The baggage train stretched out for nearly six miles and required the services of five hundred workmen with picks and axes to level the road in front of it.

The King had brought his greyhounds along and thirty falconers to take care of his falcons, for it was a literal fact that if he had not been able to hunt and hawk daily his life would almost have ceased to interest him. There was the usual complement of minstrels, the medieval equivalent of an army band, and all was music and glitter and glory as the English wound their way slowly across the unhappy French countryside.

It was because the land had been so ravaged in previous battles that the five thousand baggage carts were a necessity, and to increase the opportunities for forage the army was split into three parts. One was headed by the King, one by the Duke of Lancaster and one by the Prince of Wales. His three younger brothers rode with the Prince, and it was therefore this division that included Geoffrey Chaucer.

The English army had every reason to expect victory. They had ranked as invincible ever since Crécy, when they had put into practice the military tactics learned in the wars against the Scots and the startled chivalry of France had crumpled before the English bowmen.[3] But the Dauphin was an astute young man and well aware

---

[3] When the crossbow was introduced at the end of the twelfth century, it was condemned by the Church as a weapon unfit for Christian use. Yet it did nothing like the damage achieved by the fourteenth-century longbow at Crécy. In that battle the French lost over fifteen hundred noblemen and the English lost two.

that the French were no match for the English in open warfare.

The French therefore followed the same strategy that had proved so useful to the Scots in the days of John Chaucer's campaigning. They shut themselves up securely in their heavily fortified towns and castles and abandoned the open countryside for the baffled English to wander about in as they chose.

To complete the resemblance to the Scottish campaign it began to rain. It rained by day and it rained by night and it rained without ceasing, turning the roads to rivers. Late autumn was not the best season in which to inaugurate so elaborate a campaign, but King Edward had no reason to expect the torrents that handicapped his magnificent army.

In December the three divisions managed to meet at Reims. Reims was a holy city, for in the dove-shaped reliquary behind the abbey altar was the sacred oil that had anointed the head of each king of France since the days of Clovis. If the English claimant to the French crown could conquer Reims he would be in a stronger moral position in regard to the conquest of the rest of the kingdom.

Reims had been fortifying itself for two years in expectation of a siege, and its citizens had leveled castles and abbeys for miles around so that they could not be used by the English. The English were obliged to settle around it in a manner highly reminiscent of the way they had earlier surrounded the Scots on their mountain. The nobles were fairly comfortable, having commandeered all the neighboring villages for living quarters, but the bulk of the dripping army was not. Food ran short in the familiar way and the neighboring countryside had been plundered so repeatedly that foraging parties had to be sent as much as forty miles away.

Among the besieged citizens of Reims were two distinguished poets to match the future poet on the opposite side. The canon of Reims was Guillaume de Machaut, now an old man of about sixty-five and the most honored and influential poet in France in the fourteenth century. Among the armed defenders was his disciple, a black-haired, snub-nosed young man named Eustache Deschamps who ultimately became the most prolific versifier of the century. Deschamps was one of the most chattily autobiographical of men and left a great deal on record about his life and his feelings. It is a

46

pity that Chaucer, whose career parallels his so closely, was not occasionally willing to be a little autobiographical also. Any reader would gladly trade all of Deschamps' frank self-revelations for a single personal item from the pen of the young soldier opposing him.

By January King Edward knew that the siege was hopeless, and he raised it on St. Hilary's Day. He marched through Burgundy and the Duke of Burgundy paid him two hundred thousand florins to be allowed the privilege of remaining neutral.

Geoffrey Chaucer was captured by the French either during the siege of Reims or during this march through Burgundy. Fortunately for English literature, very few soldiers died in battle in the Middle Ages; the popular institution of ransom made a living soldier more useful to the enemy than a dead one.

Ransoming was a well-developed business, often transacted through an agent, and it was as important a part of the life of a professional soldier as account books were of a merchant's. The reason a feudal lord could afford to finance so many retainers and pay the freight charges on their equipment was that his contract gave him a percentage of the profits—usually one third—on every prisoner captured. Jean Froissart, who could be as realistic about the more prosaic details of medieval warfare as he was enthralled by its glamour, never omits to note in his chronicle when a battle or skirmish proved to be an unusually good financial investment; and the custom went to such lengths in the next fifty years that one knight openly bought up captured prisoners as a business speculation.

The Keeper of the King's Wardrobe paid sixteen pounds on the first of March to have Geoffrey Chaucer ransomed. This would be about twelve hundred dollars in modern money, not quite as much as the King paid for Sir Robert de Clynton's war horse. On the other hand, it is probable that Lionel contributed something towards the ransom also as Chaucer was still in his employ.

Leaving Burgundy, the King moved on to Paris. The Paris citizens promptly retired within their walls and were unaffected by a royal offer, delivered through the Duke of Lancaster, to give them fair battle outside. The Duke's heart was not in the offer, for he

47

was an intelligent general and anxious to abandon what was obviously a profitless campaign.

The weather struck a final blow for the French on the famous Black Monday of which the chroniclers speak with such awe. It occurred on the thirteenth of April when a violent storm struck without warning, accompanied by lightning and hail and so sudden a drop in the temperature that men died as they sat on their horses. The King of England took this as a sign that Heaven, and specifically Our Lady of Chartres, was not pleased with him, and he promised on his knees to sign a just peace.

A temporary agreement was made at Brétigny, giving Aquitaine to the English and imposing a ransom of three million gold crowns for the return of King John. Then a truce was arranged for the summer months during which the final details of their treaty could be drawn up. These matters were ostensibly handled by the Prince of Wales and the Dauphin, since King Edward could negotiate with no one below his own rank, but most of the actual work was done by the little group of court officials who were sufficiently well trained to find their way about in each other's complex legal terminology.

Chaucer had his first experience in diplomatic work that summer. The drawing-up of the treaty required a great deal of paper work and much arguing back and forth across the Channel, and in the course of the negotiations Chaucer was sent to Calais to carry letters to England and to return with the answer. The payment of nine shillings he received for his services is duly entered in Lionel's expense account.

It took sixteen baggage carts to get the captive King John from London to Dover, for his had been a very comfortable exile. Then he stayed in Calais until his impoverished kingdom finally succeeded in making a down-payment of six hundred thousand gold crowns. This was achieved by selling a princess of France to an upstart Italian family, the Visconti, who were willing to pay high to acquire royal blood in the family. Eustache Deschamps, the young poet of Reims, accompanied the princess to Lombardy, following much the same route that Geoffrey Chaucer took to the court of the Visconti some years later.

King Edward and his four oldest sons arrived in Calais in October to celebrate the treaty with France, and under a flood of ratifications and letters promissory and letters confirmatory and notarial attestations, the Treaty of Calais was finally drawn.

On its surface, the treaty was a great triumph for the English. They emerged as lords of Aquitaine and with a cash indemnity that was ten times the annual revenue of the English crown. France was so ravaged she was willing to offer anything in return for peace, and when Petrarch arrived from Italy to congratulate King John on his release he was horrified at the desolation that had spread over a once flourishing land.

Yet it was not without reason that John of Gaunt later referred to the Dauphin, in tones of deep contempt, as a lawyer. The future King of France was no gallant knight of chivalry and in fact he never fought a battle in his life. But in the flood of complicated documents that collected about the Peace of Calais, he and his advisers managed to include a slight technicality which enabled him to break the treaty nine years later. The English succeeded in collecting only a third of the ransom money and it was not long before they had lost Aquitaine.

Geoffrey Chaucer's first experience in bearing arms, like that of his father, was not on the whole an unqualified success.

CHAPTER IV

ING EDWARD was at the height of his prestige and his popularity following the Peace of Calais. He and the Prince of Wales between them, both enjoying the task thoroughly, had brought English military power on land and sea to so respected a level that the small backward island was now considered one of the major kingdoms in Christendom.

Edward was still a fairly young man in spite of his grown sons and daughters, and in some ways he was a man who never grew up. He was boy-like in his love of games and was quite willing to spend his restless energy in dancing and hunting and tournaments when political considerations made it impossible for him to go and hit Frenchmen over the head with his seven-foot sword. He was boy-like also in his erratic financial methods and in the carefree way he would slide around a political problem and leave the future to take care of itself. He had the Plantagenet love of display and his clothes were a glory of gold tissue and pearl embroidery, while his household plate and bed furniture were painted and carved with the various mottoes and insignia that showed his deep interest in chivalry.

King Edward was in fact the perfect chivalric knight, and like his oldest son he fitted almost by instinct into the chivalric mold that the feudal ages had laboriously shaped for themselves. He was a gallant warrior, a lavish spender, an uncritical son of the Church, and a gentleman who knew all the little niceties of the social code. It was for these qualities that the chroniclers praise him and they never mention, for instance, how much his political affiliations with the Flemings benefited the English wool industry. Neither King Edward nor the chroniclers were interested in such things. It was much more important that the King of England was a recognized leader in that little international set of gentlemen who upheld the tenets and the obligations of chivalry.

The social set was still international, and in contrast to the growing nationalism of England as a whole the English and French nobility were still brothers. When circumstances did not permit them the pleasure of meeting on the battlefield they met each other in tournaments or rode off side by side to war against the heathen. They had the same code, the same manners and the same speech, and King John had been much happier in London than when he returned to Paris and his unsympathetic and unchivalric son. The King of France shortly found an excuse to return to England as a hostage again and spent the rest of his life in the captivity he so enjoyed, visiting back and forth with King Edward and Queen Philippa, going hunting with them, and mourned by them sincerely when he died.

The chivalric system was one of the many tight, neat patterns which the Middle Ages had imposed upon itself, and the fourteenth century saw its dissolution beginning. It was based economically on military service in return for land, and movable business capital was now becoming as important as land tenure. In any case the medieval knight in his layers of quilting and chain mail and plate was becoming increasingly useless in a century that saw not only the effective military use of the longbow but the manufacture of gunpowder.

As the institution became more useless it became increasingly intricate and ornamental, in the same way that armor became more and more ornate as its reason for existence began to pass away. It became surrounded by complex rites and observances which had lost much of their meaning but which nevertheless gave everyone great satisfaction.

King Edward played the game of chivalry with especial enthusiasm. He had early conceived himself to be a reincarnation of King Arthur, that semi-legendary individual who had suddenly blossomed out in the twelfth century as an epitome of every civilized and chivalric virtue that a king could have.[1] King Edward even

[1] The original glorification of King Arthur was the work of a twelfth-century historian named Geoffrey of Monmouth, who was also responsible for the conviction of Englishmen that they were descended from the heroes of Troy. Geoffrey's ingenious mixture of fact, legend and imagination was an instant hit, and although some of his contemporaries

51

built himself a Round Table, although his one permanent success in that line was his Order of the Garter, which was not only a military club but a social success as well. The Order of the Garter was very exclusive, consisting of twenty-six members headed by the King, the Prince of Wales and the Duke of Lancaster. Several women in high places at court also wore the blue robes of the Garter, for even the feudal system did not entirely succeed in keeping women out of the organizations of men, and the annual Feast of St. George at Windsor was one of the major social events of the season. St. George was one of the four patrons of the Order; the other three, as solemnly listed by King Edward himself, were his royal ancestor Edward the Confessor, the blessed Virgin and the Holy Trinity. The Order could hardly have failed to flourish with such a list of patrons, and at the time of the Peace of Calais it was one of the most influential and respected in Christendom.

Among the admirers of King Edward and his court there was none more ardent than a young poet named Jean Froissart. He arrived in England shortly after the Peace of Calais to pay his respects to Queen Philippa, for he was a fellow countryman of hers and had been born in her native town of Valenciennes. He brought as his literary credentials a long historical poem he had composed on the Battle of Poitiers, and Queen Philippa was sufficiently pleased with it to take the twenty-four-year-old poet into her household as her secretary.

Froissart thought of himself as a love poet and wrote throughout his life pretty verses full of nightingales and roses. But his real desire was to write a prose history of chivalry, and the kindly Queen of England went out of her way to help him fulfil his ambition. She not only put him on a permanent salary but she gave him extended leaves of absence from time to time so that he could travel over England and the Continent and meet at first hand the warriors who had participated in the events he longed to describe. In return Froissart openly adored "the most courteous, noble and lib-

---

called him a liar he was gospel by the fourteenth century. His glorification of Arthur was seized upon by French poets and storytellers and for two centuries Arthur's prestige as the perfect hero of chivalry had been increasing.

eral queen that ever reigned in her time" and worked in excited devotion on his *Chronicles*.

Froissart said of his book, after it had occupied his attention for thirty-seven years, "The more I labor at it, the more it delights me"; and posterity has echoed Froissart's engaging estimate of his masterpiece. It is fundamentally one long hymn of joy at having been born in so wonderful a period, and both Froissart's love of color and his passion for detail (typically Flemish qualities, both of them) found an ideal outlet in describing the chivalric exploits that to him made up the whole of history. Yet even Froissart sometimes joined in the social criticism that was so characteristic a part of the writing of his day and sided with the unhappy commoners, particularly of France, whose lives meant so little to the gallant knights who rode over their fields.

The year after Jean Froissart came to England, the King of England had his Jubilee. It celebrated both his fiftieth birthday and a happy and prosperous reign. Debts were forgiven, prisoners loosed, and in a fine spirit of nationalism it was decreed that all future pleas in the law courts should be written in English or Latin instead of in French.

During the Jubilee John of Gaunt knelt before his father to be crowned with the fur cap and the circlet of gold and pearls that made him Duke of Lancaster. The Good Duke had died the previous year, universally and sincerely mourned, and when his elder daughter returned to England for her share of the vast Lancastrian estates she died of the same plague that had killed her father. This left his younger daughter Blanche the sole heir and Blanche's husband became the new Duke of Lancaster.

All this was the more gratifying to King Edward in that his eldest son had just made a singularly unfortunate marriage. Edward had never been able to fit the self-willed Prince of Wales into the economic plans he had made for his sons, since policy did not exist for the prince when it came to a matter of his own emotions. He delayed marrying until he had reached the incredible age of thirty-one and then suddenly decided to marry a woman who could hardly have been more unsuitable. Joan of Kent was two years older than the Prince of Wales, twice-married and a divorcée, and while she had been brought up by Queen Philippa her tumultuous career in no way resembled those of her two sisters-in-law. She was the most beautiful woman in England still, and, as Froissart says, the most *"amoureuse."* The Prince of Wales married her only nine months after her second husband was buried and the union required a special papal dispensation since the Prince was godfather to Joan's four-year-old son. There was first a private wedding and then a public one which King Edward attended, but it is doubtful if he ever grew reconciled to the match. It is only fair to say in Joan's favor that she was a charming woman and that later she became a potent influence for good in the kingdom; but from the economic and political point of view the Prince of Wales could hardly have made a more unsatisfactory match.

His brother Lionel was meanwhile in Ireland, struggling with the problems he had acquired by obediently marrying the heiress of Ulster and Connaught. The Irish were known to wear neither boots nor breeches and were popularly supposed to be cannibals, and Lionel was wholly unsuited to be their Lord Lieutenant. The chief memorial to his efforts was the notorious Statute of Kilkenny, whose aim was to keep the Irish from polluting the civilized English as far as possible and not only prohibited intermarriage but even the Irish game of quoits.

The year after the Jubilee Lionel lost his wife. The Queen took Elizabeth's eight-year-old daughter under her own protection, and Lionel was not left for long in the profitless state of being a widower. This time his marriage was an openly commercial transaction. The Visconti family, having already bought a French princess, were now ready to bid for an English prince. They offered in exchange two cities of Lombardy and two hundred thousand gold florins, the purchase money being known technically as the bride's dowry. The Pope, who had cause to dislike the Visconti brothers, fought hard against the match, pointing out that their social standing was too inferior to mate with English royalty. But the King and his Council pointed out in turn that there were several English princes to be married off and that as far as the question of birth went the Visconti family was very wealthy. Thus did the gentlemen of Christendom concern themselves less with gentility than with finances when a choice had to be made between the two.

Lionel journeyed to his wedding in Lombardy with a large retinue which included the enraptured Froissart. Literature was further represented at the elaborate festivities by the sixty-four-year-old Petrarch, who was at that time the intellectual leader of Europe and a close friend of the Visconti brothers. The feastings and celebrations stretched out five months through the hot Italian summer, and when Lionel died in Milan in October his death was probably caused, not by poison as his outraged friends insisted, but by a longer bout of eating and drinking than even a Plantagenet could endure. His widow married again and her new husband was promptly slain by an hostler in the mountains of Parma.

It used to be conjectured that Chaucer also went to Italy in Lionel's retinue and that he may have met Petrarch during the wedding festivities. There seems to be an irresistible desire to arrange for the meeting of literary men who happen to be born in the same century and later become giants to posterity, but this particular conjecture has since been proved wrong.

There is documentary proof that Geoffrey Chaucer was still in London when Lionel went on his wedding trip in May. In July of the same year Chaucer went to the Continent, with two horses and an allowance of £10 for traveling expenses, but there is nothing to indicate that he crossed the Alps or that his journey had anything to do with Prince Lionel.

It is much more likely that Chaucer went abroad on a mission for King Edward since he was now in the King's service. In 1360 he had been in Lionel's service, carrying letters relative to the Peace of Calais between England and France, but by 1367 he had evidently been in the King's service for some time; for in June he was given a pension by King Edward of twenty marks each year for life. The following year, that of Lionel's wedding, he was issued Christmas robes as one of the King's esquires. These robes were issued to everyone in the King's employ, from his judges to his carpenters, and constituted a twice-yearly gift that arrived as regularly as their salaries. The presence of Chaucer's name on the list shows him to have been an accredited member of the King's household.

55

Chaucer was a king's esquire and he was listed as a *valettus*, or valet of the chamber. Two centuries earlier this would have meant he was one of the attendants who served the king in his bedchamber just as the keeper of the wardrobe would have meant the individual who cared for the king's personal wardrobe and jewels. But all this had changed by the fourteenth century under the rapid expansion of the central government.

What had once been the king's personal household was developing by the fourteenth century into the administrative end of the English government. The Great Hall at Westminster, which had once been the king's living room, was now the law court for Common Pleas, the King's Bench and Chancery, with shops and booths lining its crowded walls. The wardrobe had divided itself in two and operated as separate units; the great wardrobe was for maintenance and storage, including as a subdivision a factory and repair shop for armaments in the Tower, and the central wardrobe was an accounting and administrative department whose staff of clerks had a permanent office at Westminster over the Great Hall.

In the same way that the king's living room had become a law court and the king's wardrobe had become a supply depot, a king's *valettus* had lost his original function as valet of the chamber and was turning into a governmental agent. Chaucer and his fellow esquires were in a general way the medieval equivalent of the modern civil service, performing a good many of its diplomatic functions as well as lesser errands throughout England and abroad. An esquire might be sent about the country as a purchasing agent, to act as a custodian of horses, or to borrow or convey money, and especially he would be used on foreign diplomatic missions. No permanent resident embassies of any kind were established until the following century, and all the work that was later performed by embassies had to be done by government envoys sent especially for the purpose.

For a position of this kind Chaucer probably needed a more advanced education than he could have received in a London grammar school, and it is possible that during the seven years for which there is no documentary information he spent some of the time finishing his education. The inference is plausible, but exactly where he went to school will have to remain a matter of conjecture.

If Geoffrey Chaucer had been born fifty years earlier and was contemplating a career in the royal service, he would have gone as a matter of course to either Oxford or Cambridge and then into holy orders. The Church was the one great door through which all educated men were expected to pass into professional life. Even by the middle of the century most of the officials in Edward's court, both in major and minor positions, were still churchmen. But this situation, like so many others, was changing rapidly in the fourteenth century and Chaucer himself is an outstanding example of a phenomenon that would have been inconceivable a century earlier: a lay official.

It is possible, as a great scholar of the English administrative system has insisted, that Chaucer was educated at Westminster, going through some kind of an apprenticeship in the royal household under a senior officer in the civil service. On the other hand, this sort of education seems to have been given primarily to men who were going to work in the permanent offices of the government in Westminster and London, since it consisted of learning the technique of governmental procedure and how to make out official forms.

It seems more likely on the whole that Geoffrey Chaucer received the one kind of education available in medieval England that was neither ecclesiastical nor bureaucratic and that he went, for a time at least, to one of the law schools of Holborn.

The fourteenth-century records for the Holborn law schools are lost, but it is known from the records of Lincoln's Inn for the following century that king's esquires were frequently admitted for study, although they were not bound by all the rules that applied to regular students. The Inns of Court and the Inns of Chancery in Holborn were not in any case used exclusively by men training for the legal profession; the sons of county landowners were frequently enrolled in the courses by their fathers to equip them to be men of affairs.

The possibility that Chaucer received part of his education at Holborn is strengthened by a note in Speght's biography of the poet in 1598. Speght reports that a Master Buckley had noticed in the records of the Inner Temple that "Geoffrey Chaucer was fined two shillings for beating a Fransciscane fryer in Fleetstreete." William Buckley was the custodian of the records of the Inner Temple in Speght's day and it seems likely that he knew what he was talking about. The offense for which Chaucer was fined the regulation two shillings was a not infrequent one in a day when both the Franciscans and the Dominicans were as powerful as they were disliked. A once noble evangelical movement had gone down into corruption, and if the friar in Fleet Street was anything like the fat, outrageous Huberd who rode with the Canterbury Pilgrims a beating was undoubtedly what he deserved.

The legal Inns were voluntary organizations along much the same lines as the city guilds, except that they were not under the jurisdiction of the City of London but under that of the chief law officers of the Crown. The Inns supplied room and board and a legal training that was chiefly oral, with public readings and debates delivered in the hall before the assembled students. French was the correct legal language in spite of the King's Jubilee statute, but already English and French were growing thoroughly mixed in ordinary legal procedure.

Holborn was one of the most congested suburbs of the city of London and almost certainly the dirtiest. The shore of the Fleet was crowded with various manufacturers, like the tanners, that had been exiled from the city itself; and the river was deep enough for deliveries of heavy freight like coal and lime to be made as far up as Fleet Street, which stretched its crowded length at right angles to the polluted water. There was none of the rural peace that greeted the ecclesiastical students of Oxford and Cambridge; but Holborn turned out competent lawyers and men of affairs, and a future diplomat and justice of the peace like Geoffrey Chaucer would have found the education it offered very useful.

At any rate, Chaucer received his education somewhere, for by 1368 he was equipped to take his place as a servant of the Crown and to do his part in the expanding administrative system that was gradually changing a royal feudal court into a modern government.

Chaucer's career was similar to that of most of his fellow esquires. Like him they came of middle class stock and had entered the royal service either through connections their fathers had with court or through some previous service of their own with one of the King's sons.

The wages of an esquire averaged sevenpence halfpenny a day. This would be about eight hundred dollars a year in modern money and was supplemented by annuities (such as the twenty marks given Chaucer) and by gifts of land and salaried positions. In addition the king's esquires were given board and room as long as they were in the royal household, and grants twice a year of summer and winter clothing.

A king's esquire usually married either the daughter of a country gentleman or one of the well-born young ladies who served the Queen as the demoiselles of her chamber. In King Edward's court at least a dozen of these young ladies married esquires, and among those honored was Geoffrey Chaucer.

His wife's name was Philippa and she had perhaps been named after the Queen; for her father was a Flemish knight of Hainault, that last outpost of feudal chivalry in the great industrialized areas of Flanders. His name was Sir Gilles de Roet and he had served both the daughters of the Count of Hainault, first as an official in the court of Marguerite, Empress of Germany, and then as an official in the court of her sister Philippa, Queen of England. As a countryman of the Queen, like Jean Froissart, he enjoyed her special favor, and as far as the somewhat inadequate records show he was a man of some importance.

Sir Gilles de Roet had a second daughter whose name was Katherine. She was married to an English knight named Sir Hugh Swynford but the reason she was famous in her own day and achieved space in all the chronicles of the period was because she became the one great love in the life of John of Gaunt. Katherine was a beautiful woman (at least she is so described on Gaunt's tomb) but it could hardly have been her beauty alone that held the Duke of Lancaster so securely to her side. He was not free to marry her until he was fifty-six and she ten years younger; and no event more shocked the upper-class ladies of England and France tha.1 the marriage whereby Chaucer's sister-in-law became second only to the Queen.

It used to be the custom to speak of John of Gaunt as Chaucer's patron, but this he was not. In the strict sense of the word Chaucer never had a patron. He was a hard-working public official and fully earned the perquisites he received. But John of Gaunt was not even his employer. It was Chaucer's wife, not Chaucer, who was employed by the Duke and stayed at his palace of the Savoy and received the expensive New Year's gifts. In the small grants that Chaucer received from the Duke of Lancaster his name is usually linked with that of his wife, and Chaucer's position in regard to John of Gaunt seems to have been merely that of the brother-in-law of the woman the Duke loved.

The one link that connects Chaucer with the patronage of John of Gaunt was the fact that he wrote a poem commemorating the death of the Duke's first wife, the Duchess Blanche. There is no evidence, however, either in the poem or elsewhere, that the Duke asked Chaucer to write *The Book of the Duchess*. It is at least equally possible that Chaucer loved and admired Blanche, as Froissart did, and wrote the poem out of affection rather than to order.[2]

The exact date on which Geoffrey Chaucer married Philippa Roet is not known. The first document that speaks of them as married is the joint pension that John of Gaunt conferred upon them in 1374. By that time Geoffrey and Philippa were living together in their own establishment in London and Philippa was no longer employed at court. As long as she had an official position of her own, first in attendance upon the Queen of England and then in attendance upon the second Duchess of Lancaster at the Savoy, Philippa Chaucer received payments under her maiden name. Neither the royal nor the Lancastrian expenditure accounts made any effort to discriminate between the single and the married state

[2] It was an age in which even the most independent of poets was usually obliged to address his works to some sort of patron to obtain a hearing; yet there is no hint of such a thing in Chaucer's work. Only two of his writings contain a serious dedication—one to a ten-year-old boy and the other to two friends of his in London.

of the various ladies to whom payments are recorded and no date can therefore be set for Philippa's marriage except that it was before 1374.

There used to be a certain amount of speculation concerning the marriage and the conclusion was reached that it was an unhappy one. Of this there is no evidence. There are no personal papers of Chaucer's extant, and his poetry, unlike that of Deschamps, never deals with his private life and emotions.

What brought Chaucer's readers to this conclusion was a misunderstanding of medieval literature. One of the most popular subjects for poetry in the Middle Ages was the medieval equivalent of the mother-in-law joke, the joke of the dominant wife; and it is difficult to find any fourteenth-century poet, even the somewhat solemn author of *Piers Plowman*, who does not indulge in it in one form or another. It was a literary fashion to insult the institution of marriage and it had nothing to do with the personal lives of the poets themselves.

This can be illustrated in the case of a writer like Eustache Deschamps. Deschamps indulges in the most violent attacks upon the subject of marriage, and it is almost impossible to read his scurrilous invectives without becoming convinced that his own marriage was deeply unhappy. Yet, on the contrary, Deschamps' marriage was a very happy one and he did not hesitate to say so. There is one very attractive ballade to his wife in which he expresses gratitude for her hard work, pliant disposition and sweet temper, and when his daughter married he advised her to try and model herself upon the perfections of her mother.

Deschamps, like Chaucer, was merely following one of the most deep-rooted of medieval literary conventions when he wrote against women and against marriage, and the fact that he followed this convention more violently and more extravagantly than Chaucer did merely means that he lacked Chaucer's instinctive good manners as a writer.

In any case it is useless to search in Chaucer's poetry for clues to his private life. He was one of the most impersonal of poets and it is almost impossible to find him speaking for himself. It is a loquacious eagle speaking or a wifely hen or a fat cloth-maker from the suburbs of Bath, and it is obviously impossible to recon-struct Chaucer's personal life from such diverse elements as these.

Yet if one more guess may be hazarded in a field in which too much guessing has been done already, it might be suggested that Chaucer's attitude towards marriage was not dissimilar to his at-titude towards the Church. Both were institutions so fundamen-tally safe and impregnable that any number of minor, disrespectful jokes might be indulged in about them. It is worth remembering that Chaucer insulted himself in his poetry with equal freedom—according to his persistent account he was a tubby man and not at all bright—and Chaucer respected himself and his art as deeply as he respected the Church and as he respected marriage. He could be reverent enough when he chose and if the spirit of the occasion seemed to warrant it. But he resembled his beloved Ovid in that reverence was not one of the more consistent aspects of his art.

CHAPTER V

IT WOULD be pleasant to know when Geoffrey Chaucer first began to think of himself as a poet. Perhaps he began writing as early as Boccaccio, who was scribbling what he calls "little inventions, slight as they may have been" when he was seven years old. Or perhaps Geoffrey Chaucer flowered late. At any rate there must have been some moment when his love of reading and his reverence for the art of poetry suddenly fused with something in his own spirit and the young Englishman became a "maker." [1]

When John Chaucer sent his son Geoffrey to court he had no reason to expect that a poet would be the result of a long line of wine dealers, and yet under the circumstances he could hardly have chosen a better career for his son.

It was not possible at that period to make a living out of writing poetry. The nearest anyone came to it was John Lydgate, who not only accepted poetical commissions from any members of the nobility who would give them but wrote verses for corporations or for private citizens who wished to decorate the walls of their parlors with them. Yet even Lydgate had the bare necessities of living provided for him, for he was a monk at Bury and therefore automatically assured of room and board in the monastery.

If a man wished to write, the obvious solution was to take holy orders. Francis Petrarch did this, and Jean Froissart, and Guillaume de Machaut, holding minor positions in the church that gave them an income so that they could go on with their writing.

Even this device did not remove the necessity for soliciting patronage, and a patron was not always an unmixed blessing to a writer. When Queen Philippa of England died, Froissart found a French patron and the shift of tone in his book of chronicles is unmistakable. Perhaps Froissart himself did not notice this, for he insisted that his history went "straight forward, without coloring

---

[1] Chaucer kept the great words of "poet" and "poetry" for the classics and for Dante. He himself and his contemporaries were "makers."

one side more than another," but in spite of all Froissart's good intentions he could not help being influenced by the man who paid him.

Such a state of affairs would have been insupportable to Geoffrey Chaucer, and he was fortunate in being able to earn his own living with no help from anyone. Even the most enlightened of patrons could not have kept up with Chaucer's extraordinary literary development and it might have resulted in injury to his work if he had been obliged to ask a medieval nobleman to finance him.

The one disadvantage of Chaucer's career as a civil servant was that it naturally did not give him much time for writing. But to balance this he had not only financial independence but also an opportunity to meet all sorts and conditions of people. Chaucer had his share of office work as Comptroller of the Customs and as Clerk of the Works, but even in these positions he was in contact with a great variety of human beings, from wool merchants to masons and from highway robbers to shipmen. He was in close contact throughout the whole of his career with the brilliant international courts of two kings, and his work as a diplomat brought him in contact not only with the culture of France but with the new poetry that was flowering on the other side of the Alps. If Chaucer's career as a civil servant had done nothing more than send him to Italy, it would have been worth it to him.[2]

This is not to say that it was Chaucer's career as a king's esquire that made him a great poet. His French contemporary, Eustache Deschamps, had exactly the same advantages, held the same sort of positions, knew the same people, lived in the same sort of environment, traveled in the same places, and came from the same middle-class stock. Yet when Deschamps went to Italy, for instance, he returned unaffected and went on writing the same interminable ballades he had been producing before. For Deschamps was not Chaucer.

[2] Chaucer's career was in striking contrast to another English poet who held a government post. This was Thomas Hoccleve, a devoted admirer of his, who found himself stuck in a minor clerical position in the Office of the Privy Seal. Hoccleve spent his career surrounded by red wax and parchment and was not even supposed to talk at his work.

It is curious how many surface literary qualities the two men had in common. Both were good at metrics and knew how to handle the tools of their trade. Both introduced new words into the vocabulary. Both had a well-developed sense of humor. Both were deeply interested in the life about them and had a quick and vivid sense of detail. Both were expert in the fashionable, contemporary verse forms, ballade and roundel and virelay. Both admired and imitated the prominent French master, Guillaume de Machaut. Both alternated between the stylized, romantic treatment of love then in fashion and a realistic treatment verging on bawdry. Both, moreover, started at precisely the same place in their poetic development. But Chaucer grew into a major poet and Deschamps remained a clever journalist, spending a lifetime of scribbling that thoroughly justifies his own rueful admission, "I talk too much."

Chaucer began his literary career at the same point as Deschamps because there was in literal truth nowhere else for him to begin it. The only modern poetry he could find to read was French and belonged to the fashionable court type. If he read it with more ardor and imitated it more closely that its pallid qualities justified, at least he learned the technical tools of his trade by apprenticing himself to a writer like Machaut. Nearly every great poet works with a borrowed technique until he finds one of his own, and Chaucer could have found worse masters than the courtly poets of France.

Apart from the French, there was almost no modern poetry available to him. Latin was becoming the language of the schoolroom, the Church and the classics, and as a medium for contemporary writing its prestige was beginning to fade. Italian was probably still unknown to Chaucer and in any case it is doubtful if there was a manuscript of Dante or of Petrarch available to him.

As for English, there was almost nothing in that unfashionable and unpoetic language which could be expected to attract an eager young writer at the court of Edward the Third. The few books he saw in his native language were almost certainly romances, translated out of their original French half a century after they had been written.[3] These handsomely illuminated volumes supplied the upper classes and the wealthier tradesmen with the kind of popular fiction that could be read in the garden in summer and in groups around the fire in winter, bringing into their prosaic everyday lives the glamor of Thebes or Troy and the chivalric magic of King Arthur's knights.

There was one contemporary movement in native English verse, a movement that had originality, vitality and poetic force. But it was not being written in the South Midlands dialect which Chaucer knew as English and he would have had difficulty in reading any examples of it. As a matter of fact, even if Chaucer had been able to read *Piers Plowman* or *The Pearl* it is doubtful if they would have attracted him. They constituted a final attempt to bring back into poetic use the old-fashioned alliterative verse of the Saxons—an effort, as it were, to assume that for literary purposes the Norman Conquest had not occurred at all. Excellent as was some of the work done in this style, the movement was an essentially abortive attempt to reproduce and perpetuate an antique way of writing whose reason for existence had vanished; and Chaucer's Parson was perhaps right when he disrespectfully referred to the alliterative school of the North as "rum, ram, ruf." Even if Chaucer's whole outlook, both through his schooling and his environment, had not been French, there was very little to interest him in contemporary English poetry.

What the French were able to give an ardent young poet was little enough. The great lyric inheritance which a modern English or French poet accepts as a matter of course was then nonexistent. To put a modern young writer in Chaucer's place it would be necessary to isolate him with a copy of minor eighteenth-century verse in his possession.

The comparison with eighteenth-century technique is not as improbable as it sounds. When Chaucer was a young man the literary ideals were elegance and correctness, a deep interest in suitable methods of expression and an utter indifference as to the vacuity

[3] A romance, in its literal meaning, means anything written in one of the Romance languages.

of the contents, an implicit obedience to a host of rules and the less originality the better.

These ideals are well illustrated in the literary textbooks that were current when Chaucer was a young man. Most of them had been written in the previous century, but their rules were still followed with reverence.

The textbook which particularly impressed Chaucer was the *New Poetry* of Geoffrey de Vinsauf. Later on, when Chaucer was writing *The Canterbury Tales,* it was with somewhat ironical courtesy that he referred to Geoffrey de Vinsauf as his "deere maister," but at the beginning of Chaucer's career his respect for him was not ironical, and he studied the long Latin hexameters of his master with reverent earnestness.

The medieval period might well be called the Age of Rules. There were feudal rules, religious rules, social rules, business rules, and there were also literary rules. John Chaucer ran his business under a network of restrictions that would have made a nineteenth-century importer turn pale, and his son Geoffrey entered upon his own trade of poetry under a similar kind of bondage.

It is true that the fourteenth century saw all these rules beginning to be broken, cracking under new forces that proved to be too strong for them. The sons of John Chaucer's business colleagues did not conduct their affairs in quite the way their fathers had done, and Geoffrey Chaucer did not obey the textbooks on rhetoric all his life. But in his youth they seemed to him an excellent guide, and throughout his career their influence can be traced in his work.

Geoffrey de Vinsauf was one of several schoolmasters at the University of Paris who wrote textbooks on rhetoric, and he and his colleagues like Matthew de Vendôme, John de Garland and Evrard l'Allemand laid a heavy, pedagogical hand upon aspiring young writers. The great ideal was conformity, with a surface variation to be achieved by a complex laying-on of technical devices.

None of the advice of the rhetoricians concerned itself with structure, much less with content. The chief aim was to be ornamental, and this was achieved by a long list of mechanical expedients which were classified and sub-classified in a way that would have delighted the heart of a medieval theologian. Geoffrey de Vinsauf divides the subject of Amplification into eight principal sections, headed Repetition, Periphrasis, Comparison, Apostrophe, Prosopopoeia, Digression, Description and Opposition, with Repetition being given two major subdivisions of its own and seven minor ones under that.

There were three kinds of style, High, Low and Middle, and each had the proper ornaments. These ornaments were divided into two kinds, "difficult" and "easy." The "easy" ornaments were known technically as the "colors of rhetoric" and formed an especially complex and subdivided jungle in which Chaucer wandered as fascinated as a small boy at a zoo. There were two main divisions of the colors, with over thirty subdivisions in each, not including seven sub-subdivisions under *expolitio*, for instance, or six under *significatio*.

Geoffrey de Vinsauf supplies an example for each of these, like the good schoolmaster he is; and it was doubtless interesting to young Geoffrey Chaucer to know that Rome weeping over the death of Caesar is an example of prosopopoeia and so is the farewell of the tablecloth to the table. At any rate, the information certainly did not hurt him and he seems to have read with an habitual and excellent sense of proportion that enabled him to take what he could use and to leave the rest. He later came to think of the colors of rhetoric as something rather funny, even when he used them himself. But when his "deere maister" gave him good advice, as he sometimes did, it stayed in Chaucer's excellent memory and reappeared when he needed it.

Nevertheless it was inevitable that Chaucer should outgrow the textbooks on rhetoric, for in spite of their occasional streaks of good sense the main emphasis was on a blind, unvarying obedience to rules.[4] Matthew de Vendôme goes so far as to advise his students to memorize the mechanical models of description he fur-

[4] The medieval rhetoricians did not invent these rules, which they got from the Romans. But they added to them their inimitable gifts for com- plexity and codification, and Quintilian would hardly have recognized his advice when they were through with it.

nishes them, so that they will not be tempted to wander off on personal vagaries; and Matthew's attitude is characteristic. The thirteenth century was in many things tight, strict and legalistic, and never more so than in its theories on writing. At no time was the poet permitted to wander in the misty world of dreams which the Romantic Revival conceived of as belonging to the Middle Ages. It was Addison rather than Coleridge who would have been congenial to the theories of Geoffrey de Vinsauf and the other English, French and German schoolteachers who taught at the Universities of Paris and Orleans.

This was the method whereby a young fourteenth-century poet of the sixties might be expected to write, and a more curious beginning for the author of *The Canterbury Tales* it would be difficult to imagine.

As for the verse forms that were ready for Chaucer to use, here again he entered a world that was small, rigid and full of rules. In the thirteenth century there had been a certain amount of creative experimentation among the poets of France (their heritage, perhaps, from the great twelfth-century renaissance) but the sophisticates of the fourteenth century considered this sort of thing rather careless and old-fashioned. They lavished their attention instead on refining and making still more intricate certain staple verse forms like the ballade, the roundel and the virelay, and the mark of a good poet was not the reach of his spirit but the dexterity of his craftsmanship.

This had been brought about largely through the influence of Guillaume de Machaut, now the elderly canon of Reims but still the most honored poet in France.[5] Machaut was a superb technician and it was his delight to invent innumerable variations for a few fundamental forms and to handle them with almost dazzling proficiency. He was capable of turning out a bewildering array of ballades and *lais* and a kind of short narrative verse known as the *dit*, all polished to a gleaming luster that could not hide a funda-

[5] He was also a musician, one of the best of all the medieval composers, and some of his scores still survive. He wedded his words to his music in a fashion among poets that unhappily went out with Thomas Campion.

mental hollowness in the tone. Machaut once congratulated himself for using a stanza which employed the same rhyming sound at each of its eight lines and for being able to turn out a hundred of these stanzas without the same rhyme sound used twice. To Machaut this was poetry, and it was poetry to admiring disciples of his like Eustache Deschamps and Jean Froissart.

In one way at least Machaut's way of writing proved to be very useful to Geoffrey Chaucer. An intricate verse-form like the ballade must be extremely well done if it is to be done at all. Any amateur touch of strain or any forced inversion for the sake of the rhyme scheme spoils it immediately. It supplies, in other words, an excellent training in technique, and by the time Chaucer could turn out a presentable ballade in the manner of Guillaume de Machaut he had taken the first step in learning to be a writer. Technical proficiency did not make him a poet, any more than mastery over the scales would have made him a musician; but it gave him control of his tools, and as soon as he had found what he wanted to say the tools lay ready to his hand and could be used without fumbling.

One reason for a certain poverty in the prettily shaped verses of poets like Machaut and Froissart was that they had only one subject to write about and on this subject they had nothing new to say. Their theme was love; and love was a subject that the Middle Ages had managed to stylize and reduce to a formula in the same tidy way that everything else in the medieval period was treated.

This was something of an achievement; for love is one of the most personal, unexpected and uncontrollable of emotions and at first glance it would not seem to be susceptible to a set of rules. However, there was only one kind of love which was considered suitable for a poet to write about. This was "courtly love," a stylized game that had begun in Provence in the twelfth century and was ideally suited to a graceful, artificial writer like Machaut.

Whatever relation courtly love may have had to real life, it had an enormous effect on literature. When any poet wrote of love it was this idealistic, chivalric, romantic love that he meant, and Chaucer's work is colored through and through with its strange, bright dyes. Exactly the same note can be found in any Eliza-

70

bethan sonneteer rhyming his mistress's eyebrows, and it can still be found in any popular piece of sheet music rhyming "moon" with "June." This literary tradition is so ancient by now that it seems to be a part of natural living, and it is difficult to realize that it did not exist before the twelfth century.

The reason it failed to come sooner was partly because the Church, which exercised considerable control over letters, disapproved of any manifestation of passion except in connection with religion. But a more important reason, perhaps, was that before the twelfth century romantic love would have lacked an audience. European literature, like European life, was geared to the feudal system, and the men who fitted this system no more wished to be told love stories when they settled down to be entertained in the evenings than a small boy of today would read romantic fiction in his spare time. The small boy will read anything from King Arthur to Superman just so it celebrates masculine feats of strength and daring, and his intellectual prototype, the knight or baron of the earlier Middle Ages, had exactly the same sort of literary tastes. Women did not count and therefore their literary tastes were not represented.

By the twelfth century, however, the golden age of masculinity was passing away. New influences were making themselves felt from the Orient and tastes were beginning to change. Poets became more interested in pleasing wives than in pleasing their husbands, and through one of the most sudden shifts in literary fashion ever to be recorded epics went out and romances came in.

One woman in particular had a great deal to do with the shift. This was Eleanor of Aquitaine, successively Queen of France and Queen of England. She was the granddaughter of the southern troubadour, William of Poitou, and she translated to her northern court the love songs of the lyric south. They became a good deal less Platonic in the process, but their central note of flattery was unchanged.

Woman, according to Eleanor's poets, was a rare and delicate creature, half goddess and half saint. The lover's chief privilege was to spend an adoring life in her service, giving to her the unquestioning devotion that a vassal might give his lord or a Christian his God. It is easy enough to see what such a portrait of herself would mean to the average woman, hemmed in as she was in real life by all the feudal restrictions that made her so inferior to her husband, and she listened to the poets with the same sort of delighted self-identification with which a city boy imagines himself flourishing a six-shooter on the Western plains.

In the courts of Eleanor and of her daughter, Marie of Champagne, the pages and squires were expected to wash their hands and comb their hair and learn to excel in the soft arts of love instead of spending all their time thinking of hawks and spears. They were not supposed to do less fighting, however, but more, their valor intensified because they fought for the guerdon of a fair lady's love. The Church disapproved of this sort of motivation in military matters, but on the subject of romantic love the Church fought a losing battle. The poets, in fact, set up a parallel religion of their own, with a god of Love, and saints, and observances, and various penances which the suppliant must undergo until he finally reaches the heaven of his lady's love.

The whole thing (inevitably) was put down in a book of rules. It was written by one Andrew, the chaplain in Marie's court, and called *The Art of Polite Love-making.* Andrew was well aware that his book was directly contrary to the teachings of Holy Church and spent the last third of it retracting everything he had said before; but it was the first two-thirds that was popular. Here Andrew gives advice to an imaginary young man named Walter who wishes to enter society but does not know how to conduct himself. He gives many sample conversations and itemized rules, but the basis of the book is the theory that courtly love is the root of civilized living. "Nothing in the world is done that is good and courtly unless it springs from the fountain of love." This love can only be practiced by aristocrats, since common people have neither the leisure, the money, nor the delicate sensibilities to master its intricate rules; it must be free, and therefore it is better if its practitioners are not married; it must be the most overwhelming and exclusive of emotions; and it must be consummated.

The basis for Andrew's book of rules was Ovid's *Art of Love,*

72

which was one of the most popular and earnestly studied books in the whole of the Middle Ages.

Ovid's irreverent little treatise had actually no relation to romantic love. The *Art of Love* is a flip, witty, entirely pagan production, showing a thorough knowledge of women's underwear, cosmetics and transformations, full of advice on such subjects as letting one's potential mistress win at games and how much to pay her maid, and ending on a note so candidly indecent that no modern editor has cared to translate it. But after the Middle Ages had laid their reverent, transforming hands upon him the cheerful Roman would not have known himself. Lives of him were written to prove that he was really a Christian poet living at Sulmona, and while at first glance his *Art of Love* did not seem to be the work of a Christian poet, it was when the medieval commentators were through with it. Ovid was "moralized" as they called it. That is, each of his statements was given an allegorical rather than a literal meaning, and by the time the Middle Ages had finished with the *Art of Love* it could be read (and was) in the most sheltered convents.[6] Andrew the Chaplain did not of course give Ovid the religious treatment he was accorded elsewhere, except in the sense that all courtly love was a religion, but he did present him in an incense-laden atmosphere that was wholly alien to the practical and realistic Roman poet.

While Andrew the Chaplain was the codifier of the new system of courtly love, its chief popularizer was another member of the court of Marie of Champagne named Chrétien de Troyes. He was a translator and admirer of Ovid, but his chief influence was exerted through his romances, rhymed tales of courtly lovers that filled much the same need in the Middle Ages as the romantic novel does today. Chrétien, as a Frenchman, was fond of analysis,

---

[6] There is no need to smile at the Middle Ages for this. Any Protestant may find the same thing in the King James Version of the Bible, where an Oriental love-drama of considerable outspokenness, the *Song of Songs,* has been allegorized by seventeenth-century captions to make it appear that the poet was intending to portray Christ's love for the Church.

73

and supplied his characters with long meditations on the state of their feelings. But he and his successors also gave their heroes and heroines enough violent adventures to fill a dozen books, until finally there was the inevitable happy ending in which Love Conquers All.[7]

This was the sort of book that polite society in England and France had been reading for nearly two centuries when Chaucer first took up his pen to be a courtly poet, and this concept of love had soaked so thoroughly into the collective mind of his audience that no one could have told where literary tradition left off and real life began. Froissart, for instance, assumes in his *Chronicles* that every fourteenth-century knight always went forth to battle because of the love of some beauteous lady, in spite of the direct evidence he had to the contrary. He was typical of his century in his firm conviction that all courtly joy comes from love and battle (*"d'armes et d'amours"*), now so firmly united in the popular mind that they were inseparable.

The new philosophy satisfied in men an innocent idealism and in women an equal need to be admired, and never again did the twelfth-century French conception of love slacken its hold on European literary history. Most of Chaucer's own poetry is so completely in its tradition that some of his best work, like his own great romance of *Troilus and Criseyde*, can only be completely appreciated if it is looked at in the odd, delightful kind of moonlight that came into being two centuries earlier in France.

In the thirteenth century romantic love crystallized in a poem called *The Romance of the Rose*. Of all the books produced in the Middle Ages this was one of the most loved, the most imitated and the most influential, and Chaucer was not the only poet who made it his handbook. It found devoted readers in every state in Europe and any man of culture would have recognized a quotation from the *Rose* immediately. The poem was at first very unpopular with the Church, but by the time Chaucer was born even St. George's Chapel at Windsor possessed a copy of this famous and influential work.

The first part of *The Romance of the Rose* was written by a

---

[7] It was Vergil who first wrote, "*Omnia vincit amor*," and the phrase might almost be called the slogan of courtly love.

Frenchman named Guillaume de Lorris. It was his idea to use the most popular of medieval literary forms, the allegory, to describe how a young man fell in love and how he sought the love of his lady in return. The young man is allegorized as a Dreamer who enters a garden of roses, and the story concerns his effort to pluck the most beautiful rose of all.

Guillaume possessed an unusually sure and graceful touch with allegory, and he records the progress of the love affair under a series of symbols so effective that they immediately became stock figures in every poet's repertoire. He did not invent all of these, any more than he invented the inevitable golden hair and blue eyes and rosebud mouths of his ladies. He inherited most of his images from the twelfth century, but it was his skill in combining them that made his book so popular and so influential. There was hardly a poet in the fourteenth century, for instance, who wrote a love poem without enclosing it in the framework of a dream.

Guillaume's dream occurs on a May morning and through it the poet finds his way to the garden of courtly love. Sir Mirth holds court there, his clothes embroidered and slit in the current fashion, and fair ladies with names like Courtesy and Gladness attend him. The Dreamer is admitted by an especially beautiful lady named Idleness, equipped with gloves and mirror, for a courtly lover needed as much time in which to practice his art as a man learning an intricate dance.

The garden is ruled over by the god of Love, whose head is crowned with flowers. The dove, the nightingale and the skylark sing to him, and he is as beautiful as one of the angels of the Lord. His arrows strike the Dreamer to the heart and his new subject learns from him all the rules that he must obey as Love's faithful vassal. He must avoid discourtesy and dress neatly and wash frequently and be good and kind to everyone and honor his lady and keep his love secret (all Ovid's rules, in fact, made innocent and all Andrew's rules turned to poetry). In the end he will be admitted to the heaven of his lady's consent, although in the meantime he must expect to suffer.[8]

[8] The amount of agony a courtly lover was expected to endure was remarkable, and Guillaume quite frankly compares it to the toothache. It was frequently severe enough to incapacitate its unhappy victims and its path-

The Dreamer has an assistant in Fair-Welcome, the son of the Lady Courtesy. But they are thwarted by the villain of the piece, a black-browed giant whose name is Danger. Danger is used here in its secondary meaning of stand-offishness, and in the vocabulary of all courtly poets, including Chaucer, it meant the lady's reluctance to commit herself to a course of action from which she could not retreat.

The Dreamer's efforts to consummate his love affair continue with varying degrees of success, each symbol typifying one of the moods of the chosen lady. Finally Fair-Welcome is imprisoned in a tower built by Jealousy and the hero languishes outside, bewailing the turn of Fortune's wheel. Here the book breaks off suddenly, apparently left unfinished by the death of its author.

While Guillaume did not finish the action of his tale he left a complete handbook of courtly love for future poets to imitate. His section of *The Romance of the Rose* was well worth the admiration it evoked, for the dream that took place on a May morning was the work of a good poet. Guillaume had a quite unmedieval respect for structure and proportion, and he succeeds in bringing his delicately tinted abstractions to life, from the picture of the god of Love crowned with flowers to that of Danger sleeping under a thorn with a twist of hay for a pillow. His work is reminiscent of the craftsmen who made the secular ivories of the period, mirrors and combs and caskets skillfully carved with knights and ladies and roses and tournaments and very pretty within their limitations. Guillaume was essentially a worker in miniature, and his talents were well suited to the stylized dance of love he was portraying. Perhaps more than any other writer he succeeds in conveying its odd, essential innocence. He calls it a love

> As pure as men but meet in dreams,
> Where all is fair and nought is wrong. . . .

---

ology originated in part in the medieval medical books, which all recognized "the sickness of love." Its pangs occasionally brought a note of accidental humor into the romances, as when Queen Guinevere fails to realize that two young people have fallen in love; from their symptoms she assumes they are both seasick.

And the framework of a dream is well suited to the mood of the first section of *The Romance of the Rose*.

Not so the second section. About forty years after Guillaume de Lorris' death another French poet applied himself to the manuscript of *The Romance of the Rose* and set out to complete it. His name was Jean de Meun, nicknamed "Clopinel" or "the Halt," and in all France there could hardly have been a writer more unlike the ornamental and courtly Guillaume.

Jean de Meun was a bourgeois, with no interest in structure and almost none in romantic love. He picked up Guillaume's neat little framework and loaded it with a jumbled, talented, incredible rush of opinions concerning every subject on earth. He was as characteristic of the lively, mocking, skeptical spirit in the Middle Ages as Guillaume was of its stylized rigidity, and the combination of the two men inside the covers of a single book made *The Romance of the Rose* in one sense a summary of the whole medieval period.

Specifically, Jean de Meun was characteristic of the collector's instinct that was so strong in the thirteenth century. It was then that Vincent de Beauvais attempted to pack all recorded knowledge into three magnificently unwieldy volumes and produced a universal encyclopedia the like of which was not attempted again in France until the eighteenth century. Jean de Meun was the true son of this age of accumulation, and he succeeded in packing into Guillaume de Lorris' careful little framework a series of conversations and arguments between different members of the cast that made the book five times its previous length with scarcely any plot advance at all.

This may sound dull but Jean de Meun was never that. He may have had no sense of construction but he had a wicked sense of humor, a lively eye for detail and an enthusiasm for ideas that is irresistible even when Jean is most long-winded. With apparent ease he manages to balance himself upon half a dozen different points of view concerning life, love, art, morality and economics, and in the course of his headlong career he deals with every subject that has fascinated poets before his time or since.

To read Jean de Meun's section of *The Romance of the Rose* is

77

almost like reading an anthology of familiar quotations. This would be Herrick's "Gather ye rosebuds . . ."

> Woman should gather roses ere
> Time's ceaseless foot o'ertaketh her,
> For if too long she make delay,
> Her chance of love will pass away.

This would be Robert Burns' contention that a man's a man for a' that:

> An upright heart
> Doth true nobility impart,
> But mere nobility of birth
> I reckon as of little worth.

This is an Elizabethan or Cavalier poet on the subject of love:

> 'Tis reason all unreasonable,
> A raving madman calm and stable,
> A peril sweet, delightful fear,
> A heavy burden light to bear.

This is a seventeenth-century Puritan, aware that life is

> A vain and fleeting worldly show . . .
> Since things corruptible amain
> Must unto dust return again.

This is Pope, warning against speculating on the Infinite:

> To solve the question how
> Predestination doth allow
> God's prescience, and how man's free-will
> May co-exist with both and still
> Survive and work, is not a thing
> Suited to lay folk's questioning.

This noble thought, however, does not prevent Jean from going on to speculate on the subject of free-will for four hundred and ninety lines.

Like Hamlet, Jean is fond of pointing out that a king is born as naked as a beggar, and that his corpse is worth no more by a dab of tar than any other man's. Like Rousseau, he is in full sympathy with the idea of the noble savage, and spends much time mourning the great days before civilization set in, when everyone ate nuts and berries and no one quarreled.

Jean de Meun did not of course invent these ideas of his, any more than Burns or Herrick or Rousseau invented them after him. They were the product of his voluminous reading. When Chaucer, in his turn, echoed Jean on the subject of the innocence of primeval man in his ballade called *The Former Age* he was following a tradition that in this case came straight from the fourth century. But it was probably Jean who first set Chaucer to thinking about it, as he set him to thinking about so many things, and his direct influence upon the poets that followed him is almost incalculable.

Jean de Meun was deeply interested in love, as he was in everything, and he approaches it from a dozen different angles. He approaches it as humorist, as moralist, as dramatist, as Christian, as aphorist and as pagan, and the only point of view he does not take towards love is the romantic one of Guillaume de Lorris.

On the whole Jean de Meun comes closer to the spirit of Ovid than do any of his contemporaries, and some of his advice on the subject of love-making is strongly reminiscent of that urbane and unsaintly Roman.

> To win the Rosebud, make it seem
> That love Platonic is your dream.

If you cannot cry to order, try onion juice. Give presents all round and the walls of Fair-Welcome's dungeon will collapse like a Christmas cake. If you must give other women presents don't let your Chosen One know of it, and under no circumstances try to give her any advice.

> For every woman thinks she plays
> Her part by nature perfectly,
> And interference hateth she . . .
> Rarely it haps she doeth right
> But woe betide the witless wight
> Who counsels her.

79

Jean acquired the reputation of being a confirmed cynic where women were concerned, and rather unjustly. He was well aware of what the average woman has to put up with once the ardent lover becomes the complaisant husband.

> Now no more
> He worships her as heretofore,
> But dead is joyousness; she dare
> Scarce laugh, so 'whelmed is she with care . . .
> Obedience is her only choice.

Twice Jean makes a very strong plea, almost certainly the result of his middle-class background, for equality in marriage. He did not share Milton's views on the necessary subjection of Eve to Adam, and was convinced that a woman could be a man's friend as well as his wife. A man and woman should

> . . . each in awe
> Of other stand, as saith God's law . . .
> Think you a man gains woman's love
> Who sets himself as lord above
> Her will and ways? Fair love falls dead
> When seigniory exalts its head.

But these just and sober comments are easy to forget, and the first thing any reader thinks of in connection with Jean de Meun is the vivid and rowdy little sketches with which he illustrates the shortcomings of the feminine sex. There is, for instance, the bed-time tirade of a jealous husband who is convinced that his wife has been chasing other men while he was away on business and who accumulates in an array of outrageous detail every charge that had been leveled against women since the days of St. Jerome. Even more effective is the monologue of the old hag who has been set to guard Fair-Welcome in prison, mourning the days of her vanished youth and giving a most Ovidian string of advice on the best way to catch a man. She is by no means the Wife of Bath, but there are unmistakable signs that she was one of the chief literary ancestors of that immortal old reprobate.

Jean did not originate the literary fashion of making fun of women and emphasizing their shortcomings, although there is no doubt he did a great deal to encourage it. The attack on women had been begun in sober earnest by the Church in an effort to inculcate the ecclesiastical ideal of chastity, and for centuries the church writers had been picturing women as the root of all evil, luring innocent men down the flowery path to hell as they had been doing ever since the days of Mother Eve. The delighted poets picked up this picture and enthusiastically added details of their own. A woman not only sent a man to hell after he died but on earth she squandered his money, she nagged him in bed, she lorded it over him in public, she talked all the time and she was as faithless as an alley cat.

This portrait of women was painted over and over again by poets who at the same time were tenderly hymning the feminine sex as a combination of queen and saint. Men like Chaucer and Deschamps had no difficulty in keeping these two views of the same sex in different compartments in their minds, and neither did their audiences. They had already been well trained by finding Guillaume de Lorris and Jean de Meun living amicably side by side in *The Romance of the Rose*.

When Chaucer first set out to be a poet it was naturally the first section of *The Romance of the Rose* that attracted him. It belonged to the ornamental tradition of courtly love that writers like Machaut had taken for their own, and Chaucer followed where his masters led. Along with nearly every youthful poet of his generation he entered the garden of the *Rose*, and the impression made upon his mind by the gentle, orderly fantasy of Guillaume de Lorris never entirely left him. But as Chaucer grew older and found out better what he himself wanted to say, it was the lively, realistic vigor of the second section of *The Romance of the Rose* that became of increasing interest to him; until at last, when he sat down to write *The Canterbury Tales*, it was not the shadow of Guillaume de Lorris that stood beside him but the grinning ghost of Jean de Meun.

CHAPTER VI

CHAUCER's earliest love poems are lost. According to his own testimony he wrote a great many "ballades, roundels, virelayes" on the subject of love, but the few that remain are too expertly written to have been the product of his extreme youth.

Chaucer did not value his fugitive pieces as Froissart did. Froissart eventually gathered together all his own love poems and had them illustrated and beautifully bound. With this gift he pleased a king and, as Froissart remarked with quiet complacency, he "ought to have been pleased, for it was handsomely written and illustrated, and bound in crimson velvet, with ten silver-gilt studs and roses of the same in the middle."

Chaucer treated his love songs with less consideration and now they have vanished. They evidently passed from hand to hand around the court, and on the evidence of Chaucer's friend, John Gower, they were very popular. Gower, a well-known poet himself, says that everyone was pleased with the love songs that Chaucer made "in the floures of his youthe."

They should have been popular; the remaining specimens attest that Chaucer patterned his ballades and virelays on the fashionable model that Guillaume de Machaut had given as legacy to all young poets. When he was young he probably turned out dozens of spring songs and Valentine songs in the manner of Gower or Deschamps, offering his heart as a New Year's gift to his lady in January and imploring her pity in June. Never was there a greater collection of lovelorn poets and fair, cruel ladies until the minor Elizabethan sonneteers followed the medieval makers of ballades and the air again became filled with cries of fasionable lyric woe.

It was probably some time before Chaucer rose above this sort of wholesale, youthful imitation to the personal dignity of a ballade like *Womanly Noblesse* or the lively wit and grace of *To Rosemounde*. At the beginning, as in his longer poetry, he imitated the mood and manner of other poets.

82

Yet, in one respect, Geoffrey Chaucer was no imitator even at the beginning of his career. He was, on the contrary, an innovator and an extraordinary one. Living at a French-speaking court, imitating French models, reading French poets, he nevertheless chose to write in English.

If Chaucer had been born and brought up in the north country, away from the influences of the Court and the universities, he might very naturally have turned to one of the native English dialects as a medium for his verse. But, as it was, his choice of a language should normally have been either Latin or French. His friend Gower, for instance, wrote his first major poem in French and his second one in Latin. A long time after, in the last decade of the fourteenth century, Gower wrote a poem in English, influenced apparently by Chaucer's success in that field, but the charming ballades that Gower produced during the same period are all in French.

The French language was the international language of culture at every court in Europe. When an Italian translated a history of Venice out of Latin into a modern language he translated it into French, "because the French language is current throughout the world and is the most delightful to read." It was the language of the poet and the gentleman as Latin was the language of the churchman and the scholar, while one's own native tongue was something old women used to buy fish or to scold their children.

It is true that this situation was changing. But it had not yet begun to change in court circles when Chaucer was a young man, any more than English was used in the schools when he was a boy, and it was for these court circles that Chaucer wrote. Until the invention of movable type there was nothing that could be called a general middle-class reading public, and in any case the tone of Chaucer's work shows clearly that he was writing for an aristocratic audience.

What led him to take the extraordinary step of writing for this audience in English is not known; Chaucer was not given to supplying autobiographical explanations of his motives. In this he was unlike Dante, who also shattered precedent by setting out to build a major literary career in the vernacular but left a lengthy explanation defending his course of action. Dante undertook to create a whole new poetical language by a carefully reasoned, intellectual process, weighing one Italian dialect after another and carefully discarding all sounds that were not pleasing to his cultivated ear. This was obviously not Chaucer's method, for he used ordinary London English in his poetry.

Perhaps part of the explanation lies in his solid, middle-class background which gave him a fundamental independence that not all the fashionable graces of King Edward's court could alter. Like all major artists, also, he possessed that solitary, inborn pride whose other name is integrity, and he accepted no final judgment on his work but his own.

> I wot myself best how I stande.

Even when Chaucer was ardently the imitator of French poets he was the most unorthodox imitator they could have had. For he wrote in English.

In choosing to write his ballades and roundels and virelays in his native tongue, Chaucer put himself under a heavy technical handicap. Complicated verse forms are excellently suited to the French language, with its smooth facility and its large number of rhyming words. The effortless soap-bubble games that a man like Froissart could play with whole strings of three and four syllable lines, all rhyming, show how easily the tricks of the school could be imitated by anyone writing in French. But English is not a language of lyric smoothness or a multitude of rhymes, as Chaucer was well aware. He once apologized for what he considered the shortcomings of a ballade of his by explaining that the attempt to render French lines into English was

> a great penaunce
> Since rym in Englissh hath such scarcity.

An even more serious disadvantage of the English language was that the poet ran the risk of a total eclipse of his literary reputation. English had changed from what had once been essentially a German language, with German genders and inflections, to some-

84

thing very different, and there was nothing to guarantee that it might not go on changing indefinitely. Fourteenth-century English might easily become as unreadable to future generations as Old English was to Chaucer himself. Moreover, even in his own day Chaucer's work could not have been read with pleasure by a man from the North, and even some of his fellow Londoners had different ideas on spelling and grammar from his own.

> For ther is so great diversity
> In Englissh and in writyng of oure tongue.

Chaucer was well aware of the risks he was running and sent up a prayer for the future safety of his work.

> That thow be understood, God I beseche!

But the risks did not sway him from his determination to write only in his mother tongue.

Chaucer must sometimes have felt in his darker moments that he was trying to build a house on quicksand, for English was one of the most unstable and the least respected languages in Christendom. Even two and three centuries later English poets were still haunted by the uneasy feeling that they were working in a medium which might betray them. As Edmund Waller put it,

> Poets that lasting marble seek
> Must carve in Latin or in Greek;
> We write in sand, our language grows,
> And like the tide our work o'erflows.

Francis Bacon had all his English works translated into Latin to preserve them for the benefit of posterity, and a member of the court of Charles the First performed the same service for Chaucer. He translated the whole of *Troilus and Criseyde* into Latin so that thereby Chaucer's fame "would be made stable and immovable for all ages."

It is true that Chaucer's poetry went into a partial eclipse for a few centuries. The principles of Middle English inflection were not understood and therefore it was believed that his lines did not

85

scan.[1] Even John Dryden, who was one of the most intelligent and sympathetic critics Chaucer ever had, was obliged to admit that his meter was very faulty; and it was not until the English scholars earned the gratitude of all readers of poetry by taking the matter in hand that Chaucer re-emerged as a master of prosody. All that he demands of any reader today is a brief study of Middle English inflection and pronunciation and the occasional use of a glossary. And he is worth it, as Mme. de Scudéry undoubtedly felt when she set out to translate his works into French at the age of ninety-two.

Chaucer's persistent use of the vernacular seems to have baffled some of his contemporaries. On the Continent at least he was not thought of as an original poet at all but as an obliging translator of foreign works into English, and when Eustache Deschamps wrote an admiring ballade in his honor he addressed it to the "great translator, noble Geoffrey Chaucer."

To a certain extent this title of translator was well earned, although it seems strange today as applied to one of the most original of England's poets. To Chaucer's contemporaries one of his great poetical achievements was the fact that he translated *The Romance of the Rose* into English—an achievement which was great at least in the sense that it must have cost him a great deal of time, labor and devotion. There is a fourteenth-century English translation of the *Rose* in existence, but whether it is Chaucer's is uncertain. More probably his version went the way of his youthful love songs, leaving him with added experience in his trade and with long passages from Guillaume de Lorris and Jean de Meun lodged firmly in his head.

Another translation he made, or at least a free rendering from the French, is a short religious poem which is perhaps the earliest specimen of Chaucer's work extant. It is based on a prayer from a very popular allegory written by Guillaume de Deguilleville called *The Pilgrimage of Human Life.* The prayer is a kind of

[1] To say that Chaucer's work does not scan is the equivalent of saying that Pope was careless when he rhymed "join" with "divine." Pope was never careless. It was the growth of the English language that betrayed him when "join" was no longer pronounced "jine."

86

acrostic, the initial letters of each stanza forming the alphabet, and Chaucer's version is called *An A.B.C.*

It is fitting that Chaucer began his literary career on a religious note, for the Church laid a definite pattern on his mind. Chaucer can never be understood as a writer unless it is remembered that his whole life was conditioned and controlled, as was that of any man in the Middle Ages, by the Holy Catholic Church. From the day of his baptism to the administration of the final rites he was in the hands of the Church. The bells he heard when he awoke in the morning, the masses he attended, the festivals on saints' days, the Easter confession—all these were the outward signs of the universal, inescapable, not-to-be-questioned authority upon which the whole of Chaucer's life rested.

He had been taught that his small and sinful earth lay between the curving shell of heaven and the fiery wastes of hell. Those upon it were all pilgrims, striving to expiate the sin of father Adam with penances, with pilgrimages and with frequent payments to the Church. Their life on earth was as unimportant as it was brief, and all that mattered was the inward state of holiness that would bring them safely to the gates of paradise while the sinners writhed eternally in hell.

It so happened that this pattern of salvation was entirely alien to Chaucer's poetic genius, as it was alien to that of writers like Boccaccio or Jean de Meun. It was not alien to them as men, for they were all good, unquestioning, medieval Christians. It was alien to them as poets. They could not fuse their talents, as could men like George Herbert or John Donne, into a real desire to praise the world within or the world to come. It was the world around them they loved, and Chaucer loved it most of all. When he thought of a pilgrim, it was not the vision of the soul as a pilgrim that set his imagination afire, as it had fired John Bunyan's. It was a specific pilgrim that Chaucer immediately thought of: a fat wife from the suburbs of Bath with red stockings and a space between her front teeth. Chaucer was not a mystic; he was a realist. And the more steadily he moved towards realism in his poetry the more steadily he moved away from the ideal teachings of his religion.

Chaucer was not only a poet of the earth but a poet of love, and the whole range of human passion had been condemned by the Church as evil. This was true even of the gay little garden of the *Rose,* and as Chaucer's poetry on the subject became more real and more profound the worse it became for him as a true son of the Church. Throughout the whole of his life the realistic, amoral and cheerfully irreverent habit of mind with which he had been born as a writer warred with the idealistic, moral and deeply reverent attitude which he had inherited as a medieval Englishman.

The knowledge of this frightened Chaucer sometimes, as it frightened every other medieval writer whose personal habits of thought brought him into conflict with that immovable base of his civilization, the Holy Catholic Church. There is real passion in Jean de Meun's statement that he is ready to make amends if the least criticism of the Church is found in his work, for he bows himself entirely beneath her rule. And Boccaccio grew so terrified when he looked back over the literary productions of his misspent youth that he very nearly decided to burn everything that he had written and retire to the sheltering confines of a monastery.[2]

The same conflict between his training and his literary inclinations went on in Geoffrey Chaucer throughout the whole of his life, and its bitterness can be gauged by the strength of the two warring elements within him. It was the second that triumphed throughout most of his career, and without it the world would not have had the great pagan masterpiece of *Troilus and Criseyde* or most of the characters in *The Canterbury Tales.* But Chaucer publicly repudiated his *Troilus* and he repudiated nearly all the stories in *The Canterbury Tales.* He prayed that Christ would forgive him for these and for many other poems he had written on worldly subjects, and that

[2] Boccaccio was finally dissuaded by Petrarch, that great humanist whose interest in the world around him has given him the title of "the first modern man." Petrarch was so unmedieval that he once climbed a mountain for no devotional reason at all but simply to look at the view. Yet the pull of his century proved to be too strong even for Petrarch and he ended his day of sightseeing in the mountains "angry with myself that I should still be admiring earthly things who might long ago have learned . . . that nothing is wonderful but the soul."

only his works on holy subjects or those imparting moral lessons might be remembered.

It is hardly likely that a poem like the *A.B.C.* would be remembered for other than devotional reasons, for its literary value is inconsiderable. Its one real interest lies in the meter that Chaucer chose to employ. The original French used the popular four-stress line in which *The Romance of the Rose* and a great many other works of a similar kind had been written. But in his adaptation Chaucer chose, with his curious independence, a five-stress line, and he seems to have introduced it almost singlehanded into the history of English poetry. It was the line in which Shakespeare did most of his writing, and Milton, and nearly any other English poet that might be named, and Chaucer himself grew to value it above all others. If the dating of the *A.B.C.* is correct, it shows how early he developed the line that grew to be his favorite.[3]

The five-stress line was not, however, the one that Chaucer normally used at the beginning of his career. In his youth he remained faithful for the most part to the four-stress line of *The Romance of the Rose*, and the first long poem of his that is extant is written in this meter.

This is *The Book of the Duchess*, which Chaucer composed after the death of Blanche of Lancaster in the autumn of 1369. He wrote it as an elegy, and whether he wrote it to please John of Gaunt or himself it is unquestionably one of the least mournful elegies ever written. This does not mean that Chaucer did not love the Duchess or regret her death. But he preferred to emphasize not the sorrow of her death but her loveliness while she lived and the choice is characteristic of him.

The Book of the Duchess is a very courtly and aristocratic poem, French in everything but its language. The meter is that of *The Romance of the Rose* and the spirit is the fashionable one of Guillaume de Lorris. It was obviously written at a period when

[3] The early dating of the *A.B.C.* is based on a note in Speght's edition to the effect that Chaucer wrote it for Blanche, Duchess of Lancaster, for use in her devotions. Speght is not an infallible authority, but there is nothing inherently improbable in this particular tradition.

Chaucer was deep in the works of Machaut, and the whole poem, in fact, is a careful patchwork of words and phrases taken from the French models that Chaucer admired in 1369.

As a good and obedient follower of the cult of the *Rose*, Chaucer placed *The Book of the Duchess* within the framework of a dream; and with equal obedience to literary fashions he pictures himself in the opening lines as being racked by sleeplessness through the pangs of unrequited love. These opening lines come straight from Froissart, who got them in turn from Machaut, but Chaucer managed to vitalize the faded convention so successfully that at one time there was a quite determined effort to discover the name of the lady over whom the poet was supposed to be in such pain.

The restless lover picks up the *Metamorphoses* of Ovid "to rede, and drive the night away" and encounters the tale of Ceyx and Alcyone. With a blithe, medieval disregard of the principles of balance and construction Chaucer interrupts his own story to re-tell that of Ceyx and Alcyone, and it takes him a hundred and sixty lines. As a lover of Ovid it gave him real pleasure to retell the story of the drowned king who appears to his wife in a dream, and in any case it supplied him with a pretty opening for his own sub-sequent invocation to the god of Sleep.

The invocation is worth noticing, for it is the first sign of Chaucer's separating himself from his French masters and occurs at a time when he is trying to imitate them very closely. The master in this case was Machaut, who wrote an invocation to the god of Sleep, offering him a bed stuffed with the plumes of gyrfalcons if he would bring rest to the tortured lover.

Both Froissart and Chaucer admired this passage and imitated it. But Froissart substituted a ring for the feather bed, being evidently under the impression that a ring was more courtly and dignified, while Chaucer not only retained the bed but pictured it so clearly in his mind's eye that he knew the coverlet was of excellent black satin and the pillowcases of Brittany linen. Even as early as this he had somehow acquired the art of visualizing his material objectively and realistically, and he could never have spent his career in the pretty, unreal, poetic atmosphere that satisfied Machaut and Froissart so completely.

The poem continues with the poet's dream. He dreams that it is May (of course) and that he has been wakened by the little birds singing on the tiles of his chamber roof. His room is a true dream-room of romance, for the windows are set with colored glass telling the story of the siege of Troy and on the walls are painted the events described in *The Romance of the Rose.*[4] Outside the window a hunt sweeps by in the clear blue morning air, and with the easy inconsequence of a dream the poet takes his horse and leaves his painted chamber to join the huntsmen.

Chaucer knew his hunting terms well, as anyone might who had listened to the interminable technical discussions of the sport that went on in King Edward's court and who was, like any fourteenth-century courtier, a sportsman himself. But the best touch of realism here is the puppy who has been left behind by the other hounds and does not know what to do. The animal has the conventional, romantic function of leading the dreamer to the flowery mead, but it is nevertheless an actual little English puppy.

> He com and crepte to me as lowe
> Ryght as he hadde me yknowe,
> Held down his hed and joyned his eres,
> And leyd al smoothe down his heres.

The ancestor of this puppy appears in Machaut, as did the ancestor of the feather bed, but again the fantastic and the conventionalized has become the real and the familiar. Chaucer knew beds and he knew puppies; and he described them as he knew them no matter how many medieval books of rhetoric might tell him he was wrong.

The puppy introduces the dreamer to a mourning knight, and from then on the poem is fully in the conventional tradition of courtly love. The knight is a very idealized John of Gaunt, and the poem presents his relationship to Blanche as conforming in every detail to the current romantic conception of knight and lady. There is a long description of Blanche, but nothing to show what she

---

[4] This last item, however, is a realistic rather than a conventionalized detail. Westminster and other great residences had their walls covered with painted pictures, frequently copied from the romances, in the same way that wallpaper is used today.

really looked like. She is merely the regulation lady of romance; and the fair complexion, smooth neck, white hands, red nails, straight back and all the rest of it form a catalogue so familiar that any poet of the period could write it with his eyes shut.

There is an odd charm about this section of *The Book of the Duchess* which is derived in part from the undeniable charm of its models. There is, morever, a certain spontaneous innocence in the way the young poet tried to introduce everything he admired in his recent reading in order to do honor to the great lady he had known. If *The Romance of the Rose* contained a pleasing simile, Chaucer put that down. If Machaut thought of an effectively turned phrase, Chaucer put that down also.[5] And yet out of this respectful patchwork of his models Chaucer created something that was obviously his own and could have been written by no one else.

Chaucer was only following the usual medieval custom in this reverent echoing of what he admired in the work of other men. Machaut did exactly the same thing, and so did Froissart and Deschamps. Imitation was literally the sincerest form of flattery in the Middle Ages, and the excellence of a poet was judged in part by the amount of careful reading of approved models that he could prove he had done.

Equally fashionable were the classical examples which the poets liked to introduce into their work to illustrate the matter in hand. Chaucer could not, for instance, say merely that John of Gaunt was strong and wise. He had to be as strong as Hercules and as wise as Minerva. Machaut had been chiefly responsible for the current craze of making a decorative display of erudition with examples drawn from the classics, but it was naturally a popular fashion in a period in which books were scarce and readers liked to have as much culture as possible packed into a single poem. There was an

[5] Chaucer followed Machaut so closely that at times he produced what was almost a literal translation. For instance, these lines in Machaut:

Car je la vi dancier si cointement
Et puis chanter si tres joliment,
Rire et jouer si gracieusement . . .

become in Chaucer:

I saw her daunce so comlily,
Carole and singe so swetely,
Laughe and playe so womanly . . .

and examples of this sort could be multiplied.

almost superstitious reverence for classical lore in the Middle Ages and it was considered impossible to get too much of it.

Equally medieval, and produced by the same set of circumstances, are the instructive little bits of information that Chaucer tucks into his poem whenever he gets the opportunity. For instance, he interrupts a discussion of the love songs with which the knight wooed his lady to remark that Tubal was the first to discover the art of song, unless the Greeks are right in claiming the honor for Pythagoras. It is true that Chaucer's attempt to be helpful goes a little astray here, since it was Jubal he meant and not Tubal, but the intent to convey instruction is clear enough and these sudden chunks of learning were exactly what a medieval reader liked and expected.

The Book of the Duchess is a thoroughly youthful production, and its charm is in part the charm of youth. Its medievalism is engaging because it matches the spirit of the poem as a whole, and it has the clarity and grace that Chaucer found in his French models. The poem also foreshadows the very original poet that was slowly being born: in its sudden flashes of realism, like the puppy and the feather bed, in the naturalistic ease of the dialogue, and in its typically Chaucerian sense of happiness.

There is another aspect of Chaucer's maturity which is forecast in *The Book of the Duchess*, and that is the attitude which he assumed towards himself in his poetry. It was fashionable at that time for the poet to disparage his own work in a graceful kind of way, as Chaucer does at the end of the poem when he says humbly that he has put his story in rhyme as well as he can. But it was not the literary fashion for the poet to insult himself as thoroughly as Chaucer manages to do.

The dreamer, who is supposed to be the poet himself, is presented as a well-meaning and kindly man but so slow in the wits that he is incapable of understanding that the knight's lady is dead, even though when he first meets him the knight is mourning his loss aloud.

> "My lady bryght
> Which I have loved with al my myght
> Is from me ded."

The dreamer does not understand what the knight means when he complains of having been checkmated by Fortune, and reproves him with solemn earnestness for making so much fuss over merely losing a chess game.

If this were the solitary example of an unkind treatment of his own intelligence to be found in Chaucer's work it might be explained on the grounds of literary exigency, since the device gives the knight an opportunity to describe at length all the details of his love story. But it is not a solitary example. In fact, as Chaucer grew more experienced in his art he entered into the game of insulting himself with increasing enthusiasm; and it was this, along with what was believed to be his stumbling and incorrect meter, that gave Chaucer for centuries the reputation of being "naive." [6]

The individual whom Chaucer represents himself as being is unquestionably naive, a trusting, foolish soul and automatically a butt. The portrait bears about as much resemblance to Geoffrey Chaucer himself, courtier, diplomat, justice of the peace and member of Parliament, as his jokes on women bear a direct resemblance to his wife. But it was a portrait that Chaucer increasingly enjoyed and it appears at its highest point of development in *The Canterbury Tales*.

As to why he enjoyed the joke, the full answer to that would require a much closer acquaintance with the private mental habits of Geoffrey Chaucer than even his friends possessed. But a possible answer, perhaps, might lie in the fact that one of the chief ends of his art was delight, both his own delight and that of his readers, and of all forms of entertainment he considered a joke on Geoffrey Chaucer one of the most delightful.

[6] Another reason, possibly, was Middle English spelling, since for some reason "litel child" looks more innocent to the average reader than "little child."

CHAPTER VII

HE YEAR in which Chaucer wrote *The Book of the Duchess* was not in other respects a profitable year for England.

By 1369 the good old days of which subsequent chroniclers were to write so wistfully were drawing to a close. The story-book chivalry of King Edward's court was beginning to tarnish and the King, growing old, was striving to renew his youth with a certain demoiselle of the Queen's household named Alice Perrers. The Queen too had been growing old and was increasingly misshapen with dropsy.

It was a wet year with many crop failures, and the plague came back to England as it always seemed to do in times of heavy rains. The chronic war with France began again also, bringing with it no splendid victories like Crécy and Poitiers but only higher taxes and an interminable series of arguments in Parliament as to why higher taxes had not brought victory.

The direct cause for the resumption of the war was the fact that the Prince of Wales had been made ruler of the conquered territory of Aquitaine. Edward of Wales had all the qualities desirable in a chivalric knight, but none of them fitted him for statesmanship. He and his new wife Joan kept a court in Aquitaine that for princely magnificence startled all Europe, and most of the money had to come from taxes levied on the conquered. With the same striking lack of tact that his younger brother Lionel displayed in Ireland, the Prince of Wales decided that the local lords were not fit to obtain appointments at his court, and the local lords finally revolted against taxes which they had no share in spending.

The men of Aquitaine appealed to Charles V, the plain-featured and unchivalric but canny Dauphin who was now King of France. Charles repudiated the Peace of Calais, resting comfortably on a technical point that had escaped the notice of the English commissioners. Both sides issued extracts from the treaty to point out that the fault lay entirely with the opposition, learned doctors wrote treatises on the subject, and high church dignitaries toured the two kingdoms to arouse popular sentiment against the wicked English and the wicked French respectively. King Edward took back his old title of King of France, and the Hundred Years' War, which was as chronic as the plague, reopened.

Geoffrey Chaucer served again that year as a soldier, although in no such brilliant array as had gathered at Dover ten years earlier to conquer France. The documents describe him only as *equitanti de guerre,* but he was probably in the small expeditionary force headed by John of Gaunt that landed at Calais in July. The Duke of Burgundy marched out to face the English at Tournheim and the old, familiar comedy was re-enacted, with each army drawn up on a little hill and heralds going back and forth to discuss the possibility of a pitched battle on the ground in between. The French reluctance to attack worked in favor of the English, who were outnumbered seven to one, and in the end it was the French who retreated.

It was while the English were at Tournheim that they heard of the death of the Queen. It was at Windsor, in August, that her good, honorable, hard-working life had come to an end. She had borne King Edward twelve children, and kept her temper and ignored his amatory vagaries; and she died with his hand in hers and their youngest son weeping bitterly by her bedside. She was faithful to the end to the motto of her Flemish family: *Ich wrude muche* (I work hard) and her final instructions concerned her business accounts and the payment of her debts. Her funeral had the magnificence befitting a great and good queen and among the sober throng of mourners who attended it were Geoffrey and Philippa Chaucer, clothed all in black. The Queen was laid to rest in a marble tomb decorated with alabaster figures of her relatives and contemporaries and with a space beside her for her husband when he should come.

Less than a month after the Queen's death her well-loved daughter-in-law died also. The Duchess Blanche was twenty-seven when she died and had given birth to seven children, only three of whom survived her. John of Gaunt buried his wife in an alabaster tomb near the high altar of St. Paul's, with her effigy carved and painted upon it, and Chaucer wrote *The Book of the Duchess* to give her a memorial even more durable than the painted stone. Froissart later wrote some heartfelt lines describing how much both she and the Queen had meant to him, and there was perhaps no one in England who did not sincerely mourn the two gracious and loving women.

Meanwhile the war dragged on, apparently incapable of being forced to a decision. Little by little the English holdings in France melted away and at the end of six years they had nothing left but Calais, fortified naturally by its ring of marches and easily re-garrisoned from Dover. The Commons was darkly convinced that it was nothing but mismanagement and treachery among the government bureaucrats that had failed to produce victories like Crécy and Poitiers, although in actual fact a small country like England was incapable of raising an army large enough to hold Aquitaine.

The Prince of Wales did succeed in giving his country one more spectacular victory. It was in Spain, and its political consequences were painful. Against everyone's advice the Prince interfered in a family quarrel over the throne of Castile between Pedro the Cruel and his bastard brother Henry. Pedro had been excommunicated by the Pope and was rumored to have poisoned his wife, but the Prince of Wales won on his behalf the Battle of Najara. It was a fine victory but it did not put Pedro on the throne of Castile. All it achieved was a prompt coalition between Castile and France, whose combined naval power lost England her former control of the sea. It also gave the Prince of Wales the disease that made him a helpless invalid for eight years before it killed him.

The only practical result of the English adventure in Spain was to give John of Gaunt a second wife. She was the daughter of Pedro the Cruel and had fled with her sister to Bayonne. As the elder of the two princesses she married John of Gaunt, now three years a widower, and her sister Isabella married John's younger brother Edmund. Isabella was a lighthearted and worldly individual, but her elder sister Constance was a true daughter of arrogant, devout, priest-ridden Castile. She had loved her father fiercely and when she returned to Spain many years later did not rest until she had unearthed his bones from the battlefield and had them buried with the most solemn rites.

Constance was a beautiful woman, but the marriage was never

anything more than a union of state for John of Gaunt. Through Constance he assumed the title of King of Castile, and clung to it with dogged persistence in spite of the fact that the current King of Castile did not agree with him. But in England, at any rate, John of Gaunt had his castles in Spain and the Parliament writs addressed to him always gave him his new title of King.

John of Gaunt brought his Spanish bride to the Savoy, the magnificent palace just outside London which was perhaps the most beautiful private residence in England. It was outside the west wall of London, among the great houses that lined the Thames on its way to Westminster, and its famous terraces and rose gardens sloped down to a low wall by the river. The whole wealth of the house of Lancaster had descended to John of Gaunt through his first wife, and it took the services of a special Yeoman of the Jewels and a whole staff of warders to care for the pearls and diamonds and rubies and emeralds that were in John of Gaunt's possession as Duke of Lancaster.

The new Duchess of Lancaster encountered a position at the Savoy that must have been very painful to a proud and beautiful woman. Katherine Swynford was living at the Duke's palace, her husband having been killed in the fighting in Aquitaine a year after John of Gaunt's marriage. Chaucer's sister-in-law had an official position in the household of the Savoy as the governess of his two daughters;[1] but she was apparently as openly his mistress within a few years as Alice Perrers was the mistress of the King.

John of Gaunt's irregular union with Katherine Swynford was so oddly faithful as to be almost respectable. The chroniclers, who nearly all hated John of Gaunt, write continually of his being a reckless libertine, but it always turns out that it is his connection with Katherine Swynford that they mean. With the exception of one incident in his youth the Duke is known to have had an affair with no other woman, and he testified to the Pope that he had no relations even with Katherine Swynford as long as his first wife,

[1] Governess is perhaps not a very good translation of *magistra*, which applied to a lady of high rank who did not actually give lessons but who was responsible for the general upbringing of the young aristocrats placed in her charge.

98

Blanche of Lancaster, was living. John of Gaunt had three sons by Katherine to whom he gave the name of Beaufort (i.e. "well-made") from a castle he owned in France, and he educated them carefully for the high posts in Church and State that they ultimately filled. The Duke seems to have been at heart a family man, and his record with Katherine is one of an unfaltering devotion that finally culminated in marriage. As for Katherine's relations with the children of his first marriage, she was the governess of Philippa and Elizabeth, and the son, Henry, loved her well enough to ultimately call her "Mother." [2]

Under the circumstances it is not surprising that a place was found in the Savoy household for Katherine's sister, Philippa Chaucer. Philippa had left the royal service after the death of the Queen, and in the Savoy she became one of the demoiselles in attendance upon Constance, the new Duchess of Lancaster. In 1374 she left this position and moved to London to be with her husband, who had just been given a government post in the city. But the preceding year Philippa was still at the Savoy, and among the New Year's gifts that the Duke gave various ladies was the gift of a silver buttoner and six silver buttons to Philippa Chaucer.

Geoffrey Chaucer himself was not in England that winter. He had left London on the first of December to go on a diplomatic mission to Italy, and he probably spent his New Year's Day near the snowy passes of the Alps.

Chaucer was on his way to Genoa, which was the chief commercial city in western Italy. Its naval dockyards were capable of launching six-hundred-ton transport vessels and its navy consisted of twenty-five thousand men. England had signed a treaty with the city the previous January and there was talk of establishing a special trading port for the Genoese merchants somewhere along the English coast.

King Edward sent a commission to discuss the matter of a trading port with the Doge and the municipality. Of the three members of the commission two were Genoese, a naval expert named

[2] He was by then Henry IV and the new King of England. He did not need to recognize his father's third wife unless he chose, much less to call her by so affectionate a title.

Jacobo de Provano and a fellow countryman of his named Johannes de Mari. The third member was Geoffrey Chaucer.

This was not by any means the first time that Chaucer had been abroad, but it was probably the first time he went to Italy. Whatever the trip may have done for Genoese trade it had a pronounced effect upon Chaucer's development as a poet and is worth describing in detail.

Chaucer and his fellow commissioners probably took the direct route from London to Dover known as the Dover Road. This was the southern end of Watling Street, one of the main traffic arteries in the kingdom, and Chaucer was thoroughly familiar with it long before he sent his Canterbury Pilgrims to travel upon it one green April morning.

It counted as a three-day journey from London to Dover, with overnight stops at Rochester and at Canterbury. Horses could be got on the hire system at twelvepence a day, but the King's commissioners and their retinue certainly brought their own.

Medieval roads were better on the whole than they are usually credited with being. Social historians, mindful of the number of contemporary complaints about them, are sure they were very bad, but economic historians, mindful of the amount of freight that went over them in all kinds of weather, are convinced they were fairly good.[3] No English road was ever really trustworthy in bad weather until inexpensive surfacing was developed in the nineteenth century, and horseback riding in an English December could not be called a pleasure, but Chaucer probably had a reasonably comfortable time of it. The inns at all three of the overnight stops were excellent, and that sterling medieval article of clothing, the hood, could be trusted to keep the wind and the rain out of the necks of the three commissioners.

At Dover they took ship as soon as the wind was in the proper

[3] It cost threepence halfpenny a ton to freight wine overland in winter in England. This price included the cost of loading and unloading and wine is a difficult article to pack. It also included the cost of the carter's lodgings, the feed for his horse and insurance against theft. If wine could be freighted at a profit at this figure, the roads over which it passed must have been kept in reasonably good repair.

quarter and the horses had been loaded aboard. The commissioners would not expect the shelter of a cabin, for only the largest ships had anything of the sort, but there might be a canvas awning on deck stretched over wooden hoops to shelter them from the wind and spray. Their baggage would also stay on deck, among the ship's tackle.

The English ships were much smaller than the Italian ones and averaged a hundred and fifty tons with about a hundred men to a crew. Like all medieval boats they were shaped like deep dishes, with heavy forecastles and poops. Their shapes made them relatively unsinkable, but they must have jerked around like chips of wood in the rough waters of the English Channel.

The helmsman waited for a following wind, set his course in the general direction of Calais, and corrected any minor errors when he sighted the coast of France. It took about twelve hours to cross the Channel, unless there was a storm or an encounter with pirates. These pirates were English as well as Spanish or French, like the "good felawe" who rode with the Canterbury Pilgrims, and they were one of the problems, like weather, that beset all medieval passengers impartially.

Deschamps speaks rather snappishly of an inn in Calais, where he could not sleep because the horses trampled in the stable next to him and the sea beat endlessly outside. He reserves his admiration for the French inns, with their clean pillowcases and alert service. Deschamps was not in any case a very cheerful traveler and moans aloud over the horrors of winter at sea and a dreadful trip over the comfortless, storm-ridden passes of the Alps, with the inns charging unreasonably high prices in the mountains for poor food and drink. Chaucer took the same trip as the French poet but his sole comment on it was the expense account he presented to the Exchequer on his return. It cost him thirty shillings, which would be over a hundred dollars in modern money.

It probably took the King's commissioners about seven weeks to reach their destination, traveling at the rate of a hundred miles a week. This would have brought them into Genoa to begin diplomatic negotiations with the Doge about the first of February.

During the discussions Chaucer was detached on "secret business" and sent to Florence. This was the important part of the trip as far as his development as a poet was concerned, for it was his first contact with a kind of writing that was neither classical nor French.

It is a mistake, however, to look back upon Florence with the special literary associations that the passage of centuries has given it, thinking of it only as the city of Dante's birth and Petrarch's influence and Boccaccio's devotion. As well think of Brooklyn as a lyric city because Walt Whitman lived and worked there.

Florence of the fourteenth century was a large industrial city, twice the size of London. It was the banking center of all Europe. Only Flanders rivaled it in cloth manufacture, and nearly thirty thousand people depended for their livelihood on the clothing industry. This had turned into a really capitalistic enterprise, with bitter class feeling already being generated beween capital and labor, and a workers' revolt blazed up only six years after Chaucer's visit. In spite of Boccaccio's praise of the city it does not seem to have been an especially pleasant place to live, judging by the speed with which its wealthier inhabitants built country estates for themselves just outside its grey walls. It was the center of a pushing, fast-growing mercantile area and when Dante lived in Florence he had hated its commercialism bitterly.

Dante was long since dead when the English commissioner named Geoffrey Chaucer arrived in Florence in the spring of 1373. The swarthy, restless, unhappy exile had been buried more than fifty years earlier, and his bowed figure walked no more in Ravenna. Yet already Dante was beginning to cast a shadow over the city that had exiled him, a shadow that was to grow gigantic in the coming years. Florence had exiled him as a politician but was forced to accept him as a poet, and Chaucer must have heard talk of him wherever books were mentioned at all.

The increasing enthusiasm over Dante as a writer crystallized that summer of 1373 into a petition to the Signoria that the *Divine Comedy* be expounded by some competent authority in a series of public lectures. The lecturer chosen was Giovanni Boccaccio, who was now an old man in his sixties but who still loved Dante with the enthusiasm of a boy.

With a striking sense of the fitness of things, Boccaccio decided to give his lectures in Italian instead of Latin. Boccaccio had abandoned the vernacular in his own work, in devoted imitation of his friend and master, Francis Petrarch, and had given his last years to writing a work of heavy scholarship in Latin.[4] But Boccaccio was still convinced that serious poetry could be written in one's own native language, and it was this aspect of Dante's work that he chose to underline by giving his own lectures in Italian also. He was bitterly criticized for it in some quarters, but a literary leaven had begun to work in Florence that could hardly have escaped the notice of the English commissioner visiting the city in the spring.

It is true that Chaucer had already made up his own mind independently to use his native tongue in his poetry, but it must have been a memorable day for him when he discovered that the great Florentine also had had the same idea. Once Chaucer had encountered Dante he could not have rested until he had a copy of the *Divine Comedy* in his own possession, and he read it with an intent thoroughness that shows how deeply Dante must have interested him.

No human being could have been more unlike Chaucer either as a personality or as a writer than the author of the *Divine Comedy*, with his tremendous, tragic, all-embracing reach as a poet and his peevish, ambitious, intemperate, melancholy existence as an individual. The poet of heaven and hell had almost nothing to say to the poet of earth, and Chaucer knew it.

Chaucer had what Boccaccio lacked—a very clear idea of what was right for him as an artist. For all his admiration of Dante he was never tempted to imitate him.[5] Chaucer kept to his own road, the road that eventually led him into writing another kind of Comedy altogether, and at no time did Dante influence the bent of the English poet's mind. He did, however, contribute to Chaucer's

[4] Petrarch himself had been interested in the vernacular in his younger days, when he was writing sonnets to Laura, and he still believed that his native tongue had literary possibilities that might be worth exploring. But he pinned his own hopes of personal immortality on a massive production, named *Africa*, which he wrote in Latin.

[5] This is not to say that Boccaccio tried to imitate Dante. He tried instead to imitate Petrarch and bowed his gay spirit to the ill-fitting harness of classical scholarship because he was sure that whatever was right for Petrarch was right for him.

growth, for Chaucer was as wise in recognizing what he could use from another poet as he was in keeping fundamentally to his own independence.

Dante was an intensely medieval poet, and it is worth noting that Chaucer was not impressed by his medievalism. The two aspects of his work that caught Chaucer's attention are two in which Dante foreshadowed the poets of the Renaissance. One was his use of the vernacular rather than Latin, and the other was his brilliant new use of the art of description.

Chaucer was accustomed to the French manner of description, which aimed at ornament rather than realism. The French have always liked analysis and their instinct was invariably to present a person or an object to the reader by analysis rather than in a single visual image. Dante's method was precisely the opposite. He was master of the art of specific realism, of seizing the exact detail which will make the image come alive in the reader's mind. He does not explain; he presents, whether he is describing the croaking of a frog or the movement of a flock of sheep or the appearance of a wound in a man's head.

This is the Renaissance method rather than the medieval one. It is foreign to the medieval fondness for types, for dealing with the general rather than with the specific, and it must have struck a reader as alert as Chaucer as a startlingly new method of presentation. It happened also to coincide with his own interest in concrete detail, for he was the writer who had already put linen pillowcases on Machaut's rhetorical feather bed.

It would probably not be correct to say that Chaucer learned from Dante a new way of using description. Chaucer was a writer of slow, careful development and he found his own idiom as a writer in the same way that he had already chosen his own native language—by himself. But it would be correct to say that Dante convinced Chaucer of the rightness of his own independence. Here was a poet who refused to conform to rules, who wrote in his own mother tongue and in his own way, and yet whom even a reluctant Florence was beginning to acknowledge as the greatest of her sons. To a young English poet who was beginning to break rules himself it must have been a great comfort to find a man like Dante.

CHAPTER VIII

GEOFFREY CHAUCER returned to England in May, bringing with him some valuable material that did not show in his luggage.

He was apparently considered a successful diplomat, for shortly after his return he was sent down to Dartmouth to investigate a dispute between the Mayor of the port and a Genoese shipmaster. The Genoese ship, one of the large merchandising vessels known as tarits, had been driven ashore on the English coast and the Mayor of Dartmouth was accused of robbing it of its cargo. The cargo was probably alum, which was the main import from Genoa and indispensable to the dyes in the English cloth industry. Dartmouth itself was a hotbed of pirates who called themselves shipmen; and when Chaucer remarks dryly of a certain Shipman of his own,

> For aught I know, he was of Dertemouthe

there was no one in his audience who would have lacked an instant mental picture of that particular Canterbury pilgrim.

The following year Chaucer received the back pay due him for his mission to Genoa in wages and expenses. The payment represented nearly two thousand dollars and was nine months late, for the Exchequer moved with a slow dignity in these matters. Chaucer's official life, like that of everyone else who worked for the government, was that of being chronically owed. To receive payment in the same year was a real burst of speed, and government employees like Chaucer, who sometimes were obliged to advance wages out of their own purses, must have wondered what the large staff of clerks and accountants in the Department of the Exchequer did with their time.[1]

---

[1] Other government departments had the same lethargic qualities. Philippa Chaucer had some fur-lined garments due her at Christmas and they were finally delivered to her by the wardrobe department in March, when the greater part of their usefulness for that year had departed.

Up to the year of his return from Genoa, Chaucer had no official position with the government except that of being a king's esquire. In June of 1374, however, he received for the first time a permanent, salaried, government position. He was made Comptroller of the Customs and Subsidy of Wools, Skins and Hides in the port of London.[2]

The revenue derived from the customs duty on the export of hides and woolfells was not large; but the export duty on raw wool was the chief financial mainstay of the English government. It was literally golden fleece that moved in a heavy stream from the pastures of England to the looms of Italy and Flanders, and London was chief of all the English ports where customs officials were stationed to levy a tariff on it as it passed.

No poem has ever been written to English wool, but when a government ordinance of 1353 called it "the sovereign merchandise and jewel of the realm of England" some minor official was combining a lyric note with a sober statistical fact. Wool was indeed the chief jewel of England, the one really valuable export article in a country that was predominantly agricultural. It was with the revenue from wool and the bait of the wool staple that King Edward financed his wars and bribed his allies; and it was not until a corporation of English merchants acquired a monopoly of the wool trade that the King found a creditor he could not bankrupt as he had already managed to bankrupt several individual financiers and two of the greatest banking houses in Italy. King Edward might well have chosen for his motto the little verse of praise that a wool merchant engraved on the windows of his new house:

> I praise God and ever shall,
> It is the sheep hath paid for all.

The export duty collected on each individual sack of wool was not large, but it amounted to a huge sum in the aggregate. For in-

[2] According to the copy of this patent enrolled in the Exchequer, Chaucer was also made Comptroller of the Petty Customs on wines, cloth and other merchandise. But he apparently was not actually given this additional minor post until 1382.

stance, four years before Chaucer entered the customs service the City of London loaned the King five thousand pounds, which would be the equivalent of about $375,000 in modern money, the City to be repaid out of the receipts from the wool customs. The whole sum was repaid by this method in seven months.

On the twelfth of June Chaucer went to Westminster to take his oath of office, administered by the Court of Exchequer in their upstairs office to the right of the entrance to the Great Hall. Chaucer took the oath in French, swearing that he would live in London and keep his customs accounts without falsification and in his own handwriting, so help him God and the saints.

Chaucer also received from the Exchequer his half of the cocket seal neatly secured within a little purse. The two Customs Collectors had one half of the seal in their possession and Chaucer as Comptroller had the other half. The cocket was the seal used to stamp the parchment receipt given to each wool merchant as soon as he had paid the port duties, and no wool could go down the Thames from London without the full seal stamped upon it.

When Chaucer took his oath to live in London, his residence had already been chosen for him by the government and a lease had been signed a month before. The lease was signed with the City of London, for the lodgings given Chaucer and his wife were municipal property—a house over one of the city gates.

These houses over the gates had originally been built for the families of the Sergeants-at-Arms who guarded the city wall. But as London became less of a military stronghold, correspondingly less attention was paid to the original purpose of the buildings. By Chaucer's time they were leased by various city officials and seem to have been considered very desirable residences. As far as can be ascertained, Chaucer was the first royal official to occupy one of them, although another king's esquire was given a similar lease eight years later. There were no restrictions upon Chaucer's occupancy except that he was to keep the premises in good repair and not to sublet them; and the city, of course, reserved the right to take over the building at once in the unlikely event that London was attacked.

Chaucer's gate was Aldgate, the nearest of all the city gates to his place of business and only half a mile from the customhouse on the Thames. It was one of the four original gates of the city but had been almost entirely rebuilt the previous century so that it was now a solid structure of stone and Flanders tile. The second story was Chaucer's home and beneath it arched the two heavy curves of the gate proper. Each arch had its portcullis, almost never used, and a gate which William Duerhirst, the porter, closed at night and opened again the next day. The first thing the Chaucers heard in the morning was the rumble of the carts over the stones, coming in from the country and stopping at the gate each day to pay the small tax that helped pave the city streets.

The house over Aldgate gave Philippa Chaucer her first real home and Geoffrey Chaucer a chance to settle down and spread out his books. Living over Aldgate would be about the equivalent of living on the second floor of a modern duplex, except that the Chaucers had the advantage of the whole place to themselves as well as a garden and a cellar.[3] Their position not only gave them more light than the average London householder but also what must have been a beautiful view. Their west windows overlooked the tile roofs and church spires of all London, with the gilt cross of St. Paul's rising in the distance, while through their east windows they could see as far as the green fields and woods of Essex. It was a direct walk down Leadenhall to Cheap, the great shopping street of the city, and on Leadenhall the tallest Maypole in town went up on the first of May, overtopping even the steeple of the parish church.

Chaucer mentions this residence over Aldgate in the only autobiographical remark concerning his surroundings to be found in his poetry. He says that as soon as his day's work was over he did not look for "rest and newe thynges" but hurried home at once and buried himself in "another book." He was not even interested, he says, in what his neighbors were doing. All he wanted to do was to read, and he behaved exactly like a hermit except that he was not precisely a man of "abstynence." Having a home of his own had

[3] Londoners were accustomed to climbing stairs. In many three-story houses each floor was inhabited by a different family under a different freehold, to be reached usually by an outside stair.

evidently made it possible for Chaucer to indulge in an orgy of reading, and he read with the passion of a man who suddenly realizes how many kinds of books there are in the world and how few of them he has read.[4]

The poem from which this autobiographical passage is taken is called *The House of Fame*, and the mark of books is clear upon it even without Chaucer's testimony. The poet had obviously been reading in all directions, with the excited curiosity that was characteristic of him, and it was because he read with such delight that *The House of Fame* is never dull. Even the soberest bits of information received a sudden twist in his mind that made them into something quite different. As for the range of his reading it covered histories and stories and poems and scientific treatises and embraced everything from the *Aeneid* to Dante's *Divine Comedy*.

John Lydgate, in making a list of Chaucer's work, says that he "wrote" Dante in English and there has been some attempt to show that by this Lydgate meant *The House of Fame*. If this was Lydgate's intention, he could surely not have read either poem. There are echoing phrases and devices here and there in *The House of Fame* that show Chaucer had been reading Dante and reading him carefully, but the tone of the two productions is a world apart. Chaucer, for instance, has a guide to *The House of Fame* as Dante had a guide through the Inferno; but if the stately Vergil who guided Dante bears any resemblance to the chatty Eagle who guides Chaucer, then the heroes of the Greek tragedies are close kin to Sam Weller.

It is quite possible that Chaucer considered at one time the idea of rendering the *Divine Comedy* into English, since his first instinct with any book he admired was apparently to translate it into his own tongue. Yet if he ever planned such a translation nothing came of it as far as extant manuscripts are concerned. Certainly the

[4] Dante felt the same sort of excitement where books were concerned. He once spent three hours in Siena during a festival, hearing none of the noise because he was deep in a book. And although he was a man who valued his own dignity, he stretched out on his stomach on a bench in front of an apothecary's shop because he had just acquired a new book and could not wait until he got home to read it.

lively *House of Fame* is not Chaucer's attempt to reproduce in English the dark and massive splendor of Dante's masterpiece.

What Chaucer actually was attempting to do in *The House of Fame* is open to question. There are some indications that he intended to make it a love poem, branched off on another aspect of his subject and failed to return. Or possibly he had no clear plan of the poem in his own mind and merely intended to ramble along in the easygoing medieval way on the general subject of "fame" until he was through. The end of his poem would naturally give the best clue as to what was in Chaucer's mind when he began it, but the end of *The House of Fame* is missing.

This is not the only one of Chaucer's poems that is unfinished, and in fact there is no poet, in all the history of English literature, who left so many poems undone. This was partly the result, no doubt, of an exceptionally busy public life, which obliged Chaucer to fit the herculean labor of being a major poet into his spare time. Partly it was the result of his steady development as a poet, for when he had outgrown a former way of writing he saw no reason to turn back the clock and finish what no longer interested him. Partly also it was the result of his incurable optimism; he cast his *Canterbury Tales*, for instance, in so ambitious a framework, involving a hundred and twenty tales in all, that he would have needed at least another decade to finish it.

In the case of *The House of Fame* there is another possible explanation that can be advanced for the unfinished state of the manuscript. Chaucer was already well into the third book, which is as long as the first two books combined, when the poem breaks off; and since Book III is his "litel laste book" the poem must have been very near its end. It is quite possible that the manuscript became mutilated and that the concluding lines that Chaucer composed have since been lost. On the other hand, the poem is such a rambling affair that it is equally possible that Chaucer had no clear idea of where he was going and left *The House of Fame* unfinished because he could not think of a way of finishing it.

The first book of the poem is a conventional and circumspect production. Chaucer chose the same meter he had used in *The Book of the Duchess*, the smooth old meter of the *Rose*, and there is the same device of enclosing the story in a dream. In careful obedience to the books of rhetoric Chaucer starts off with a proem, moves on to an invocation, and then settles down for about three hundred lines to retell the story of the *Aeneid*. It is done lightly and prettily enough, but any competent French poet could have done as well.

The second book, on the other hand, is pure Chaucer. No one else could have done it. The whole thing comes suddenly to life with the arrival of an Eagle to take the startled dreamer on a visit to the upper air and consists of a kind of conducted tour to which Chaucer was subjected by that remarkable fowl. The Eagle arrives like a cannonball, constituting perhaps the first use of artillery for literary purposes in English, and his personality is as original as the manner of his appearance.

The Eagle subjects his dazed listener to a series of lectures delivered with an aplomb and with an instructive flood of supplementary detail that mark the bird as a born platform orator. Later, Chaucer was to create a hen of somewhat the same didactic tendencies, but the Eagle could have out-talked even the charming Pertelote. His attitude towards "Geffrey" is the charitable one which any right-minded bird might be expected to assume towards a born idiot, and Geoffrey takes it with meekness for he well knows that the Eagle is a far more intelligent individual than he.

The conversation that takes place between Geoffrey and the Eagle should be read to be appreciated, but a few of the highlights of the tour can be mentioned. The Eagle's flood of conversation is natural in an accomplished talker who has maneuvered his audience into a receptive position (Geoffrey is dangling in the Eagle's claws and has no wish to be dropped), but he does all he can to make his dazed companion feel comfortable. He bids him rouse himself in a much kinder tone than the one that wakens Geoffrey in the morning and while he admits that Geoffrey is no light weight to carry around through the air, he wishes it understood that the whole expedition is strictly for the poet's own good.

It occurs to Geoffrey's wavering brain that it is possibly Jove's intention to turn him into a star, but the Eagle says, no, not yet. The trip has been scheduled because the poet has used his wit, such as it is, in writing love songs until his head aches without knowing very much about "Love's folk." The Eagle adds the severe strictures on Chaucer's hermit-like habits after work which can perhaps be taken as autobiographical, and promises to bring him to a certain House of Fame where he will hear all the tidings of love.

Geoffrey incautiously remarks that he does not see how all these tidings can be enclosed in a single area, and lets loose upon himself a flood of instructiveness from the delighted Eagle, who has obviously been waiting for just such an opportunity.

The Eagle is particularly well posted upon physics and the properties of sound. Sound is only "air ybroken," and this broken air travels in steadily widening circles, like ripples in water, until it finally reaches the House of Fame. It is a long lecture, and a complicated one, and the Eagle points out at the end with considerable pride that he has delivered it without using any hard words at all. Has he not treated his difficult subject

> "Withoute any subtiltie
>   Of speche, or great prolixitie
>   Of termes of philosophie,
>   Of figures of poetrie,
>   Or colours of rethorike?"

"Yis," says Geoffrey meekly, and the Eagle gives a crow of triumph.

> "A ha!" quod he, "lo, so I can
>   Lewedly to a lewed [ordinary] man
>   Speke."

It is the final triumph of this accomplished bird that he is capable of modifying his language so that even Geoffrey is capable of understanding him.

This treatment of "Geffrey" is of course a continuation of the mock self-characterization that Chaucer began in *The Book of the Duchess*, except that here it is much more cleverly handled. Chaucer does not say that Geoffrey is a well-meaning but somewhat feeble-minded individual. He shows that he is, through the rather ostentatious patience with which the Eagle lectures him, as a broadminded bird willing to make every allowance. This is characterization by suggestion rather than by statement, a method that Chaucer was later to bring to such heights that only Shakespeare excelled him at it. It is just possible that he got the original hint for his technique from Jean de Meun, but, if so, it was only a hint and Chaucer developed it in his own way.

The tour continues with the Eagle pointing out various points of interest along the route. They are now so high in the air that the earth is only a "prikke," and the Eagle does not wish his passenger to miss anything along the route. He bids him notice the "airissh beastes" that generate the wind and hail, and points out the Milky Way that some call Watling Street.[5]

The Eagle also makes a determined effort to give Geoffrey a lesson in astronomy. Geoffrey protests he does not want a lesson in astronomy; he is much too old for schoolwork. The Eagle points out hopefully how useful it would be, when Geoffrey was reading poetry and encountered references to the Bear and to Orion, to know their exact places in the heavens. "No fors," says Geoffrey briefly, which seems to be the exact medieval equivalent of "Nothing doing." The Eagle philosophically abandons his project since in any case they have arrived at the House of Fame. He bids his pupil a kindly farewell and the second book ends.

The third book is somewhat confusing, and it is difficult to see what kind of an ending Chaucer could have given it to pull it together into an orderly whole. The root of the trouble seems to be that Chaucer was thinking of the word "fame" in two different ways, both as "tidings" and as "reputation," and he could not make up his mind whether he wanted to write about "tydynges of Love's folk" or the thirst of mankind for personal immortality. Possibly he intended the first and then grew more interested in the second, to which he gives most of his attention. At any rate, although he claims that the contents of the third book were all planned out "in myn hed," the plan never took very clear shape on paper.

The chief interest in the third book, apart from the ingenuity

[5] Watling Street was the road Chaucer took to Dover when he went to the Continent. It was supposed to be as thick with travelers as the Milky Way was thick with stars.

shown in the descriptions of the wall of ice and the revolving house of twigs and so on, lies in the opportunity that the subject gave Chaucer to roam about in his reading. He takes a personal tour through the authors who were popular in the Middle Ages which is quite as extensive in its way as the Eagle's tour through the sky.

Chaucer surveys with particular affection the tellers of tales.[6] He begins with Josephus, whose history of the Jews was oddly popular in view of the savage way contemporary Jews were treated. Then he lists the historians of Troy, including an "eye-witness" like Dares the Phrygian and ending with the great English expert, Geoffrey of Monmouth. The only name on the list whose veracity is suspect is Homer's. Homer was "favorable" to the Greeks, which was the wrong side from the English point of view. For the English had been assured by Geoffrey of Monmouth that they were descended from Aeneas, and Aeneas came from Troy. Chaucer presents this point with deep gravity, but it is a gravity that is somewhat suspect also.

Chaucer continues his list with the great Roman historians: Vergil, and Ovid whom he loved, and Lucan and Claudian whom he admired. Then he can see a vast crowd of more recent writers stretching out in front of him, thick as rooks' nests in trees, and drops the attempt to itemize them all.

By this time the lady who owns the House of Fame has made her entrance. She can give immortality to any man she chooses, and an excited crowd of petitioners surrounds her wherever she goes. Chaucer shows in this section an unusually strong sense of the fickleness of personal reputation and the uselessness of any man's spending his life in pursuit of so flimsy and unreliable a prize. When a passer-by stops to ask him if he has come to the House of Fame in the hope of snatching a little personal renown for himself, Chaucer gives him an answer that goes far to explain his own success as a writer:

[6] In the Middle Ages these writers were also called "historians." In that period any story which a poet or prose writer told was supposed to be based on fact, and to the medieval mind the word "fiction" would have been an exact synonym for "falsity."

"Sufficeth me, if I were dead,
That no wight have my name in hande.
I wot myself best how I stande."

Chaucer could never have been the strongly creative writer that he was if he had tried to write with one ear cocked attentively for the applause of posterity. He stood before the tribunal of his own mind and wrote to satisfy himself; he had nothing to do with the tyrant whom he personifies as ruling the House of Fame and distributing her favors with a calm disregard of justice.

At this point it apparently occurred to Chaucer that he had done nothing about the love tidings he was supposed to have come to hear. Therefore the Eagle makes a brief and somewhat subdued reappearance and drops him into a revolving house of twigs which is full of confirmed talebearers like sailors and pilgrims.

In one corner of the house of twigs is a place for love tidings, and everyone is racing towards this corner. They climb over each other and tread on each other's heels and stamp the way men do when they are catching eels, to listen to what a certain man in authority has to tell them. But no one will ever know what the man in authority had to say, for at this point the poem ends.

The suggestion has frequently been made that Chaucer intended this final speech to announce some kind of love tidings connected with Edward's court, such as the betrothal of John of Gaunt's daughter, Philippa, or the marriage of his nephew Richard. This would be an excellent way to give the poem an exact date if it could be proven, but it is a hazardous occupation to try to link Chaucer's poetry with contemporary events.

Chaucer was like Deschamps. When he wished to deal with contemporary events in his poetry he labeled them clearly and made them unmistakable to any well-informed reader. *The Book of the Duchess* is strewn with puns that link "White" to "Blanche" and "rich hill" to "Richmond" and "long castle" to "Lancaster" in case some reader might fail to realize what duchess it was that had died. In *The House of Fame* there is nothing of this kind, not even the vaguest hint that Chaucer was concerned with court activities.

It is altogether natural and legitimate to wish to date *The*

House of Fame. All the light that can be thrown on Chaucer and his poetry is little enough, and even the smallest ray of illumination is cause for gratitude. But the theory that Chaucer undertook to write *The House of Fame* to flatter someone at court would indicate that the Eagle was right in his assumption that the poet was a little feeble-minded. An accomplished court poet wishing to announce a royal betrothal would not insert it at the tail-end of his poem as a kind of an afterthought, and after the scrambling, undignified kind of introduction that is given to it. The theory becomes untenable if it is remembered that Chaucer's "Geffrey" is a fictional character and bears no resemblance to Geoffrey Chaucer.

CHAPTER IX

HAUCER's new position in the London customs service did not prevent the King from sending him on diplomatic missions abroad. The only difference now was that a deputy was appointed to keep Chaucer's accounts for him while he was out of England.

The next foreign mission of which there is record came in December of 1376, two and a half years after his appointment to the customs. He went to France in the company of Sir John Burley "on the King's secret affairs."

Sir John Burley belonged to the King's intimate circle, and at this time he was Captain of Calais.[1] What he and Chaucer accomplished on this special mission is not known, but it was probably concerned with the two-year-old truce with France that was now drawing to a close.

There was need of peace between the two countries as far as England was concerned, for her home affairs were in a tangled state. King Edward had just held a second Jubilee, commemorating fifty years of reign, but there was none of the proud excitement that had marked the birthday Jubilee he held earlier.

The game of chivalry was tarnishing, and the men who played it had lost their youthfulness of heart. The Prince of Wales had died in June, after eight years of invalidism had given him time to compose in French verses his pathetic epitaph:

> I am poor and bereft; I lie under earth . . .
> Were you to see me now, I do not think
> You would believe that ever I was a man.

[1] An Exchequer writ of the previous year indicates that Burley and Chaucer may already have been acquainted. The officials of Calais were cited to appear before the Baron of the Exchequer in regard to a business matter, and Chaucer went surety for the appearance in court of the Treasurer of Calais. If Chaucer knew the Treasurer well, he probably knew the Captain also.

King Edward himself was a tired old man who had lost interest in the pageantries of kingship. The reins of government had for a long time been slack in his hands, and after the shock of the death of his eldest son he gave up all pretense of being a king. He retired to his beautiful manor house at Sheen, and when Parliament assembled in January it was presided over by his grandson. This was Richard, the only surviving son of the Prince of Wales and Joan of Kent, and at this time ten years old.

There had been talk of arranging a marriage between Richard and the small Princess Marie of France to form a permanent peace between the two countries, and the December mission of Geoffrey Chaucer and Sir John Burley may conceivably have been in the nature of a preliminary negotiation. In February a formal delegation, headed by the Bishop of Hereford, arrived in France to discuss the marriage, and at the same time a private delegation arrived also.

This private delegation was a confidential one consisting of three men. One of the three was Geoffrey Chaucer. The other two were Sir Guichard d'Angle and Sir Richard Stury.

It is not easy to recreate the minutiae of a long-vanished and very complicated political situation, but on the whole the three confidential envoys seem to have been chosen to strike a working balance between the two major political parties in England. Sir Guichard d'Angle was a member of the party of the late Prince of Wales, a party that had been fighting Alice Perrers to gain control of the realm ever since she had taken up her unofficial guardianship of the King and all his possessions. Sir Richard Stury, on the other hand, shared with Lord Latimer the distinction of being the chief political lieutenant of this same Alice Perrers; while Chaucer, who apparently never meddled with political factions, was on speaking terms with both sides.[2]

Sir Guichard d'Angle had been born a Gascon, but he thought of himself as an Englishman except that he asked to be buried on home soil when he died. He was a close personal friend of the

---

[2] The Bishop of Hereford's delegation had a prominent lawyer upon it, and Chaucer would have been even more useful to his own delegation if the theory about his legal training at Holborn should be correct.

Prince of Wales, who had made him Marshal of Aquitaine and the guardian of his son Richard.[3] He was experienced in marriage negotiations for he had arranged the dual wedding at Rochefort between the two princes of England and the two princesses of Castile; and when John of Gaunt's marriage party arrived in England it was Sir Guichard d'Angle whom King Edward hurried to greet. Deschamps says that everyone loved him, laying particular stress on the Gascon knight's gallantry, his good nature, and his accomplishments as a singer and dancer. Froissart loved him also and characterizes him as the perfect knight, "gay, loyal, gallant, prudent, secret, generous, bold, determined, enterprising."

Sir Richard Stury was a different sort of man altogether, and seems to have been chiefly a brilliant politician. His personal influence and prestige were less than Sir Guichard's, but his political importance was much greater now that the Prince of Wales was dead. The Prince hated him to the end and greeted him from his deathbed with the bitter remark, "Come, Richard. Come and look on what you have long desired to see."

The Prince had had good cause for bitterness, for he knew that Alice Perrers had beaten him. His party had temporarily stripped her of power when the Good Parliament was in session the previous spring, but her hold on the King was stronger than his. She had returned from her temporary exile and reinstalled her lieutenants at court; and the bishops who had sworn to excommunicate her if she broke her oath and returned to court had remained tactfully silent ever since.[4]

Alice Perrers must have been a remarkable woman. She was feminine enough, with her little dogs and her gloves embroidered with daisies, but her abilities were those of an exceedingly adept politician. The fourteenth-century chroniclers raise their voices in

[3] That is to say that Sir Guichard was Richard's *magister*, holding the same relationship to the young prince that Katherine Swynford held to the two daughters of John of Gaunt.

[4] There is a persistent theory that Alice Perrers was affiliated with John of Gaunt, a theory apparently derived from the efforts of the chroniclers to link two unpopular figures together. Yet John of Gaunt not only consented to her banishment but persuaded King Edward to grant him her forfeited estates.

such a passion of fury against her for daring to oppose their beloved Prince of Wales that it is difficult to get the exact truth about her; they report, for instance, that she was of base extraction and a weaver's daughter when she actually came from a respectable land-owning family in Hertfordshire. Particularly venomous is the influential chronicler of St. Albans, a circumstance which is traceable to a dispute Alice Perrers had with the Abbot of St. Albans over the possession of a certain manor. Yet in any case the language the chronicler uses towards her is by no means as vindictive as the language he uses towards John Wyclif.

In her own day she was evidently looked upon with respect. Wyclif was not too proud to be under her protection. The Pope was not too proud to approach her, along with other influential people in England, when he wanted a favor done for his brother; and the only formal charge her enemies ever brought against her was that she interfered in the operation of the law courts by sitting beside the judges and influencing their decisions.

At any rate, it was never any disadvantage to Sir Richard Stury in his subsequent career to have been associated with her. When young Richard came to the throne, Stury continued as a knight of the chamber under the son of his old enemy. He was a member of the royal council and served on various diplomatic, judicial and administrative commissions. He has been called a timeserver; but he risked the royal displeasure by publicly backing an unpopular religious movement and could not have been entirely without convictions. He had at least one of the qualifications of a born politician—an excellent memory; for he met Jean Froissart again after a lapse of nearly a quarter of a century and recognized him instantly.

These were the two diplomats with whom Chaucer was associated on his trip to France in the spring of 1377, and the fact that he constituted the third member of so small and influential a group of envoys indicates how safely he could afford to make jokes about himself on paper. Only a man of known intelligence can call himself a fool.

The formal negotiations over the marriage of Richard and Marie were held at Bruges and the confidential ones at Montreuil.

Chaucer, of course, was at Montreuil. The rough draft of a treaty was hammered out, to be presented for approval to the Kings of England and of France, and the commissioners parted with an agreement to meet again on the first of May.

Chaucer and Stury sailed for England together and went to report to the King at Sheen. This was a manor a few miles southwest of London on the banks of the Thames (it is now called Richmond) and later on in his career Chaucer was to become personally responsible for the maintenance of its parks and gardens and vine-shaded galleries.

King Edward lay dying at Sheen, surrounded by bedclothes and doctors, while Alice Perrers sat beside him and told him that very soon he would be able to ride out again with his hawks and his hounds.[5] It was almost certainly to Alice Perrers that Chaucer reported, for the King had no longer anything to do with the details of governing England.

On the first of May Chaucer returned to France in the company of Sir Guichard d'Angle. Stury was no longer with them, but there was a host of English dignitaries headed by the Bishop of Hereford and the Earl of Salisbury. The stateliness of the proceedings seems to have somewhat hampered the negotiations, for the English commission met at Calais and the French at Montreuil and all discussions between them were carried back and forth by messengers.

It was difficult in any case to reach a decision. The French wanted the English armaments at Calais dismantled, while the English were convinced that the twelve Aquitaine towns offered as Marie's dowry were inadequate. The area had been reconquered by the French so recently that the English still had a firm conviction that Aquitaine belonged to them.

The discussion ended suddenly before the month was out with

[5] This was numbered among her many sins by the implacable chroniclers, for she should have spent her time warning the dying King to consider the state of his soul. But it is easy to see why the frightened old man clung to her and why she did not need the services of the Dominican friar who, the chroniclers were convinced, prepared magic potions to lure the King into loving her.

the death of the Princess Marie. Some of the English delegation left at once, Chaucer luckily not being among them, and were murdered by French pirates in the Channel. The whole engagement took place directly under the eyes of the enraged Captain of Calais and there were only four survivors. The English commissioners were supposed to have been granted protection by the King of France, but the truth was that no government had any control over the action of its own shipmen and the English should have waited until a convoy was formed before they attempted to cross the Channel.

In June, King Edward died at Sheen. He was buried in Westminster Abbey next to his wife as she had requested, with his great sword beside him and his hands clasped in prayer. In time, his long and prosperous reign was going to seem to Englishmen to have been a glow of increasing triumphs and a haven of good will, but in the year 1377 they turned with real relief to his grandson Richard as the new ruler of England.

Richard was a beautiful child, inheriting not only the usual good looks of the Plantagenets but the special grace of his mother, Joan of Kent, who was still the loveliest woman in England. It was Richard's misfortune, however, that his father and mother had more in common than their very decorative appearance. They shared equally, and passed on direct to their son, the sensuous, extravagant love of splendor that had brought them to disaster in Aquitaine and helped bring Richard to disaster in England. The Prince of Wales endowed his son also with an unstable emotional temperament that was capable of the most gallant heroism when conditions were favorable and of almost insane rage when they were not.[6] In the end Richard's inheritance from his parents destroyed him, and his career is the saddest of all the Plantagenets'. The crowds that gathered before his coronation to watch him ride through London called him in admiration another

[6] The Prince of Wales ordered the death of three thousand men, women and children after the siege of Limoges, directing the slaughter from his litter, and even the admiring Froissart was deeply shocked. "I know not why the poor were not spared. . . . God have mercy on their souls, for they were veritable martyrs."

Absalom, and with more accuracy than they knew. He was as beautiful as Absalom, clothed all in white with his golden hair loose on his shoulders, and the end he came to was as needlessly tragic.

John of Gaunt supported his ten-year-old nephew loyally, although he would have been the new king himself if Richard could have been removed from the scene. If Gaunt had possessed the evil character the chroniclers liked to attribute to him, the least he could have done was to attempt to seize the reins of government from Richard's hands. Instead, he helped form a very reasonable sort of coalition government to see the youthful ruler through his minority. He served as head of the Committee of Claims the week before the coronation, decreeing who should serve in various honorary offices during the celebration and deciding the delicate problems relating to pedigree and politics that arose.[7]

The coronation was preceded by a magnificent procession, involving everyone of any importance at all in the City and the Court, that trailed its colorful way behind the trumpeters from the Tower of London to Westminster. The house fronts and streets were decorated, the conduits ran wine for three hours, and the goldsmiths outdid all the other city pageants by devising a metal angel who leaned down from a portable castle to offer the young King a crown.

Richard was put to bed early that night, but he was worn out when he left Westminster Abbey the next day after the coronation services. His tutor picked him up and carried him the rest of the way and one of the King's shoes, the holy ceremonial shoes of Edward the Confessor, slipped off the small feet. There were some who were greatly disturbed by this and took it for an omen.

The tutor was Sir Simon Burley, brother of the Sir John Burley with whom Chaucer had traveled to the Continent the previous winter. He was a hot-tempered, extravagant, overbearing man, but he had been the favorite schoolfellow of the Prince of Wales and

[7] Among those who appeared before the Committee of Claims was a ward of Geoffrey Chaucer's named Edmund Staplegate who wished to hold the office of Butler at the coronation. The committee ruled against him and the post went to the Earl of Arundel.

Richard loved Sir Simon Burley as much as his father before him had done.

Chaucer took his part in the new government along with the rest. The various annuities that had been granted him by King Edward were confirmed and he took up the customs accounts that his deputy, Thomas de Evesham, had been keeping for him while he was abroad.

Less than a year later Chaucer needed the services of a deputy again. He was sent to the Continent on a diplomatic mission, but this time he went not to France but to Italy.

Chaucer went to the court of Milan, to discuss "certain affairs touching the expedition of the King's war." The war was the chronic war with France, which had reopened after the failure of the marriage negotiations, and the English government was turning to Lombardy for financial and military aid. The Visconti family ruled in Lombardy, the two upstart brothers who had been rich enough to buy both a French princess and an English prince. Bernabo Visconti, who ruled at Milan while his brother ruled in the neighboring city of Pavia, had acquired a new son-in-law in Sir John Hawkwood, the most brilliant general in Europe. It was under orders to confer with Bernabo Visconti and Sir John Hawkwood that Chaucer journeyed to Milan.

Chaucer traveled with Sir Edward de Berkeley but each of them had a full retinue, Sir Edward's consisting of ten men and Chaucer's of six. The party left England May 28, 1378, and the journey must have been a pleasanter one than Chaucer's first trip to Italy. Summer is a better time for crossing the Alps and Chaucer was going to a more attractive city than crowded, commercially minded Florence.

It would be idle to suggest that either of the Visconti brothers was a virtuous individual, but like the later Italian tyrants of the Renaissance they both possessed a whole-souled interest in art, literature and public order. They and their ancestors had made Milan into a beautiful city. It was built on a green plain, crisscrossed by the remarkable system of canals that made it possible to ship the goods of Lombardy all over Europe. The walls of the city were built of the famous rose-colored local brick and the castellated battlements were called *merlato* because they looked a little like a blackbird's open beak.

Behind the rose-colored walls stood a well-run city. The gutters were new, the streets were paved with stone, and thieves were almost nonexistent. Each inn was responsible for checking its guests and notifying the official registrar of a new arrival and the Visconti had a private postal system whose privileges they sometimes extended to individuals. Letters were stamped at the post office without being opened unless Bernabo had some reason to suspect their contents.

As a center of culture, Milan stood high among the cities of Italy. It numbered among its citizens six hundred notaries, eighty schoolmasters, and fifty professional transcribers of manuscripts. When Genoa and the other northern cities wanted any literary work done they came to Milan. Bernabo himself was deeply interested in literature and was building up his personal library at Milan as his brother Galeazzo was doing at Pavia.

The great hall of the palace, where Chaucer probably first met Bernabo, was itself a tribute to the cultural interests of the family. Giotto had done the frescoes, which encircled the walls under a roof of blue and gold and showed Hector and Aeneas and Charlemagne and other heroes of antiquity mingling their painted shapes with legendary but equally heroic members of the Visconti family.

The lord of this magnificence, Bernabo Visconti, was almost larger than life himself. The Pope called him with some bitterness a "son of Belial" for he was a man upon whom excommunications had no effect at all. During Bernabo's sudden attacks of rage only his wife could go near him (for he loved his wife deeply in spite of his thirty-six illegitimate children), but he had an odd passion for justice and almost invariably judged the rich more harshly than the poor. A flamboyant, lively, uninhibited individual, he had a great fondness for practical jokes and usually found his butt in some ambassador to his court, for the dignity of the species as a whole seemed to fascinate him. Possibly some of the dislike the Pope felt towards him was caused by the fact that Bernabo once made the papal ambassadors eat the whole of a document they had brought him, up to and including the wax seals.

Bernabo's son-in-law, Sir John Hawkwood, was a much more respectable gentleman. As a professional soldier he fought on various sides in the endless inter-city wars—for Pisa and against Pisa, for the Pope and against the Pope—but always to the accompaniment of a chorus of universal admiration for his talents. He was the first to fight in the winter in Italy, evidently not considering it winter in comparison with his native Essex, and he was not only a talented soldier but an honorable one. Unlike most of the men of his trade he never sold out his current employer and he treated his own men with scrupulous fairness.

Chaucer probably enjoyed himself at Milan. There is no reason why he should have been intimidated by Bernabo Visconti, in view of his own lively sense of personal independence and his ability to see a joke, while his long diplomatic training and experience with court life would have made him feel entirely at ease in the great palace hall beneath the beautiful frescoes of Giotto.

As a poet Chaucer had every reason to be interested in the court of Milan. The late Francis Petrarch had lived in the city for eight years as a close friend of the family, and as godfather to Bernabo's son Marco he had composed a special poem in Latin hexameters for the christening. It is not likely that Chaucer was able to resist the impulse to make a pilgrimage to the west part of town to visit the house where Petrarch actually lived and wrote, and to stare out the great man's own window across the green countryside to the distant line of the Alps. For Chaucer admired Petrarch deeply, as did every other writing man in Europe, and it would have been well worth a special trip to the Vercellina gate to visit his house.

Another activity which almost certainly occupied Chaucer's spare time was that of looking for Italian manuscripts. His subsequent poetry shows that Dante had roused in him a deep interest in books in the Italian vernacular and it was in Italy that these were most likely to be found. Even the well-equipped bookstores of Paris did not deal in local Italian manuscripts that were of no interest to outsiders, and it was only in Italy that Chaucer could readily buy works in the Italian tongue. If Bernabo Visconti learned that his English guest was unaccountably interested in poems in the local vernacular, he could easily have put him in touch with the booksellers with whom he himself had dealings all over northern Italy, and they in turn could have offered Chaucer whatever they had in stock.

It was probably in some such way that Chaucer came into contact with two Italian poems that had a profound effect on his future development as a writer. One was an epic called the *Teseide* and one was a love story called *Il Filostrato;* and they were both the work of Giovanni Boccaccio.

There has been a tendency to put twentieth-century knowledge against a fourteenth-century background and to feel that Chaucer must have known that these two poems were written by Boccaccio. But all the evidence goes to show that Chaucer encountered them in an unsigned manuscript.

Boccaccio had now been dead for three years, and his reputation among his contemporaries was very different from the reputation he has today. If Chaucer knew him at all in a personal way it was as the elderly lecturer who had been scheduled to give a talk on Dante the season following Chaucer's own visit to Florence. If he knew him in a literary way it was as the scholarly author of that monumental Latin treatise, *De Casibus Virorum.*

Neither Chaucer nor any other fourteenth-century reader had any reason to link this scholarly writer of Latin prose with the lively, experimental Italian poet that Boccaccio had been in his youth. Boccaccio himself had lived to be deeply ashamed of the pagan love stories he wrote when he was young and unregenerate, and it was to expiate these early sins of his that he thought of retiring to a monastery.

Even his best friends were not familiar with the poetry of Boccaccio's youth. Boccaccio was devoted to Petrarch and said of him, "I have been his during forty years or more"; yet even Petrarch only encountered Boccaccio's final masterpiece in the vernacular, the *Decameron,* by accident. Petrarch read it the year of his death, twenty years after it had actually been written, and Boccaccio's earlier works in the vernacular he never read at all.

Some of Boccaccio's stories became well-known, but their author did not. One of the *Decameron* stories, that of the patient Griselda, circulated all over Europe, but everywhere from Holland to Spain it was attributed to Petrarch. When Chaucer translated the same story into English as one of his Canterbury tales he attributed it to Petrarch as the continental translators had done. The same thing was true of some of Boccaccio's lesser works, and when a fourteenth-century French writer found a copy of *Il Filostrato* in Sicily he announced firmly that it had been composed "by a Florentine poet named Petrarch."

Chaucer was almost abnormally careful to give credit where credit was due and his list of literary acknowledgements is a long one. He mentions by name every poet to whom he was indebted, from Ovid to Petrarch, and the only name he fails to mention is Boccaccio's. The most likely explanation is that he never heard of it and that he encountered his work in one of the unsigned manuscripts in which the poetical step-children of Boccaccio's youth drifted aimlessly around Italy.

It is useless to speculate what effect Boccaccio's masterpiece, the *Decameron*, might have had upon Chaucer if he had encountered it. He was able at any rate to do wonders with the two lesser works of Boccaccio that came his way.

The new sort of writing that Chaucer found when he read the *Teseide* and *Il Filostrato* did not give his mind an immediate illumination. It was not with a sudden leap that the *Teseide* became the Knight's Tale and that *Il Filostrato* bloomed into *Troilus and Criseyde*.

Chaucer was an artist of slow growth, moving carefully and experimentally along his own chosen line, and there was a period of uncertainty in his work when he first began to think over this new material that had come his way. There are two shorter poems written about this time that show he had been reading the *Teseide*. One is *The Parliament of Birds* and the other is *Anelida and Arcite*; and the impact of Boccaccio upon these two poems is curious. In the first, Boccaccio's influence is superficial and the poem is a successful example of Chaucer's courtly French technique. In the second, Boccaccio's influence is much stronger and the poem is an unfinished failure. It is as though the French mode to which Chaucer had previously been accustomed was cracking under the new and heavier weight that was being put upon it.

128

The Parliament of Birds is completely within the French poetical tradition and could equally well have been written if Chaucer had never been to Italy at all. There is an occasional echo of the *Teseide*, as there is of a dozen other poems, but the background is still that of the garden of the *Rose*. The story is enclosed in the familiar framework of a dream, and the theme is one long beloved by the poets of France. It is a development of the pretty legend that on St. Valentine's Day all the birds gather before the goddess of Nature to choose their mates.

Nevertheless, Chaucer had progressed a long way since he wrote *The Book of the Duchess* in earnest youthful imitation of the French models. He was no longer an apprentice to the French school of writing but a qualified master, and he now had the poetic strength and experience to control his material instead of letting his material control him.

A striking example of his development as an independent artist is the stanza form he used in *The Parliament of Birds*. The usual vehicle for narrative verse was the four-stress couplet of *The Romance of the Rose*, which Chaucer himself had used in *The Book of the Duchess* and *The House of Fame*, and which Chaucer's prominent fellow poet, John Gower, used as a matter of course when he finally made up his mind at the end of the century to write something in English. But Chaucer himself had already grown dissatisfied with the pretty, tripping, jog-trot meter which he himself calls "light and lewed [ordinary]" and the result of his dissatisfaction was a new stanza form. It was the seven-line stanza with five stresses to the line that is now called "rime royal."

Chaucer probably got the original hint for this stanza from his reading in French. Poets like Froissart and Machaut were constantly experimenting with the structure of their ballades and they occasionally used a stanza of seven lines instead of the usual one of eight. If this seven-line stanza were to be freed from the usual rules surrounding the ballade—the address, the refrain, the envoi, the restricted number of stanzas and the set number of rhyming words—the result would be Chaucer's rime royal.

On the face of it, the ballade stanza would seem to be a highly unsuitable medium for narrative verse. A successful ballade consists of a graceful circling around a fixed point, with the technical dexterity of the poet in constant evidence. A successful narrative stanza, on the other hand, should take its place unnoticed in the continuous forward movement of the story itself, with the poet's technique so dexterous that it does not show at all.

Chaucer had already been making experiments with his new stanza. There are in existence two otherwise typical examples of the routine French poetic form known as the "Complaint" in which Chaucer tried out rime royal. In one of these, *A Complaint to his Lady,* Chaucer also tried his hand at Dante's meter of *terza rima.* He found the Italian form unsatisfactory, but the variant he made out of the French ballade stanza became in his hands one of the finest and most flexible narrative stanzas in English literature, reaching finally its full flower in *Troilus and Criseyde.*

Geoffrey Chaucer was an exceedingly careful, thoughtful artist, and the signs of the developing craftsman are as clear in his work as the signs of genius. He took his trade of poetry seriously, working at it with intentness and intelligence, and he must have done a great deal of revision on some of his poems before the final result satisfied him. He might well have said of his career as a poet what he says of love at the beginning of *The Parliament of Birds:*

> The lyf so short, the craft so long to lerne,
> Th' assay so hard, so sharp the conquerynge. . . .

Chaucer was not one of the smooth little poets, who write easily and whose work easily passes away. He worked hard and worked slowly, developing from within himself, and however well he knew his craft there was always more to learn.

There are signs in *The Parliament of Birds* that in spite of his success in handling the French conventions Chaucer was already growing restless within the pretty confines of the garden of the *Rose.* The poem is still enclosed within the framework of a dream, but the book that sets the poet dreaming does not belong to the storybook world that sets Chaucer dreaming in his two previous narrative poems. It was this time an actual book on dreams:

> Tullyus of the Dream of Scipioun.

In Marcus Tullius Cicero's book on the state there was a description at the end of the dream of Scipio. This was picked up in the fourth century and given a long commentary by a writer named Macrobius, and the production as a whole became the most popular book on dreams in the Middle Ages.

It is not, however, the general subject of dreams that concerns Chaucer in his résumé of the contents of Cicero's book. It is rather the smallness and unimportance of the earth as Scipio saw it in his dream, the "litel erthe" that is worth no man's love because it is so full of torment.

It is not too much to say that this conception of the world haunted Chaucer. Both his reading and his religion told him it was correct and as a good Christian he would have agreed instantly with Jean de Meun's restatement of the same proposition:

> Wretched the fool who deems that this
> Poor earth our only city is.

Yet even while Chaucer's head told him that this was true his heart vehemently denied it. It was not a "poor earth," the one he was privileged to live upon. It was a wonderful earth and full of wonderful people—some of them evil and some of them foolish but all of them interesting. The man who had it in him to write *The Canterbury Tales* could never have believed, as he writes here, that the life span is only a kind of living death,

> that oure present worldes lyves span
> Nis but a manner death.

Chaucer wrote this as the good Christian which of course he was. But he never succeeded in combining his Christianity successfully with his poetry, and the result is a constant intrusion of an off-key note into even his most perfectly unified work.

Once *The Parliament of Birds* recovers from this sudden excursion into moral philosophy the tone of the poem is exquisitely maintained. It is a distinctively Chaucerian tone, consisting of a graceful and practiced handling of the courtly love tradition combined with the inability to keep a wholly straight face in its presence.

The little story that Chaucer worked out for his poem was, unlike most of his plots (and Shakespeare's), his own invention. It has some incidental allegorical trappings that come mostly from Boccaccio and from that dean of French allegorists, Alanus de Insulus.[8] But once the goddess Nature has been safely established upon her hill of flowers the story becomes wholly Chaucerian.

All the birds come together before Nature to choose their mates, the falcons versed in the idealistic theories of courtly love while the lower orders of wood and barnyard fowl are bred to a more realistic point of view. The little plot gave Chaucer an opportunity to make affectionate fun of the conventions of courtly love without antagonizing its most conscientious practitioner—for who would expect sense from a duck or a goose?

The first bird to choose his mate is a royal falcon, who delivers a highly correct and aristocratic speech. He is as anxious to be the humble servitor of his lady as was the original Dreamer in the garden of the *Rose.* He has two rivals, however, who are equally ready to serve the same lady, and the three falcons spend the whole day pressing their respective claims as lovers in stately and ornamental diction.

The common birds do not like this at all, since they cannot choose their own wives until the aristocrats have finished; and the air is filled with their wails. They want to go home and wish that the falcons would stop arguing.

"Have done, and let us wende!"

Particularly excited are the goose, the duck and the cuckoo, and they go, "Kek kek! kokkow! quek quek!" as though they have just flown out of the pages of a medieval psalter.[9]

Nature is somewhat excited herself by now and she calls out,

[8] It is worth noting how carefully Chaucer gives full credit to "Aleyn."
[9] The artists who decorated the psalters for the noble families of England had both a respect for reality and a strong sense of fun. In the Gorleston psalter there is a picture of a duck in difficulties, with a passionate "queck" issuing from its beak, that for both humor and accuracy comes a close second to Chaucer's easily insulted fowls in *The Parliament of Birds.*

132

"Hold youre tonges there!" When peace is finally restored it is agreed that a full parliament should be held to discuss the matter. Each group of birds will have its accredited spokesman: a falcon for the birds of prey, a goose for the water birds, a turtledove for the seed-eating birds, and a cuckoo for those who eat worms.

The question sometimes arises as to whether any of these four groups of birds were intended to express Chaucer's own views on the subject of love and it has been argued both that Chaucer admired courtly love as the falcons did and that he held it in the same scorn as the goose. This is forgetting that Chaucer was an objective writer. He does not speak in his own person in *The Canterbury Tales* when the Canon's Yeoman gives his views on alchemy or the Wife of Bath her views on husbands, and no more is he taking sides in *The Parliament of Birds* when the falcon and the cuckoo have so hot an argument it nearly breaks up the meeting. Chaucer had learned already the art of presenting characterization through dialogue, and while he was not yet capable of carrying it to the heights he achieved in *The Canterbury Tales* the method used and the point of view behind it are exactly the same.

Chaucer himself was at one time a member of Parliament, and his fellow members had a right to be a shade uneasy in the presence of so observant a man. Chaucer knew accurately the very tone of public debate—the large contempt for everyone's opinion but one's own and the self-generated mood of excitement in which tempers are so rapidly lost. It is easy to deduce from his poem why actual medieval sessions of Parliament were such stirring events and why the House of Commons sometimes quarreled with the House of Lords.

The first speaker in Chaucer's parliament is a feathered equivalent of a member of the Westminster House of Lords, and his mental processes are those suitable to his class. He first brings up the possibility of trial by battle and the three rivals shout, "Al redy," as a single bird. Their representative is obliged to reprove them for this. What he wishes to recommend, once he has recovered the thread of his discourse, is that the lady should marry the best-born of the three.

The waterfowl then put their heads together and elect the goose to be their speaker. The goose begins with a strong unsolicited testimonial to her own brains and then gives it as her verdict that if the falcon's lady will not love him let him love someone else.

The turtledove, who represents the seed-fowl, is very much upset by this crude and realistic advice; for it is the turtledove's opinion that a true lover should be faithful to his lady forever. The duck, who has not been asked for his opinion, considers this merely funny, for in his philosophy there are more fish in the sea than ever came out of it.

The cuckoo then reports for the birds that eat worms, and the cuckoo is in something of a temper. It is his theory that if the falcons cannot stop arguing they ought to stay single and give the other birds a chance to mate in peace. This brings forth a series of insults from the "gentil" falcon that no gentleman should have permitted himself. The cuckoo is a murderer of hedge-sparrows, a gluttonous destroyer of worms, and a boor who is quite unfit to marry anyone at all.

At this point Nature takes a hand and closes the debate. She decrees that the lady shall make her own choice, and the lady falcon asks for a year of grace in which to make up her mind. Then the lesser birds choose their mates and a special group sings a little song in honor of St. Valentine before they depart. This is a roundel, the only example that is extant of the many poems that Chaucer wrote in this meter, and a very charming one. It is fitted, like the songs that Shakespeare wrote for his plays, to an older tune.

> The note, I trow, ymaked was in Fraunce.

Then the poet awakens and characteristically picks up some "othere bookes" to read. He intends to go on reading, and hopes that "som day" he will make a better writer of himself. And with that the poem ends.

A very strong effort has been made to date *The Parliament of Birds* by assuming that Chaucer wrote the poem to celebrate an actual historical marriage or engagement. Usually the royal falcon is made out to be King Richard but there the unanimity ends. The lady falcon has been variously identified as Marie of France,

Philippa of Lancaster and Anne of Bohemia. Even more difficulty has been met with in an attempt to identify the other two suitors, and the guesses have ranged from William of Hainault to Frederick of Meissen or John of Blois.

The probable reason why no satisfactory historical parallel can be found to the love suit in *The Parliament of Birds* is that none exists. The situation is the same as that which applied to *The House of Fame*. If Chaucer had desired to compliment King Richard and some intended bride, he could have devised a much more suitable plot than one that shows his courtship squabbled over in public and still unsuccessful at the end of the poem. When Deschamps satirized the court of Charles VI under the guise of birds, showing Charles as an eagle, one of his uncles as a falcon, and the upstart courtiers as various kinds of lesser birds, he had no difficulty in making his meaning perfectly plain. Chaucer was certainly not a less skillful poet than Deschamps, and if he had wished to write a similar court allegory using the device of birds he was capable of making his meaning equally clear.

It is exceedingly risky to assume an historical meaning in *The Parliament of Birds* when Chaucer himself gives no reason in the poem for assuming that any such meaning exists. All that can safely be said is that it is a poem in honor of St. Valentine's Day, and a delightful one.

If *The Parliament of Birds* is a success in what it sets out to do, *Anelida and Arcite* must be counted as a failure. But it is a highly interesting failure. It apparently marks Chaucer's first attempt to make use of Boccaccio's work in other than a superficial way, and the attempt injured his old way of writing without as yet contributing anything new to it. A minor writer would probably have abandoned his experiments with the new Italian way of writing at this point, but Geoffrey Chaucer was not a minor writer.

The Italian poem with which Chaucer was working, Boccaccio's *Teseide*, was the first attempt in the Middle Ages to write a full-length classical epic in the vernacular. The epic style happened to be entirely foreign to Boccaccio's own particular genius but he struggled with it with dogged determination and managed to produce twelve books stuffed with the usual epic materials of Olympian machinery and catalogues and invocations and the rest of it. Boccaccio based his poem on the story of Thebes, which had already been celebrated by Statius in his *Thebaid*, a poem which Chaucer knew well. Boccaccio modeled his own epic on the *Thebaid*, which in turn had been elaborately and conscientiously modeled upon the *Aeneid*, and the result was a stiff and elaborate affair which obeyed implicitly the classical rules of the epic.[10]

It was inevitable that Chaucer should be impressed by the epic machinery that chokes the *Teseide* and that he should have been momentarily tempted by the idea of using epic material himself. But he realized early that the epic style did not belong to him and he never finished his sole experiment in the epic manner.

Anelida and Arcite opens with great pomp and circumstance. Chaucer begins with an epic invocation to Mars, god of battles, praying that he may assist the poet with his tale. Then there is a second invocation to Polyhymnia, the muse of serious poetry, who lives with her sisters under the unfading laurel by the well of Helicon.[11]

After this very correct beginning the poem continues in a correct manner also. Duke Theseus is returning from his triumphant war against Thebes, and there is an opportunity for a listing of the nobly resonant names in which any writer of epics may delight.

> Amphiorax and Tydeus,
> Ipomedon, Parthonope also
> Were dead, and slayne proud Campaneus.

At this point the heroine of the tale makes her appearance. She is a queen named Anelida and from the first Chaucer has no idea what to do with her. Anelida's story is practically finished before it is begun; for she loves a knight named Arcite, and Arcite is untrue to her, and there is nothing Anelida can do but mourn.

---

[10] Boccaccio was most conscientious about this. For instance, the *Aeneid* consists of twelve books and 9896 lines. Boccaccio saw to it that his *Teseide* consisted also of twelve books and 9896 lines.

[11] Helicon was not actually a well. It was a mountain. But medieval authors did not have the advantages of modern ones and they had to get their classical information where they could find it. Boccaccio had already made the same mistake about Helicon.

Chaucer gives her lament, and it is a lovely thing. But it has nothing to do with epic material or with the mood of the poem; even the meter is entirely different. It is an example of the old French form known as the "complaint," and to a reader who has settled himself to read a classical epic the interruption is baffling.

Then Chaucer picks up again his weight of epic material but without enthusiasm. He composes one very inferior stanza in which Anelida falls down in a faint, gets up again, and goes off to sacrifice at the temple of Mars. Chaucer announces that he will next describe the temple of Mars, but he does not. The poem ends here, and with it Chaucer's sole attempt to write in the epic manner.

The laborious and stumbling use that Chaucer has made here of the *Teseide* is in interesting contrast to the brilliant and assured technique that is his when he is writing Anelida's Complaint. He had tried his hand at this popular French verse-form before, notably in the *Complaint to his Lady* and the *Complaint of Mars,* but these two poems were chiefly interesting for their experiments in versification. Anelida's Complaint is no experiment. It is a finished work of art, and one of which Chaucer had a right to feel very proud.

Chaucer chose for her lament an exceedingly complicated rhyme scheme,[12] and then handled it in a way that was peculiarly his own. Any experienced French poet would have been capable of inventing as difficult a form and of using it with equal dexterity, but Chaucer's distinction lies in something further: he made his intricate rhyme scheme sound like ordinary speech. He would not even permit himself the use of inversion, and the effortless, unforced, conversational flow of the lines gives an illusion of prose speech to what is in reality very intricate poetry.

Not only does the Complaint sound like real speech but Anelida sounds like a real woman. Hers is no artificial, stylized passion neatly bounded by a French rhyme scheme; it is that of an actual human being in actual pain. Anelida passes through all the familiar stages, from hurt pride to fear to a self-abasement that is

[12] In one section there is a passage of 16 lines with only two rhyme sounds.

unpleasant to watch in so great a lady, and all the time at the back of her mind she is aware that she can no more keep Arcite faithful to her than she can keep April from raining. Yet for all that she gathers together everything she possesses in an effort to keep him, and it is a measure of the sympathetic reality of the characterization that it is difficult not to dislike Arcite intensely.

Chaucer was already a master in the arts the French could teach him, as the Complaint of Anelida shows. Later on he was to become a master of the secrets of the Italians and when he turned again to the *Teseide* he laid upon it a practiced and unerring hand. He stripped the *Teseide* of all the epic machinery and extraneous material that had once fascinated him, cut Boccaccio's twelve books down to the actual story, and retold the whole thing with intelligence and grace in what is now the Knight's Story in *The Canterbury Tales.*

By that time Chaucer had acquired from Boccaccio the one gift that was of value to him—the gift of story construction. He did not get this from the *Teseide;* he got it from another poem of Boccaccio's called *Il Filostrato.*

Il Filostrato has not a very high reputation today as a work of art, having been overshadowed by the *Decameron.* But it remains a brilliantly constructed tale of young love produced in a period in which good narrative construction was very rare. Chaucer recognized it instantly for what it was. It combined in his own mind with his own developing gift for characterization, and produced one of the literary masterpieces of the world in *Troilus and Criseyde.*

Troilus and Criseyde seems so effortless a work of art that it is difficult to remember how much hard work went into writing it and how many years of reading and thinking and experimentation preceded the finished product. It is therefore of great value to have a poem like *Anelida and Arcite.* It marks the period of transition that was inevitable while Chaucer was struggling with a new kind of technique and shows a stage of the journey he took from France to Italy on a personal and literary mission much more important than his horseback ride to the city of Milan in the service of the King.

138

CHAPTER X

HAUCER returned from his trip to Milan in the autumn of 1378, arriving in London on the nineteenth of September. He took over his duties as Comptroller from Richard Baret, who had been serving as his deputy in his absence. Baret had held various posts in the wool customs, and only the previous year had been appointed custodian of the customhouse.

The customhouse was a building rented by the government on Wool Wharf, on the east side of town between London Bridge and the Tower. Its facilities were apparently inadequate for the amount of business that had to be transacted there and five years later a man named John Churchman built a permanent customs office on the same wharf, renting it by the year to the government for a profitable sum. Chaucer and his colleagues must have found this a much more satisfactory arrangement, for the three-story building was built expressly for housing the customs. The ground floor had the weights and balances for weighing the wool, the second floor had the counting house for the staff and the customers, and the top floor had two private rooms for the convenience of the customs officers.

There were three major officials in the wool customs, the rest of the staff consisting of subordinate members like the clerk of the wool-beam, the weighers, searchers, packers and so on. The two most prominent officials were the two Collectors, who did the actual levying of the customs duties and the collecting of the money from the wool merchants. They presented the Exchequer with an annual statement of their receipts, and it was Chaucer's business, as Comptroller, to prepare a counter roll of his own to give the Exchequer officials a check upon the accuracy of the Collectors.

The jurisdiction of the customhouse extended from Tilbury on the west to Gravesend on the east, and the three customs officials were responsible for every wool ship on the Thames within that area. As a competent officer Chaucer could have given immediately the name, place of lading, burthen, owner, tariff and customs payment of any given ship in the whole London district.

In order to maintain its authority over the port, the customs office had a boat of its own and the full-time services of a boatman. If any wool merchant tried to slip by without paying the tariff his goods were forfeit to the government and the full price of the wool was paid to the officer who had apprehended him. A merchant named John Kent, for instance, tried to export a shipment of wool to Dordrecht without paying the customs duty. Chaucer forestalled him and was granted as his reward the value of the wool. The sum amounted to £71 4s 6d, which would be about five thousand dollars in modern money.

Chaucer's salary was probably a comfortable one, although it was not as large as that of the two Collectors. In addition, he and his colleagues received a special annual bonus "for their assiduous labour and diligence" and Chaucer's share formed an addition of four or five hundred dollars a year to his regular wages.

If Chaucer showed special diligence he must have been a very hard-working official, for the post of Comptroller of the London wool customs was not an easy one. When he closed his books on Michaelmas Day, a year after his return from Milan, the records show that a total of one thousand, two hundred and twenty wool merchants had come to Wool Wharf to have their wool weighed and taxed during the twelve-month period. The customs duties that had been collected from them amounted to £23,781 8s 3¾d, which would be about one million, five hundred thousand dollars in modern money. There was, however, no "about" where Chaucer's accounts were concerned. He was responsible for the accuracy of his accounts down to the final three farthings.

Keeping accounts in the fourteenth century was no easy matter in itself. All the computation was done in Roman numerals, which prevented any addition or multiplication from being done on paper.[1] The preliminary figuring was done on a board marked

---

[1] The Arabic numerals had been known in Europe for nearly two centuries, but the Middle Ages did not believe in change. Even as late as 1299 and in the greatest banking center of the West, Florence, the use of the new numerals instead of the old alphabetical system was forbidden by law.

out with parallel columns signifying pounds, shillings and pence, with thin discs of metal on it that could be moved about to the appropriate positions.[2]

A further complication was the variety of coinage in circulation, which was difficult to reduce to its equivalent value in pounds or marks. Only the Italian florin had a really standard value, but a chronic medieval shortage of ready cash meant that the merchants were forced to deal in a mixture of foreign coinage no matter how severely the government frowned upon the practice. Another solution frowned upon by the government but resorted to by the merchants was that of paying part of their customs dues in installments, a method of operating upon the credit system that made the bookkeeping even more complicated for Chaucer and his fellow officials. The government attempted in 1382 to bribe the wool merchants into abandoning this practice by offering them exemption from a new subsidy of half a mark if they would pay their regular dues in cash. The subsidy was a special tax imposed by Parliament, and it gave extra work to Chaucer and the two Collectors because it had to be entered separately in the accounts and could not be included in the normal customs receipts.

The office of Collector must have been a well-paid and very desirable position, for it was held by some of the most important men of London. The list of Collectors during Chaucer's twelve-year period of service in the customhouse, from 1374 to 1386, reads like a *Who's Who* of the most prominent business and political figures in the city.

Particularly closely associated with the office of Collector was the triumvirate that at this time really governed London. It was composed of three merchants named William Walworth, Nicholas Brembre and John Philpot. Of the three, Walworth had the least connection with the customhouse, for he served as Collector only a year while Chaucer was Comptroller. Brembre and Philpot, on the other hand, served jointly with Chaucer for six years, and after Philpot's death Chaucer was Brembre's Comptroller for two years longer.

[2] The Exchequer department originally used a painted cloth to indicate the columns. This cloth was called *chequy* in French and gave the department its name.

141

It is not too much to say that these men managed London among them. Walworth was mayor in 1374, Brembre in 1377, Philpot in 1378, a man of their own choosing the following year, Walworth in 1380 and Brembre in again for three terms from 1383 through 1385. They owed their political strength to the fact that they were the heads of the wealthy and aristocratic food guilds, which were being bitterly but unsuccessfully opposed by the clothing guilds.

This local feud between the food guilds, headed by Walworth, Brembre and Philpot, and the clothing guilds, headed by John of Northampton, is worth mentioning only because John of Gaunt supported John of Northampton. The theory still persists that Chaucer owed something in his public life to the patronage of John of Gaunt, but it is evident that as far as Chaucer's twelve-year service in the customhouse is concerned he was in the opposite camp. Only one member of John of Gaunt's faction succeeded in getting a post in the customhouse while Chaucer was there and he served as Collector for only a year, being dropped as soon as King Richard came to the throne.

Part of the power of the Brembre-Walworth-Philpot triumvirate came from the fact that it was backed by the King. The three merchants were not only close friends of Richard's, but it was their wealth that supplied him with the huge loans that he needed. Whenever the matter of finances comes up in the patent rolls the names of these three are almost invariably linked with it. They were not, however, eyed with the mistrust that the Commons usually accorded the King's friends, and when two special treasurers of war were appointed to administer a new levy and make sure that it was not diverted to nonmilitary purposes, it was Walworth and Philpot whom the Commons appointed.[3]

Walworth was a member of the immensely powerful Grocer's Guild, and part of his wealth had been made in speculation. He engrossed (that is, he bought up and monopolized) various kinds of foodstuffs and held them for a rise in the market. Brembre belonged to the Fishmonger's Guild, which controlled what was

[3] It was in their official capacity of war-treasurers that they paid Chaucer the money that took him to Milan.

142

really the basic food of the city. It is difficult to form a just estimate of the character of either one, but they seem to have been clever business men with the kind of ruthlessness that often accompanies efficiency in making money. Nicholas Brembre, at any rate, was bitterly hated, and when his enemies ultimately petitioned for his execution they indulged in a singularly bad pun and called him a "bramble" in the fair realm of England.[4]

An entirely different sort of man was John Philpot, who was fully as rich and fully as clever as the other two. Philpot was one of the best-loved men in England and the pride and joy of the Grocer's Company for centuries afterwards. All the chroniclers unite in his praise, for he was an intelligent philanthropist and a true patriot. Like many other Englishmen, for instance, he was distressed by the slack handling of the navy, for John of Gaunt's naval campaign of 1378 had been a failure and the French were making hit-and-run raids along the English coast almost at will. But John Philpot did not waste his time criticizing the government. He outfitted a naval squadron of his own, and this private fleet not only recaptured all the English vessels that had been lost in an enemy raid on Scarborough and the Isle of Wight, but fifteen French and Castilian vessels as well. Similarly, when there was an invasion scare in London and the city planned to stretch an iron chain across the Thames, one of the sixty-foot stone towers that supported it was financed by a tax of sixpence to the pound on city rentals and the other was paid for by John Philpot out of his own purse.

It is recorded that John Philpot was a man of jolly wit, and he must have been a delightful person to know. Chaucer was not deeply attracted to business men as a class, if his portraits in *The Canterbury Tales* can be taken as any indication, but it is not fanciful to assume that John Philpot was a good friend of his. His name appears with those of several other prominent men who

---

[4] This petition against Brembre was the first to be presented to an English Parliament in the English language. It is quite likely that this epoch-making use of the vernacular was caused by nothing more than the unwillingness of the petitioners to abandon their pun once they had thought of it.

were Chaucer's friends in a legal release that was given Chaucer in 1380 by one Cecily Chaumpaigne.

This particular document aroused a certain amount of discussion when it was first discovered, for it released Chaucer of every sort of action "*tam de reptu meo, tam de alia re vel causa.*" Very little is actually known about fourteenth-century law, and a premature conclusion was reached that Chaucer had been cited for rape. Later on, a further documentary discovery made this theory untenable, for it consisted of deeds of release by Richard Goodchild and John Grove to Chaucer, and by Cecily Chaumpaigne to them, with a bond by John Grove to pay her ten pounds. The whole episode illustrates the danger of jumping to conclusions, and all that can be said with certainty about the matter is that Chaucer was evidently involved in the eighties in some kind of an abduction suit.

Another distinguished Londoner whose name is linked with Chaucer's on a legal document is Ralph Strode. He went surety with Chaucer in 1382 for the peaceful behavior of a wealthy fellow Londoner. Earlier than that he went bail with John Wyclif for a mutual friend, and unless Wyclif knew two Ralph Strodes it was this same Strode with whom he had a religious controversy at Oxford. Strode was a thorough conservative and had almost no meeting point with Wyclif, but the controversy between Wyclif and his "dearest friend" is unique among those upon which Wyclif embarked for the courtesy and good nature of its tone.

Later Strode became a distinguished lawyer, representing the City of London, and as an employee of the city he was given a residence over one of the city gates. Strode lived over Aldersgate, the next gate to the north from Chaucer's Aldgate. Like his neighbor to the south Strode was something of a literary man; while he was teaching at Oxford he wrote books on formal logic and scholastic philosophy that were still being reprinted as late as the sixteenth century, and he also wrote poetry. Chaucer must have considered him one of the most intimate and valued of his friends, for after he finished *Troilus and Criseyde* he dedicated it to two men and one was "philosophical Strode."

The other friend to whom Chaucer dedicated the *Troilus* was

John Gower. Chaucer calls him "moral Gower," for at the time Gower had just achieved fame as the author of a monumental poem on ethics, written in French, which he called the *Miroir de l'Omme* (*The Mirror of Man*).

Gower's poem had every reason to be popular in its own day, for it fitted without a ripple into the normal current of conservative medieval opinion. The *Miroir* is perfectly in accord with contemporary thinking in almost any aspect of the poem that could be named: in its preoccupation with sin, in its conscientious arrangement into divisions and subdivisions, in the fact that it is written in French instead of in English. It is thoroughly medieval also in its interest in political, social and moral reform.[5] Gower makes a wholesale attack on all the social evils that plagued contemporary society, with special reference to churchmen, lawyers and doctors —three very powerful groups that had been perennially viewed with alarm ever since the days of Jean de Meun.

Gower was a sound craftsman and a thoroughly "safe" writer in every respect. For several centuries he was considered Chaucer's equal as a poet, and at this particular period he must have ranked as his superior. For until Chaucer wrote *Troilus and Criseyde* he had produced nothing of his own to rank with Gower's monumental *Miroir*.

The two poets were evidently close friends. Chaucer left power of attorney with Gower, and with another friend called Richard Forester, when he went abroad to visit the court of Bernabo Visconti, an act of trust he would hardly have made if the two men had been only casual acquaintances.

It is easy to write about Chaucer's friends; it is unfortunately more difficult to write about his family. There is no church registry extant to testify to the names of his various children as there are public documents to testify to his friends.

If Chaucer had been less like himself and more like Deschamps, his readers would have known a great deal about his sons and daughters. Deschamps even introduces the reader to the family

[5] There is hardly any English writer of the fourteenth century who does not do his best to reform the nation, and in this connection Chaucer's poetry is in striking contrast to the general temper of his age.

nursery, with loud complaints about the expensiveness of cradles and swaddling clothes and the general difficulty of rearing children. When a son of Deschamps needs an ecclesiastical position or a daughter marries, his readers hear about the matter at once. But Chaucer is as silent about his family as he is about himself, and the names of his children can be established only by indirect evidence.

There was a certain Elizabeth Chaucer who became a novice at the Abbey of Barking in 1381. John of Gaunt contributed over fifty pounds towards the expenses that occurred in connection with her initiation and the gifts that were given on that occasion. This would be nearly four thousand dollars in modern money, and the size of the sum can best be explained by the supposition that Elizabeth was Philippa Chaucer's daughter and therefore the niece of John of Gaunt's adored mistress. There would be no Chaucer family in whom John of Gaunt was interested except the one that was related to Katherine Swynford.

There was a certain Lewis Chaucer whose name appears among the soldiers garrisoning a royal castle at the beginning of the following century. Here again, as with Elizabeth Chaucer, the dates fit in correctly, and the probability that Lewis Chaucer was Geoffrey Chaucer's son is further strengthened by the fact that Chaucer wrote his *Treatise on the Astrolabe* for "litel Lowys, my sone."

Stationed along with Lewis Chaucer in the royal garrison of Carmarthen in 1403 was a certain Thomas Chaucer, and in his case the evidence is much more direct. A contemporary of his named Thomas Gascoigne asserts in his theological dictionary that Thomas Chaucer was the son of Geoffrey Chaucer, and the testimony may be considered reliable since Gascoigne was not only a prominent figure in fifteenth-century England but a neighbor of Thomas Chaucer's in Oxfordshire. For supplementary evidence there is the fact that Thomas Chaucer used his father's seal and that he, like his sister Elizabeth, was taken under the patronage of his future uncle, John of Gaunt. He entered the Duke's service in 1389 and was given ten pounds yearly for his fee.

As the nephew of Katherine Swynford, Thomas Chaucer was first cousin to the Beauforts and they graciously called him kinsman. The Beauforts were men of high standing in fifteenth-century

146

England, for one of Katherine's sons became a duke, one a cardinal and one an earl.[6] When the tomb of Thomas Chaucer came to be designed, either by Thomas himself or by that great lady, the Duchess of Suffolk, who was his only daughter, the three Beauforts were the only men whose arms were represented upon it. The twenty coats of arms which are displayed were evidently chosen to represent all the great names of the day with whom Thomas Chaucer could claim a connection either through his mother or his wife. Among the glitter of great names on the tomb—the Beauforts, the Nevills, the De La Poles, the Burghershes and the Roets—no common name appears. Only the Beauforts were prominent enough to represent the male side of the family and all the other coats of arms represent women.[7]

Thomas Chaucer was a much richer and more prominent individual than his father or his grandfather, but his career was not unlike theirs. Like his grandfather he was connected with the wine trade, serving for nearly thirty years as the King's Butler. Like his father he was a diplomat, a justice of the peace and a member of Parliament. (He served fourteen times as a member of the House

[6] John Beaufort, Earl of Somerset, was the great-grandfather of Henry the Seventh, first of the Tudor kings.
[7] The fact that the Chaucer coat of arms was omitted from Thomas Chaucer's tomb later gave rise to the theory that he was not Geoffrey Chaucer's son. As Speght put it in the sixteenth century:

Some hold opinion (but I know not upon what grounds) that Thomas Chaucer was not the sonne of Geoffrey Chaucer, but rather some kinsman of his, whome hee brought up. But this pedigree by the hands of Master Glouer . . . that learned antiquarie, as also the report of chronicles, shew it to be otherwise.

A more modern variant of the same theory is the suggestion that Thomas was the bastard son of John of Gaunt by Philippa Chaucer. This theory, which is frequently treated more respectfully than it deserves, is based upon the favors that Philippa Chaucer and her children received from the Duke—favors which are of course susceptible of a much simpler explanation. The theory that Philippa was his mistress is in any case untenable. A court scandal of such magnificent proportions would have been seized upon at once by the chroniclers, who were only too ready to saddle John of Gaunt with any misdemeanor that could conceivably be laid upon him.

of Commons, and five times as its speaker.) Like both his father and his grandfather he married a woman of higher social position than himself. The family fortunes, from a worldly point of view, went steadily upwards through four generations of Chaucers, culminating in Thomas as the last male member of the line.

Geoffrey Chaucer stood about midway between his father and his son; he was much richer and more prominent in public affairs than his father, John Chaucer, had been, but he never became as rich or as prominent as his son Thomas.

It is not possible to estimate exactly the state of Chaucer's finances at this period of his life, but it is obvious that he was what would be called a well-to-do man. As Comptroller of the Customs he not only had his wages and an annual bonus, but the special financial perquisites that rose out of his office, like the five-thousand-dollar payment from John Kent's forfeit.

As a king's esquire Chaucer was still receiving annually the twenty marks that had been his pension since 1367. He had also been granted a daily pitcher of wine which had a cash value of £7 2s 6½d (about five hundred dollars a year). As an esquire he also received his regular gifts of summer and winter robes from the King, and in addition there was a royal gift of twenty-two pounds (about fifteen hundred dollars) in somewhat tardy recognition of Chaucer's services abroad during the French marriage negotiations.

That Chaucer had other sources of income is shown by the accidental survival of various documents. He obtained, for instance, at least two Kentish wardships, occupying about the same position in relation to the heirs as a trust company holds today. It was a profitable position; Chaucer, for instance, received £104 (nearly eight thousand dollars) from Edmund Staplegate for administering his lands during his minority and arranging his marriage. In addition to this there were the minor grants from John of Gaunt, and the annuities from both the King and the Duke of Lancaster that went to Philippa Chaucer direct and were acknowledged under her private seal.

Geoffrey Chaucer had of course many ways of spending his income but it is a safe guess where at least a part of his money went. It went for books.

Chaucer says in one of his poems that he possessed sixty books, and if this is an autobiographical statement Chaucer had a library to be proud of. Many a college library at Oxford or Cambridge had less and still considered itself well equipped, and the greatest ecclesiastical library in England, that of Christ College at Canterbury, had only seven hundred volumes.

Until the fifteenth century witnessed simultaneously the introduction of movable type and a fall in the price of paper, books were considered a luxury. They were always carefully mentioned in wills, like Sir Richard Stury's copy of *The Romance of the Rose*, and were treated almost as respectfully as the second-best bed.

The average nobleman might have a French romance or two carefully displayed along with the family psalter, but very few private individuals had the means or the intelligence to collect extensive libraries. The two great exceptions in the fourteenth century were Francis Petrarch and a chancellor of Edward the Third's named Richard de Bury. These two tracked down books with the singlehearted excitement of true bibliophiles, and were quite undeterred by the layers of dust and litters of mice under which their treasures were buried. It was said of de Bury that he never traveled without five baggage wagons behind him to carry the books he felt were too precious to leave behind.

Chaucer was not a royal chancellor, able to go rooting around Europe for valuable manuscripts. Nor did he have leisure like Petrarch's to enable him to explore the centers of Continental culture. Except for his brief professional visits to Europe, he was dependent for his reading largely on what the London booksellers could find for him.

London, unlike Paris, had no powerful university to patronize the manufacture and stimulate the sale of books. Richard de Bury felt that Paris was "the Paradise of the world, with its delightful libraries and book market." The Latin Quarter was the haunt of book lovers from all over Europe, but the same could hardly be said for London's Paternoster Row. Nevertheless, the London book dealers were numerous enough to incorporate into a guild in

1403, and some of them were prosperous and enterprising men. Oxford and Cambridge had booksellers too, and even Lincoln, which was not a university town, had a book dealer who was prominent enough to take orders for books from King John when that well-adjusted exile was living in England.

Chaucer probably acquired most of his library from commercial sources such as these, although he may have been reduced, like Petrarch, to borrowing a manuscript and copying it out when he could not secure the original. Chaucer's books were probably not the expensive, lavishly illustrated kind that were written out on fine parchment, for, unlike Richard de Bury, he was not as interested in the appearance of his books as he was in their contents.[8] Chaucer describes his personal copy of Cicero as an "olde book totorn"; it was evidently thoroughly worn out through either his own reading or that of a previous owner.

Books were not ornaments as far as Chaucer was concerned. They were necessities. It is likely that most of the books in his library were small, comfortable volumes, like the little pocket edition of St. Augustine that Petrarch carried everywhere with him; and the big ones were the kind that could have been spread out on his writing table for quick reference when he needed them.

A library of this kind would not have cost Chaucer a disproportionate part of his income, for the price of books was subject to wide variation. The Abbot of Litlington paid twenty-two pounds for his missal, but a secondhand manuscript on civil law could be bought for a couple of shillings. The average price of a book was between forty and sixty dollars in modern money, and if Chaucer was not too particular about the appearance of some of his volumes he could easily have financed his entire library out of the fine John Kent paid for trying to smuggle wool to Dordrecht.

[8] Richard de Bury gave some detailed advice in his *Philobiblion* as to how fine books should be treated. No scholar should read a book when he has a cold, unless he is aware of the uses of a handkerchief. He should not let a crying child admire the little pictures within the capital letters, "for a child touches whatever he sees." He should not use the pages to press violets and primroses, and above all he must resist any depraved impulse to scribble in the margins.

The sixty books that Chaucer had in his library almost certainly implies more than sixty authors. It was a period in which *florilegia* were very popular—selected sayings from classical authors arranged together in the form of an anthology. It was also a period of omnibus volumes, and many unrelated works of literature were frequently bound together under the same cover. A book which belonged to the husband of Chaucer's Wife of Bath had within it a treatise by St. Jerome, the love letters of Heloise, the parables of Solomon, Ovid's *Art of Love* and an assortment of other literary productions; and while the Christ Church library had only seven hundred books it listed three thousand separate writings.

The books were protected by durable bindings, usually made of wooden boards covered either with parchment or leather. The university libraries used chests for the storage of books that were not in particular demand, and Chaucer also, according to his own authority, had a "cheste" for his books. But he probably kept his particular favorites on a shelf near the head of his bed, like the Clerk of Oxford who rode with the Canterbury Pilgrims, or like the clerk in the Miller's Tale with his

bookes great and smale . . .
On shelves couched at his beddes head.

If Chaucer followed the usual medieval custom there was probably a pricket in the wall behind the bed, with a sharp point on which he could fix his candle. Then, with a dozen books within arm's reach, he was comfortably prepared after a busy day at the customs office to "rede and drive the night away," as he had been doing ever since he was a young man.

Chaucer was not only a buyer and a reader of books; he was a producer of books also. In the Middle Ages every author was his own publisher, for such commercial publishers as there were kept mostly to the classics and to university textbooks.

The medieval writers were forced into a close relationship with the medieval scribes that was seldom amicable on either side. The age-old occupation of arguing with the printer did not begin with the introduction of movable type, and both Chaucer and Petrarch had bitter experiences in their sometimes unavailing attempts to obtain accurate copies of their work.

The act of publishing was a simple one in theory. The writer delivered his manuscript to a professional scribe, who in turn was supposed to produce as many copies of the work as its author desired. Then the author would proofread the entire edition, perhaps, like Petrarch, persuading a friend to read the original aloud to him while he made the necessary corrections. Once these corrected sheets were put into circulation the book could be said to have been published, and after that it was public property. A book dealer, if he wished, could order through his own copyists as many editions of it as he pleased without obtaining the consent of the author; and a popular author had cause to be grateful if this did not occur before he had completed his own revision of the manuscripts.

This was the arrangement as it was ideally supposed to be. But the professional scribes were not well-paid men—they received twopence a day which was the wage of a plowman—and the final copies they delivered to the enraged authors usually differed markedly from the master version. Petrarch apparently had his pick of Italian scribes by virtue of his exalted literary position, but when he wanted anything of extreme importance copied, such as the letters of Cicero, he copied it himself. It was Petrarch's considered opinion that no scribe made any effort to follow the original version; once, when he hired a priest to do some copying for him, he remarked bitterly that he wondered whether he would, "as a priest, perform his duties conscientiously, or, as a copyist, be ready to deceive."

Chaucer was in a less advantageous position than Petrarch, for there were probably ten professional scribes in Italy for one in England. It is true that there were still book makers in England working with careful reverence in the fine old tradition, but this attention was lavished on the beautiful books that were written in Latin or French and was not extended to what were considered unimportant books in the vernacular. Chaucer took his chances along with the rest; and while no contemporary manuscript of his work has survived, the careless copies that were made in the following century show clearly why he ended *Troilus and Criseyde* with the heartfelt but not very hopeful prayer that no scribe would "mis-write" or "mismeter" the poem.[9]

It is not a pleasant experience for a poet to devote hard and careful work to finding exactly the right word, only to have his scribe turn it into something quite different, and in a sudden moment of irritation Chaucer expressed his feelings rather forcibly on the subject. He had employed a scribe named Adam to copy out two books he had been working on for some time, and as soon as the sheets arrived back in his possession Chaucer found he had to go over the whole thing with knife and pumice stone to undo the damage that Adam had done. It was Chaucer's wholehearted wish, expressed in seven lines of doggerel, that if such a thing happened again his scribe would get the scab.

> Adam scriveyn, if ever it thee befalle
> Boece or Troylus for to writen newe,
> Under thy long locks thou must have the scalle,
> But after my making thou write more trewe.
> So ofte a-daye I must thy werk renewe,
> It to correcte and eek to rubbe and scrape;
> And al is through thy negligence and rape.[10]

The "Boece" which Chaucer mentions in this scathing little verse is the English translation he had just made of the *Consolation of Philosophy* by Anicius Boethius.

The *Consolation of Philosophy* was enormously popular in the Middle Ages. Men as dissimilar as Dante and Jean de Meun united in loving it, and when King Alfred wished to educate his

[9] Chaucer would have appreciated Caxton. When a certain gentleman told Caxton that his edition of *The Canterbury Tales* did not match up with one that the gentleman's father loved and possessed, Caxton eagerly borrowed the book and at once put out a new edition. Caxton's anxiety to have the book "trewe and cor-recte" would have seemed to Chau-cer and Petrarch an almost unbeliev-able emotion in a printer.

[10] Chaucer was sometimes reduced to embodying warnings to his scribe in the body of his verse. When he uses the name of "Lamuel" he adds warn-ingly,

> Not Samuel, but Lamuel, say I;

and when he mentions "Dane" he adds with some asperity that he does *not* mean "Diane."

people in the ninth century Boethius was one of the four classics that he translated into English. By Chaucer's day it was looked down upon in Florentine intellectual circles as fit only for schoolboys, but in that case Italian schoolboys must have been a highly intelligent group.

Boethius wrote the *Consolation of Philosophy* while he was in prison awaiting death. The Middle Ages thought of him as a Christian martyr, but Boethius was not put to death for his religion. He was put to death for his politics and the book could as well have been written if he had never encountered the Christian religion at all. Boethius made the sixth century the last echo in the Dark Ages of the old, serene Greek habit of thought, and the master and source of the *Consolation of Philosophy* is Plato. The book records an heroic attempt to find a durable peace in the writer's own spirit, and to discover even in a personal tragedy the working of a divine plan whose final end is beneficent. Its theme is that any man can rise superior to the accidents of Fortune if he seeks safety in the steadfastness of his own soul.

Chaucer had a profound respect for the *Consolation of Philosophy*, and he translated it into English prose with the most painstaking care. He had a French translation open before him on his writing desk, a precaution he usually took whenever he prepared himself for any extended encounter with the Latin language; and he also had the commentary of a Dominican scholar named Nicholas Trivet to assist him in ascertaining the exact meaning of each sentence and paragraph.

The result is an extremely conscientious piece of work. Chaucer moved through the *Consolation of Philosophy* inch by inch, anxiously attempting to reproduce the original literally and exactly at all points, and produced a complex, Latinized English which is very unlike the clear, simple sentences that were his in his normal element of poetry. He achieved a version of Boethius that is half as long again as the original Latin and not easy reading by any standard.

Chaucer apparently felt that prose was a more dignified language for philosophy than was poetry, and he clung doggedly to prose even when Boethius himself used verse. Each section of the original begins with a lyric that Boethius permitted himself for the sake of pleasure and variety, and Chaucer turned all this Latin poetry into English prose.

Here he found himself involved in further difficulties as a translator. Poetry is a much more compact, suggestive medium than prose and Chaucer found that he was obliged to insert long parenthetical explanations to make his meaning clear. For instance, in the seventh song in Book IV Boethius says that "Earth overcome giveth the stars" and his anxious translator was obliged to add that by "earth" Boethius meant earthly desire and by "the stars" heaven. Chaucer found himself obliged, in fact, to add a parenthetical explanation of every sentence in this particular lyric, and the whole bears witness to Chaucer's firm determination to make Boethius clear to the least attentive reader.

The whole translation is conditioned by this anxiety on Chaucer's part. One of its faults as prose is that Chaucer carefully repeats nouns where pronouns would have served the purpose much better. So little faith has he in his readers that he will even pause to explain that "masculine children" means "sons" and that "from present to future" means "from time past to time coming." These are somewhat extreme examples, but they show how careful Chaucer was that Boethius should not be misunderstood in any particular.

Chaucer's attitude towards his reader is not unlike that which he took towards ten-year-old Lewis in another prose work of his, the *Treatise on the Astrolabe*. In the essay he wrote for his son he announces that he will avoid "curious endyting and hard sentences"— in other words, phraseology that is learned rather than understandable—and that he will say everything twice so that his young reader will get it once. In the *Consolation of Philosophy* Chaucer follows the same method. When he uses the word "autumn," evidently for the first time in English, he explains that he means "the latter end of summer." A little farther on he uses the same word again, and again he explains that autumn means the latter end of summer.

This is not pedantry; it is anxiety to be understood. The same wish to be quickly and easily understood is apparent in Chaucer's

poetry also, and the reason why Chaucer did not achieve his desire
in prose is because he was working in an unfamiliar medium. Chaucer could achieve clarity in his poetry, a medium over which he
had full mastery; he could merely try to achieve clarity in his
prose.

Chaucer was no scholar, and his translation is not a satisfactory
one from the scholarly point of view. He was constantly losing his
way among Latin prepositions, conjunctions and various other parts
of speech because he did not stop to consider their exact shades of
meaning, and his translation is not the work of a good grammarian
any more than it is the work of a really good writer of prose.

Nevertheless, Chaucer's version of the *Consolation of Philosophy* is an honest, sober attempt to make a great classic available to
Chaucer's own generation, and it has its moments of distinctively
Chaucerian excellence. Phrases like "love of having" or "the light
of his inward sight" could scarcely be improved upon, and occasionally there are gleams of the kind of English prose that flow-
ered three centuries later in the King James version of the Bible.

> O Father . . . shine thou by thy brightnesse,
> for thou art clearnesse, thou art tranquil
> rest to debonayre folk; thou thyself art
> beginning, bearer, leader, path and goal;
> to look on thee, that is our ende.

It is true, however, that clear straightforward English of this kind
is an exception in Chaucer's version, and that a kind of complicated
Latinity is more often the rule.

Chaucer made expert use of Boethius in his own poetry. The ballade he called *Gentilesse* is derived very largely from a passage of
Boethius on the subject, with the great difference that Chaucer is
now free to move in his familiar element of verse. *The Former
Age* is an excellent expansion of the fifth lyric in Book II of the
Consolation of Philosophy and as a ballade it is lively, colorful and
specific. These are not especially Boethian virtues, but they are
poetic ones; and at any rate they are no farther removed from
Boethius than Chaucer's prose version of the same lyric, in which a

brief sentence of five words is followed by a parenthetical explanation of thirty-one.

The most beautiful poetical transcriptions of the *Consolation of Philosophy* that Chaucer made occur in *Troilus and Criseyde,* the poem that Chaucer sent to Adam the scribe at the same time he sent his prose version of Boethius. The *Troilus,* however, is a marvel of integration from many literary sources, and Boethius was only one of the many writers that Chaucer had available in his mind when he sat down to write his great love story.

Troilus and Criseyde was a much more difficult book to write than the *Consolation of Philosophy.* But the finished version has an ease about it that seems effortless, for Chaucer was working with his own chosen subject in his own medium. It was not ideas that attracted him, but people. It was not prose in which he felt at home, but poetry.

Chaucer wrote both books because he wished to write them. His version of the *Consolation of Philosophy* was as much a labor of love as his narrative masterpiece of *Troilus and Criseyde.* But in the second it is the love that is evident, and in the first it is only the labor.

CHAPTER XI

HAUCER wrote *Troilus and Criseyde* by exactly reversing the method he had used in *The House of Fame*.

In *The House of Fame* Chaucer had an idea that interested him but he did not stop to think it out before he put pen to paper. He rambled about on the general subject of fame and the resulting poem is typically medieval in its looseness of structure. Even Jean de Meun could hardly have been less systematic.

Troilus and Criseyde, on the other hand, is a long and intricate work of art that is under the conscious control of its creator from the beginning. Chaucer knew precisely the result he wished to obtain before he began his poem, and as a mature artist he was capable of obtaining it. There were of course many revisions before Chaucer sent his final draft to Adam the scribe, but these revisions were made in the same spirit that produced the original conception of the poem.

In thinking out his poem in advance Chaucer was following one of the few good pieces of advice that he derived from the textbooks on rhetoric; for the method used here is the one originally recommended by Geoffrey de Vinsauf.

> If one has a house to build, the impetuous hand does not rush to the act; the innermost line of the heart measures the work in advance, and the inner man prescribes a course according to an established plan; the hand of the mind fashions the whole before that of the body. . . . When a plan has arranged the subject in the secret place of the mind, poetry will come to clothe the matter with words.

Chaucer was well aware of this excellent piece of advice when he sat down to write *Troilus and Criseyde;* he quotes the first five lines of it in his own poem, so accurately that he had either just read de Vinsauf's advice or already knew it by heart. Yet it hardly needs his own direct quotation from his "deere maister" to show how carefully Chaucer measured the possibilities of his poem in advance, or to prove with what concentration he planned the house he was about to build and "caste his werke ful wisely ere he wroughte."

This was not at all the usual medieval way of writing a love story. Construction is the last quality to be expected of a medieval romance and even the best of them ramble all over the landscape. Their audiences expected a reasonable amount of fighting and love-making but neither expected nor received a well-knit plot.[1]

Chaucer had been brought up on this French school of romantic fiction and he had reason to think that there was no other way of writing a love story. It is easy to see, therefore, with what a shock of delight he read the Italian romance that Boccaccio had written in his youth and called *Il Filostrato*. Boccaccio was a born story-teller, with a sense of pace and a sense of construction that was wholly unlike anything Chaucer had hitherto encountered.

Chaucer had especial reason to be impressed with the craftsman-ship of *Il Filostrato* because he would have recognized the source of the story immediately. Boccaccio took it from a very haphazard account of two lovers that was embedded at intervals in a popular history of Troy. Chaucer mentions this history in *The House of Fame*; he was familiar with it and would have compared it imme-diately in his mind with the new version of the same tale in *Il Filostrato*.

The source of Boccaccio's poem was a twelfth-century poem called *The Romance of Troy* which a French poet named Benoît de Saint-Maure had dedicated to Eleanor of Aquitaine. It consisted largely of heroic deeds of battle, but drifting in and out

[1] One of the reasons for this was the fact that the romances were deliv-ered orally in most cases and were very long-winded. When Froissart read *Meliador* to his current patron the occupation lasted him every night for ten weeks. The plot construction of a romance like *Meliador* was very like that of the modern "soap opera" heard on the radio, where the story is also told orally and strung out over an extended period of time.

through the clatter of arms were occasional glimpses of the tribulations of a pair of courtly lovers named Troilus and Briseida. Briseida loves Troilus but in the end she deserts him for a Greek knight named Diomede.

A little later on this French poem was translated into Latin prose by a Sicilian judge named Guido de Colonna, and medieval readers got the idea that Guido had been the original author of the poem.[2] It is for this reason that Chaucer mentions "Guydo" in *The House of Fame* as one of the historians whose writings hold up Troy and does not mention Benoit de Saint-Maure.

Boccaccio took the story of Troilus and Briseida, which was hardly more than a rambling anecdote in *The Romance of Troy*, and turned it into a superbly constructed lyric cry of young love and loss. Boccaccio was involved at the time in a violent love affair of his own, and he had a vivid idea of the way young lovers behave. He records in detail the early stages of the courtship, which are only implied in *The Romance of Troy*, adding another main character, whom he calls Pandaro, to bring the lovers together. But his greatest innovation was caused by his solid, inborn sense of narrative technique, which contrasts so startlingly with the usual medieval way of telling a story.

It was Boccaccio's narrative facility that struck Chaucer at once. There was nothing new in the general atmosphere of the story, for Boccaccio was as familiar with the details of courtly love as any Frenchman. But the swift, accurate plot development was his own, and Chaucer recognized its value immediately. Unlike his first baffled excursion into the *Teseide*, Chaucer knew at once what to do with *Il Filostrato*.

Chaucer used the plot construction, which was Boccaccio's strength. He did not use the characterization, which was Boccaccio's weakness. His acceptance of the first is as striking an example of his creative intelligence as his rejection of the second, for there can be no question that Chaucer was right in both.

Boccaccio's abilities did not lie in the direction of characteriza-

[2] There was naturally no way for a medieval reader to judge the relative age of a manuscript, and Latin of course was a much older language than French.

160

tion. He was a storyteller, not a delineator of character, and *Il Filostrato* is characteristic of all his work in this respect. His heroine, Cressida, has no more personality, for all her wealth and breeding, than any shallow little Italian courtesan, and she turns to her new lover, Diomede, with exactly the same sort of ease she first turned to Troilio. Her cousin Pandaro is a conventionalized young man-about-town who performs his task of go-between adequately but never comes to life in the process.

The one really good characterization is that of the hero, the passionate and forsaken Troilio. Boccaccio poured into the character of Troilio, as he himself admitted, his own longing for a fickle Italian lady named Maria d'Aquino; and Troilio is undeniably a real human being with his Italian emotionalism and his shaken, susceptible heart.

It is worth noting that the characterization of Troilio is the only one that Chaucer transferred direct from *Il Filostrato* to his own *Troilus and Criseyde*, making comparatively few changes in the process. It is also worth noting that the characterization which seemed so brilliant in Boccaccio's poem becomes almost commonplace in Chaucer's. For in Chaucer's version it is obliged to measure up against two of the most remarkable pieces of character-drawing in English literature—Chaucer's Pandarus and Chaucer's Criseyde.

In thinking out the personality of his heroine, Chaucer turned his back on the whole of Boccaccio's conception of her and made no attempt to salvage any of it. Boccaccio pictured her merely as the kind of woman who might be expected to attract his dear Troilio and might also be expected to betray him. She serves merely as a focus for the hero's emotions and has no independent existence of her own in the reader's mind.

In this one respect Boccaccio was inferior to his source, *The Romance of Troy*. Benoit de Saint-Maure might not know how to tell a story but he did have a clear sense of the fundamentally human nature of the woman he calls Briseida. He had the sympathetic imagination to realize how she would feel after she had betrayed Troilus, and with a Frenchman's interest in human emotions he gives her a dozen lines to say that are a small masterpiece of psychological accuracy. She is a thoroughly believable woman, in her regrets, in her fear of what people will think of her, in the excuses she makes to herself for her conduct, and in her pathetic resolves to do better in the future.

Boccaccio was not interested in characterization and he saw nothing of value in Briseida's speech, but when Chaucer read the same French lines his eye was instantly caught and held. He knew that Benoit's brief attempt at psychological portraiture was as right in its way as Boccaccio's innovations in plot construction, and it was from this small hint of Benoit's that he began to build up his own conception of Criseyde.

It is clear that Chaucer was greatly impressed by this passage from *The Romance of Troy*, for in his treatment of the same scene he made almost no attempt to improve upon his source. One of the most admired lines in the whole of *Troilus and Criseyde* is Criseyde's touching resolve that at least she can be true to her new lover:

> "To Diomede algate will I be trewe."

This is only Chaucer's swift poetic echo of what Benoit had the lady say two centuries earlier: "I must turn all my heart and mind to Diomede from this time forth."

The original quickening of Chaucer's imagination owed something to Benoit de Saint-Maure, but his final portrait of Criseyde has no actual literary antecedents. She owed a great deal more, in all probability, to the well-bred, gracious women he met at court. There is a friendly, colloquial ease about her way of talking that Chaucer may very well have first heard in someone like Elizabeth de Burgh or Blanche of Lancaster, and it may have been from some great lady also that Criseyde derived her tact, her courtesy and her sense of humor. But her actual birth as an individual was of course in Chaucer's own spirit, where she was formed out of his profound knowledge of the human heart and projected through his steadily increasing genius for characterization.

If Criseyde is a delightful woman, her uncle Pandarus is an equally delightful man. Chaucer ignored Boccaccio's routine Florentine gallant who performs his function of go-between without a spark of actual individuality, and in fact nothing remains of the character as Boccaccio conceived it except the name. The English poet who had already created the chatty Eagle and the well-meaning "Geffrey" and the practical duck suddenly discovered an opening for a full-length comic portrait. The joy with which he seized upon the opportunity is only matched by the complete success of the result.

Nothing like this had been done before in the Middle Ages, and nothing exactly like it has been done in any narrative poem since. It is necessary to turn to the novelists and the dramatists to find a comparable achievement, and in Chaucer's field the only comic figure that can match Pandarus is his own Wife of Bath. Both have the same irresistible reality and the same streak of broad, cheerful cynicism. The difference between them is that Pandarus knows he is being funny while the self-revelations of the Wife of Bath are unconscious. And also, of course, Pandarus is a gentleman and the Wife of Bath is by no means a lady.

Even if Boccaccio had been capable of creating such a man, Pandarus could not have entered *Il Filostrato* without tearing the story apart by the sheer weight of his reality. The fact that he fits excellently into *Troilus and Criseyde* is a measure of the enormous distance that in this respect separates Boccaccio's lyric narrative of young love betrayed from Chaucer's more mature study of real human beings.

Chaucer chose to write his poem in rime royal, the stanza he had first tried out in *The Parliament of Birds*. Rime royal is a very strict poetic form, one of the most difficult that a writer can use, but Chaucer was a sufficiently accomplished technician to find its difficulties less than its advantages. He had already succeeded in making the duck and the goose and the cuckoo talk easily and colloquially within its narrow metrical confines, and he was now prepared to do as much for the conversations of Pandarus and Criseyde.

Chaucer had by this time acquired, through a combination of natural talent, long experience and hard work, a poetic style that was perfectly suited to narrative. He is the one English poet who never raises his voice and at the same time never sinks into a wearying monotone.[3]

It is to be noted that no one ever tried to parody Chaucer's literary style; there is nothing to parody in a style as clear and as deceptively simple as water. It is only when the amateur poet tries to go and do likewise that he discovers that there is more to Chaucer's style than meets the eye.

Chaucer's lack of a "high style" and his persistent use of the terms of common speech are especially odd in a period in which it was another kind of writing that was valued. The ideal of rhetoricians like Geoffrey de Vinsauf was never to use an ordinary word if an extraordinary one could be substituted, in the same way that an eighteenth-century English poet would have scorned to use an ordinary word like "fish" if he could find a phrase like "the finny denizen of the deep."

In the course of writing *Troilus and Criseyde* Chaucer makes an ironical bow in the direction of this kind of writing. He speaks of something which he calls the day's honor, the eye of heaven and the foe of night, and then explains in a courteous aside that by this he means simply the sun. In one flick of the pen Chaucer reveals more of his fundamental conviction on the subject of writing poetry than if he had, like Deschamps, written a whole book on the subject.

Chaucer was an abnormally self-conscious artist in the sense that he was aware both of his capabilities and of his limitations. He was convinced that the middle way was the right one for him not only in his style but in his treatment of emotion, and he never attempted to deal with the heart-shaking passions that writers like Marlowe or Webster took for their own.

Chaucer was a poet of daylight and of common things, and he was well aware that he lacked the emotional force to go beyond his mental environment. He says so, in fact. He refuses point-blank to describe Criseyde's anguish when she is forced to leave her lover, on the basis that if he attempted such a thing in his writing

[3] Wordsworth achieved the first, but in many of his poems he failed notably in avoiding the second.

> It shoulde make her sorrow seeme lesse
> Than that it was.

He felt that he might "childlisshly deface" her pain through attempting to describe it, and therefore, with an honesty and a self-knowledge rare in any writer, he leaves it alone.

Chaucer knew that his art was not formed for high tragedy, and he also knew that it was unsuited to the youthful lyricism that sets the tone for *Il Filostrato*. Chaucer was not an excitable young Italian. He was a middle-aged Englishman with a knowledge of people, a respect for reality, and the fundamental sense of proportion that is sometimes called a sense of humor. He went through the story of *Il Filostrato* with a clear idea of what he wanted to do; he kept the sequence of the plot and the names of the characters, and then reformed the whole poem in his own image.

Chaucer disclaims this labor of creation. In fact, he disclaims any act of creation at all. According to his account, *Troilus and Criseyde* is a direct translation from another author and there is nothing of his own in it at all.

> Wherefore I will have neither thank ne blame
> Of al this work . . .
> For as myn auctor seyde, so sey I.

On even the smallest details Chaucer turns to his "auctor" for corroboration, and the only difference he will admit between his poem and its original is where he was unable to do the original justice.

> I can not tellen al,
> As can my auctor, of his excellence.

For anything Chaucer will admit to the contrary, *Troilus and Criseyde* is the same sort of production as the *Consolation of Philosophy*—a careful, conscientious translation of the work of a Latin author.

This author is not Boccaccio. Boccaccio did not write in Latin but in Italian and in any case anyone who had read *Il Filostrato* would know at once that Chaucer was using it only as a starting point for his own work. Nor does Chaucer pretend that the author was Boccaccio. His Latin author is a certain gentleman named Lollius.

As far as is known today, there was never a Latin writer named Lollius who wrote a history of the Trojan War. Chaucer did not invent the name, for he used it in good faith in the list he made in *The House of Fame* of the writers who bear up the fame of Troy, and an ingenious explanation has been advanced to account for Chaucer's mistaken conviction that Lollius was a real historian.[4] But however firmly Chaucer may have believed in a writer named Lollius he was of course well aware that Lollius had nothing whatever to do with *Troilus and Criseyde*.

On the other hand, the whole weight of medieval opinion was against Chaucer's claiming the story as his own. As has been said before, the Middle Ages would have considered a word like "fiction" a synonym for "falsity," and no writer of love stories would admit that the tale itself or any of the details in it were his own invention. He always got them from another author. This authority was always a very ancient one, and never dealt in fictions but always reported reliably what had actually occurred.

A characteristic example of this point of view is the introduction which the dean of French romance writers, Chrétien de Troyes, gave his most popular tale, *Cligés*.

> We find this story, which I desire to tell and
> relate to you, recorded in one of the books of
> the library of my lord Saint Peter at Beauvais. . . .
> The book, which truthfully bears witness to the
> story, is very ancient; for this reason it is
> all the more to be believed.

[4] There are two lines in Horace which read:

Troiani belli scriptorem, Maxime Lolli,
Dum tu declamas Romae, Praeneste relegi.

They mean: "While you are preaching oratory in Rome, Maximus Lollius, I have been reading Praeneste (i.e., Homer), the writer of the Trojan war." If these lines had been badly copied, as lines so frequently were, it might easily seem that Horace was characterizing one Lollius as the greatest of writers on the Trojan War.

It is true that Chaucer was not familiar with Horace (and it is a pity, for he would have enjoyed him thoroughly) but excerpts from his work were frequently quoted by other authors. John of Salisbury quotes these lines for instance, in his *Polycraticus*, and this was a work that Chaucer almost certainly knew.

Chrétien wished to receive no credit as the original author of *Cligés*. He wished to receive neither "thank ne blame" and therefore sheltered himself behind an imaginary authority in the Beauvais library as Chaucer sheltered himself behind the equally imaginary Lollius.

Chaucer found in Lollius a name that was ideal for his purposes. Lollius was an antique historian, he wrote in Latin, and his authority no one could impugn since no one had ever read him. This left Chaucer free of all responsibility for *Troilus and Criseyde*, since he was only a harmless translator. The full responsibility for the whole story rested with "myn auctor."

In Chaucer's case this convenient fiction was particularly useful. He was attempting something in *Troilus and Criseyde* that had never been tried before by a poet in either England or France. He was rejecting the pat little formula for love stories that had been current for two centuries, in which a beautiful blonde heroine meets a strong, handsome hero and the two fall promptly in love, undergoing various vicissitudes until they are finally united in a happy ending which proves that Love Conquers All.

Chaucer was not planning a love story dealing with conventionalized, sentimentalized types; he was attempting to portray real human beings and real emotions. *Troilus and Criseyde* was in this respect so alien to the reading habits of his London and Westminster audiences that it is possible Chaucer found a literary device like "Lollius" really useful in protecting him from the possible results of so risky an experiment. The Middle Ages did not take kindly to experiments of any kind and Richard's court had never encountered a love story that was not modeled on the French.

In one respect Chaucer was like the French romancers, in the sense that he was interested not only in what his characters did but in why they did it. In the French writers this interest takes the form of long chunks of analysis whose only reason seems to be to slow up the plot. Chaucer sometimes uses the analytical method himself, but with him it seems a reasonable device, as when Hardy or Meredith uses it. Chaucer has already managed to convince his reader that he is discussing real people and he has already let them speak for themselves. But, like all real people, they are intricate, and Chaucer occasionally introduces a passage of analysis to make their manner of thinking plain.

Chaucer is much less interested in his hero than in the other two main characters, for the emotions of Troilus are those of any young man in love. He first sees his chosen lady in church on an April morning and is lost from that time forth. Troilus is a lifelike young man but not a living one. He moves but he does not breathe. He is really little more than the lovesick Dreamer who wanders through the *Romance of the Rose,* and he is ardent, dutiful and heroic because these are the qualities every courtly lover must have.

Troilus was Boccaccio's favorite character, but he was not Chaucer's. It is difficult for an Englishman to take a really sympathetic interest in a lovesick youth, and even in a lyric, Italian drama of young love like *Romeo and Juliet* it is to be noted that a mocking realist named Mercutio had no difficulty in detaching the author's interest from the hero.

There is somewhat the same situation in *Troilus and Criseyde.* Pandarus is not unlike Mercutio in his amiable, ironic wit and his utter inability to be serious even in the most serious moments. Although a self-announced expert in love, he is permanently unlucky in his own love affairs; and he regards his lack of success in "the olde daunce" with a rueful grin and the good-tempered admission, "I hoppe alway behynde."

Pandarus takes real delight in manipulating the love affair of his friend Troilus and his niece Criseyde, for he is by nature a born manager. He is congenitally unable to resist the impulse to push people about for their own good, and is so expert at the occupation that he must have had years of practice in it. This was the character that Boccaccio had conceived as merely a routine go-between for the two lovers, and it is easy to see how Chaucer deepened the story by making Pandarus a real human being.

The delight that Pandarus takes in managing his friends is evident in his first appearance. He goes to visit the princely young Troilus and finds him in tears in his bedroom because he has fallen in love with Criseyde.[5] A lesser man than Pandarus would have

[5] As soon as a courtly lover had been hit by the arrows of the god of Love he was supposed to take to his bed in extreme pain and go into a kind of decline.

ordered him to brace up and behave himself. But Pandarus marvels politely that fear of the Greeks should bring one of the most gallant of the Trojan warriors to such a pass that he can think only of his sins, and expresses his surprise that dread of the foe should "bringe our lusty folk to holynesse." This misinterpretation of his sufferings annoys Troilus, as it was intended to, and in a short time Pandarus has the whole truth out of him.

Troilus is not an especially intelligent young man, and Pandarus does not feel it necessary to be very subtle in his dealings with him. But the case is contrary with his niece Criseyde, who is quite as clever as Pandarus is. When Pandarus goes to visit her as an ambassador from Troilus his method of approach is thoroughly feminine in its delicacy. He does not tell her that Troilus loves her. Instead he plays upon her natural quality of curiosity as he played upon Troilus' masculine quality of pride.

The scene between the uncle and the niece is a marvel of suggestiveness in the way it records a charming bit of surface banter with two currents of determination beneath it. For Pandarus has a secret and Criseyde is determined to get it out of him, although no onlooker would guess it from the casual way they go on joking with each other. The scene is an achievement in characterization and dialogue that is unique in any writing in English before Shakespeare.

Pandarus is not only a delightful conversationalist (especially when he is with Criseyde) but he is one of the most fluent and accomplished of monologists. He is glad to hold forth upon any subject whatever, from the lore of dreams to the art of letter writing, and, like the Eagle in *The House of Fame*, he is incapable of resisting any opportunity that presents itself of delivering a lecture. Once Troilus became somewhat peevish under a particularly erudite flood of information and was moved to protest, "I am nat deaf. Now peace, and crye namore." The reader, however, is not likely to feel that he can get too much of so wonderfully chatty a man.

Pandarus is extremely fond of proverbs and scatters them lavishly through his discourses. In this he is rather like Chaucer himself, and equally Chaucerian is his inability to resist the opportunity to make fun of his beloved proverbs by parodying the

169

somewhat obvious nature of their lore. Pandarus remarks gravely that we have it on the authority of wise old clerks that anyone who is disjointed is not whole.

> "He that parted is in every place
> Is nowhere whole, as writen clerkes wyse."

Nor is black usually white, as some equally sage old proverb would doubtless have pointed out if someone had thought of it.

Pandarus' brand of comedy is not so much humor in the ordinary sense as a fundamentally dispassionate, ironic view of life and he appears at his most characteristic in the scene in which his stage-managing is finally successful. He and a rainy night have combined to maneuver Criseyde into his bedroom, and from then on it is up to Troilus. As far as the hero and heroine are concerned, the scene is Chaucer's nearest approach to actual lyric height and Boccaccio himself could hardly have done it better. But combined with this, in a really extraordinary and very English counterpoint, is the half-sympathetic and half-mocking presence of Pandarus.

Pandarus persists in behaving as though nothing out of the ordinary is taking place. He plays the game of being merely a thoughtful host who has given up his bed to a young lady for the night and who has found himself with another young guest in the room. When Troilus kneels down by Criseyde's bed, Pandarus as a good host provides him with a cushion for his knees. Then he suggests, with his usual reasonableness, that if the two of them will move a little closer to each other they will be able to carry on a more successful conversation. Pandarus then goes over to the fireplace, taking with him the only candle in the room, and settles down for a little light reading in an "old romaunce."

The tone he maintains throughout is perhaps closest to that of the Nurse in *Romeo and Juliet*, and like that other confirmed realist Pandarus does not interfere with the lyric quality of the love story but rather heightens it by contrast. The difference between the two of them, of course, is that Pandarus is not in earnest. There was merely something in the situation that aroused his sense of the ridiculous, and he was temperamentally incapable of resisting a joke.

170

The respect that Pandarus felt for young love was as real as his respect for proverbs, but he was so constituted that he could not take either of them seriously all of the time. As for his private game of being the perfect host, he enjoyed it enough to go on playing it the following morning. He dropped in upon his niece before she was up and inquired with the most tender solicitude if the rain had kept her awake. Whereupon Criseyde blushed and went under the sheet, and Pandarus made his peace with her by suggesting mildly that she cut off his head.

Pandarus felt no regret over the seduction of his niece, and the reader is not supposed to feel that any is required. He did it, as Chaucer says, of "full good entente," and it is important not to confuse him with the connotation of the word "panderer" or with the unpleasant individual that Shakespeare made of him in his own *Troilus and Cressida*. Chaucer's Pandarus was operating honorably under the rules of the game. According to the code of courtly love, the lover was a humble suppliant who needed assistance in reaching the heaven of consummation, and whoever assisted him in reaching this heaven had the full approval of Chaucer's audience. Under this convention love and marriage belonged under separate headings; some early specialists in the subject actually condemned marriage in this connection because it put a man and woman under a legal obligation to be faithful to each other and made their love in that sense less honorable.

According to the literary convention within whose bounds Chaucer was writing, Pandarus gave his two young friends the best gift that lay in his power. Like the friend of the Dreamer in *The Romance of the Rose* he had merely been bending all his energies to the removal of "danger," that instinctive reluctance of the lady to commit herself which is like a black-browed giant guarding the rose. That night in Pandarus' house the rose is finally plucked, and Chaucer's audience was quite as pleased about it as was Pandarus himself. To anyone who had been brought up in the literary traditions of courtly love it was the equivalent of the old fairy-tale ending: "And so they were married and lived happily ever after."

Guillaume de Lorris characterized the garden of the Rose as a place "where all is fair and nought is wrong," and there is in fact a curious innocence about the whole of this convention as it was handled by the medieval poets. It has its own sort of morality, for those who serve the god of Love are exalted and purified in the service. It also has its own sort of religion. When Troilus sings a song in praise of love, it is a more or less faithful translation of the eighth lyric in Book Two of the *Consolation of Philosophy*, in which Boethius describes love as the power that binds together the whole earth and keeps it stable.[6] Troilus himself is altogether reformed by the success of his suit. He aids the poor, is courteous to the lowly, and flees pride and avarice. When he goes out hunting he spares the "smale beastes" with a consideration that only a lover could be expected to show.

All this is accurately in the tradition of courtly love. But while Chaucer was writing within the bounds of an accepted tradition he was also writing of real people, and it may be safely stated that anyone might be improved by loving Criseyde. She was a delightful person; and her author, as a matter of fact, was in love with her himself.

Criseyde was an aristocrat, but her aristocracy was like that of Shakespeare's Beatrice or Rosalind. That is to say, she did not let the fact that she was a great lady bother her much. She never made any attempt to maintain her dignity because it would not occur to her that she could lose it. It is curious that two middle-class poets like Chaucer and Shakespeare, born in a period when distinctions of birth counted for something, should have been able to portray so accurately in their women such a vital and yet elusive aspect of good breeding.

Criseyde was always serious in her dealings with Troilus, who was a good young man but not very quick in catching a joke. She kept her love of teasing for the occasions when her uncle was around. Particularly irresistible is the subject of his love affairs, which were famous for their lack of success. But Criseyde's teasing is very gentle, and Pandarus is certainly fair game. For his, as he admits himself, was a "jolly wo," and he conducted his love af-

[6] It is hardly necessary to add that Boethius was thinking of a very different kind of love from the one Troilus felt for Criseyde.

fairs in an Ovidian spirit that was much more likely to injure his purse than his heart.

Criseyde is equally willing to tease herself. In their first scene together Pandarus suggests a little dance on this delightful May morning and Criseyde pretends to be very shocked. She turns suddenly into the perfect widow, so demurely pious that she is unbearable. Her dear uncle must be mad to suggest dancing, when everyone knows that widows never do such things. The proper thing for her to do is to retire to a cave with a book to instruct her in the lives of the holy saints—this from a lady who is sitting in her "parlour" reading a romance of Thebes.

Straight-faced foolery of this kind is something that the English have always enjoyed, and Chaucer knew that he did not need to underline any of Criseyde's remarks with the statement that she was making a joke. No member of his audience was going to misunderstand the wide-eyed innocence with which she looks at her uncle when he rises to go without having disclosed his secret. She does not ask him to stay. She merely remarks that she never knew him to weary so soon of feminine company.

This oblique method is so similar to the one Pandarus himself employs that it is no wonder Criseyde and Pandarus enjoy each other. The bond of affection between them is a real one, and when Pandarus says that except for his mistresses he loves her better than any woman in the world he is carrying on a joke (which she began) to cover his own display of sentiment. It is characteristic of Criseyde that she answers not his actual speech but the emotion behind it, and expresses her own love for him in soberness and earnestness. Like all good humorists, Criseyde knew when to be serious.[7]

Her courtesy is unvarying, and it is the satisfactory kind that is based not upon surface propriety but on fundamental good breed-

[7] This whole scene is Chaucer's development of what is hardly more than a stage direction in Boccaccio's poem, to the effect that Cressida and Pandaro indulged in "laughter and soft words, many jests and very kind speeches, as are common at times between kinsfolk." To see what Chaucer does with this brief hint is an object lesson in the art of writing.

ing. When she goes to dinner at her uncle's house the night of the rain, she wants to go home again and cannot because of the storm. She therefore pretends that she was only joking when she told her uncle she wanted to leave, so that Pandarus will not realize she is reluctant to stay. For, as Criseyde tells herself reasonably, she may as well accept his invitation to spend the night and be cheerful about it as to grumble over the situation and then stay anyway.

For the rest she was exceedingly lovely to look at, had no business sense (her uncle evidently managed her affairs for her) and was an abject coward where the war was concerned. There was some excuse for this, for Criseyde's position in Troy was a difficult one. Her father was an astrologer and he had deserted to the Greek side because he was convinced that the Trojans would lose the war. This put Criseyde in the uncomfortable position of being the daughter of a traitor, although everyone loved her and she was a welcome guest at the dinner parties of Hector and Helen. She could not help trembling whenever she thought of the Greeks, and it was not until she found in Troilus a "wall of steel" that she ceased being frightened.

No novelist could surpass the delicate accuracy with which Chaucer shows Criseyde's attitude towards Troilus changing from mild curiosity to an overwhelming, self-forgetting love. The change has very little to do with Pandarus, who merely supplies a series of gentle shoves at the proper moment. Chaucer establishes this clearly, for any other behavior on the part of her uncle would have been inexcusable. Even under the courtly love system, no woman could be involved in a love affair against her will. Such a situation, moreover, would reflect upon the independence of spirit and the honesty of Chaucer's heroine.

Criseyde is not aware she is falling in love. It is only the reader who is aware of it. Chaucer makes him the guest of Criseyde's thoughts and then leaves him free to deduce what he pleases.

After Pandarus has left her alone with the news that she is loved by a prince of Troy, Criseyde undertakes to be very calm and wise about the whole thing. She goes over the whole conversation, inch by inch, and wonders why she should have been so upset over her uncle's announcement. After all, Troilus means nothing to her.

Then she hears shouting in the streets and puts her head out the window. It is Troilus riding home from the day's fighting, very handsome, very military in his damaged armor, very much embarrassed by the plaudits of the crowd. When Criseyde looks at him and considers that this is the man who is dying for love of her, she feels a faint stirring in her own heart and pulls her head in quickly. She is not yet in love with Troilus but she has lost the power to think of him with indifference.

The care and subtlety with which Chaucer portrays the gradual change in Criseyde's emotions form a curious contrast to the suddenness of Boccaccio's heroine. As soon as the Cressida of *Il Filostrato* learns that Troilio loves her she meditates as follows:

> "Who will ever desire me if I grow old?
> Certainly no one. . . . Well it is therefore
> to make provision in season. This lover
> of thine is handsome, well-bred, wise and
> clever, and fresher than garden lily. . . .
> Why not give thy love to him?"

Following this exceedingly practical meditation she meets her chosen one at night with little further delay.

Chaucer had *Il Filostrato* before him on the table as he wrote, and this passage annoyed him. Nothing could have been farther from his own conception of Criseyde, and he enters the poem in his own person at this point to defend her against even the breath of such a slander. Some people, says Chaucer darkly, may have the idea that she "lightly loved Troilus right from the firste sighte." May anyone who thinks so, he continues with partisan fervor, fail to prosper. Criseyde did not begin by loving Troilus. She began "to like hym first" and later on her liking grew into love.

After the affair is consummated, Chaucer gives Criseyde a beautiful speech in which she explains to Troilus why she loves him. It is not for his wealth, for his breeding, nor for his courage as a warrior. It is because he is a man of courtesy and self-control and possesses the Boethian quality of "moral vertu, grounded upon trouthe." A woman who values these qualities does not love quickly or lightly, as Chaucer knew.

175

The first hint of Criseyde's ultimate surrender is conveyed through a scene in her garden. The device Chaucer uses is a sudden shift in the mood of the poem at this point, so that the reader begins to feel as susceptible to the power of love as Criseyde herself is shortly going to feel.

Hers is one of those beautiful little medieval gardens, trimly fenced and green shaded, that are full of flowers and trees and sanded paths upon which long-skirted maidens may walk. One of the maidens begins to sing a love song, and there are seven stanzas of lyric, effortless evocation of the happiness, the contentment and the glory of love. Criseyde gives no particular indication that she is moved by the song and she cuts short the conversation on love that follows. But as she lies in bed that night she hears a nightingale singing in a green cedar tree beneath her window, and she knows that he sings of love.

Chaucer does not maintain this lyric note once it has served his purpose. In fact he is not above teasing his heroine in the next scene because she is so intent on trying to prove to herself that Troilus is still nothing to her. When Pandarus brings her a letter from the lovesick prince, Criseyde is sure she is not going to read it. Oddly enough, however, she finds time to look it over while she is dressing for dinner, and when her uncle is unkind enough to ask her what she thinks of it she turns bright red and hums a little song. She finally consents to write a letter to Troilus in return, but only to say that she will be a "suster" to him, and she wishes it clearly understood that she makes this concession only to give her uncle pleasure. And when Pandarus maneuvers her to the window seat with some talk of the tenants in the house across the way and then shows her Troilus riding by, Criseyde answers, "So he doth," with an elaborate unconcern that deceives no one but herself.

The two finally meet, through a dinner party that has been arranged by the indefatigable Pandarus, and Troilus is unable to do anything to further his own suit. As soon as he sees Criseyde his voice "quook" and his carefully prepared speech goes out of his head. Pandarus himself could have arranged nothing more effective. No one could fail to be sorry for Troilus at the moment, and certainly not a lady as gentle-hearted as Criseyde.

It is her pity that Pandarus plays upon from that time forward. He uses his best weapon almost brutally the night of the rain, when he comes to her with a tale of Troilus having arrived dripping and in trouble. At the climax of the episode, when Criseyde knows that she is firmly caught, she is for a moment—to use Chaucer's pitying phrase—like a small bird in the grip of a hawk. After that she loses herself in the happiness of Troilus and is deeply and self-forgetfully in love.

An exchange of prisoners results in an agreement to send Criseyde to her father and the two lovers face separation. It is not of herself that Criseyde thinks then, but of Troilus.

> "O deere hearte eek, that I love so,
> Who shall that sorrow slay that ye be inne?"

She goes to comfort her lover, remembering her uncle's statement that "Women ben wise," and she tries earnestly to be wise enough for two. This was an occupation for which Criseyde was totally unfitted, for she was a dear lady but not really very wise.

Troilus is tortured by the suspicion that his lady will meet "many a lusty knight among the Grekis," but Chaucer goes out of his way to underline the fact that Criseyde intends to be faithful. Her "heart trewe was and kinde" and she takes her departure from Troilus in true love and deep sorrow.

Troilus' presentiment is fully justified when a young Greek knight named Diomede appears to conduct Criseyde to her father's tent. Diomede is briefly but adequately characterized by Chaucer, and he is a familiar type. He is a good soldier and an almost professional lover, who can take a woman in any way but seriously. He is aware that Criseyde is very lovely, and he handles the necessary preliminaries with practiced ease as he rides beside her away from the walls of Troy. He only wants to be a brother to her, and he has never opened his heart before to a woman like this, and he only wants to be treated as her friend. And so on. Criseyde thanks him politely for his offer of friendship but she only hears "a word or two" of all that he has been saying.

Diomede has no intention of letting his "lufsom lady dear" get away for any lack of boldness on his part. Criseyde is trying to nerve herself to an attempt to steal through the armed lines, after ten days in camp, when Diomede arrives at her tent. He begins to press her a little, and then, suddenly, Chaucer's exact and loving characterization of his heroine falls apart. In five lines she betrays Troilus and takes Diomede for her lover. The story even reports, adds Chaucer sorrowfully, that she let Diomede wear her colors on his sleeve and gave him a brooch that had belonged to Troilus.

What had happened to the unhappy Criseyde and to her equally unhappy creator was that the story in which they were involved had betrayed them both. It was the story of a woman's unfaithfulness and as such had been current for two hundred years. It was too late to change it now. Criseyde's creator had been incapable of resisting the ancient plot as it came to him through Boccaccio's magic as a storyteller, and there was nothing he could do but carry it through to the bitter end.

If Chaucer had been willing to resign himself to the situation, he could easily have motivated Criseyde's unfaithfulness. He had already characterized her as an easily frightened woman, one who needed a man to lean on, and Diomede might in time have become a wall of steel to her as Troilus had once been. It is true that the situation would never have been to her credit, but Chaucer could easily have made it a believable one.

Instead, Chaucer refuses to give any motivation for her yielding to Diomede. He gives it not even one line of the kind of psychological analysis that accompanied her slowly deepening love for Troilus. It takes four books to accomplish Criseyde's seduction by Troilus, and to make it believable. Her seduction by Diomede occurs in five lines and is naturally not believable at all.

After that Chaucer's heart was no longer in his work, and in the rest of the poem he follows Boccaccio closely and almost by rote. There is nothing of Chaucer's own invention in these final scenes. He adds to his transcriptions from *Il Filostrato* the scene that had first attracted him in *The Romance of Troy*, in which Briseida regrets what she has done, but the characterization that seemed so striking in Benoit's rather commonplace narrative now seems curiously thin and pale. This is just an ordinary woman. She is not Chaucer's Criseyde.

178

Chaucer is well aware that she is not his Criseyde, and he remarks almost sullenly that in reporting Criseyde's new love for Diomede he is merely repeating what the old books say. Three times in as many stanzas he disclaims all responsibility in the matter.

> Men say—I not—that she gave hym her heart.

Earlier in the poem Chaucer had suggested to his readers the hopeful possibility that these old authorities that testify to Criseyde's guilt may be liars. If so, it is Chaucer's strongly expressed wish that the slander they have put upon an innocent woman will fall back upon themselves.

Chaucer's thorough dislike of the traditional ending of his story shows in the carelessness with which he wrote it. The greater part of Book Five reads like an earlier draft of the poem which its author lacked sufficient interest to revise. Its faults are typically medieval ones which the poem as a whole outgrew.

If Chaucer had been giving serious attention to his closing pages he would certainly have struck out the six stanzas suddenly inserted in the tale at a most inopportune moment to describe the three main characters. Apart from being wrongly placed they are not especially good descriptions in themselves, except for the open affection given to Criseyde's. In their arrangement they are too much like the descriptions that appear in the romances, formalized and conventionalized in accordance with the precepts of the rhetoricians. No reader, moreover, wants to be given at this point the names of Diomede's father and grandfather.

If Chaucer had been revising his fifth book with more care he would probably also have omitted the seven stanzas that give a detailed synopsis of the *Thebaid* of Statius. This again was the kind of rambling medieval device that would have seemed excellent to Chaucer when he was writing *The Book of the Duchess*, but which he had outgrown. It is alien in every way to the compact, intelligent vigor of *Troilus and Criseyde*.

The real excellence of the fifth book consists in what Chaucer got direct from Boccaccio—in the agony of waiting that Troilus endures while Criseyde is with the Greeks and in his pathetic attempts to assure himself that she is still true to him. This is excellent translating but it is nothing more. In fact, the creative impulse is so obviously lacking that Chaucer falls into the same kind of mood that was his when he was translating Boethius. Boccaccio has Diomede speaks of "ambages," and Chaucer is so much the conscientious translator that he inserts two lines of his own to explain in parenthesis that an ambage is an ambiguity—"double wordes slye."

The truth is that the creative interest that Chaucer experienced so powerfully in the first four books of *Troilus and Criseyde* is almost wholly lacking in Book Five. Chaucer does his best, but he cannot bring himself to any real enthusiasm for a plot from which the bright lady of his own creation has vanished.

Chaucer of course knew from the beginning that he was heading for a major difficulty with his plot and that the more he persuaded his readers to love his dear Criseyde the more strange her sudden downfall was going to be. Therefore he was obliged to invent a plausible reason for the ending of his tale if he was not to lose the trust of his readers altogether.

Chaucer refused to base Criseyde's guilt upon Criseyde's character, as a modern writer would be obliged to do. As a medieval writer he had another and better loophole of escape. He could blame it upon the stars.

Whether Chaucer himself believed in astrology there is no way of knowing. Living as he did in a pre-Copernican universe, in which the sun moved around the earth and the stars traveled across the heavens directing a crisscross of rays down upon humanity, it would be strange if Chaucer did not have a cautious respect for the influence of the planets upon the lives of men. But whether he personally believed in astrology or not he found its doctrines very useful to his purpose in *Troilus and Criseyde*. They relieved him of the unpleasant necessity of motivating Criseyde's fall through some flaw in her own character. Her fall was instead the "fatal destyne that Jove hath in disposition" and nothing that Criseyde herself might do could have averted her fate.

In order to reinforce this point, Chaucer fills the latter part of his poem with discussions of fate, free will and predestination.

The characters are deeply concerned with the question of whether an individual can control his fate or whether it is written in the stars. Troilus broods over the subject for seventeen stanzas and finally comes to a conclusion which, for the purposes of this particular poem, is supposed to be shared by the reader:

> "For all that cometh, cometh by necessitee:
> Thus to be lorn, it is my destinee."

Troilus reaches this conclusion in Book Four, which is prior to his betrayal by Criseyde. In other words, Chaucer gives a reason for his heroine's sin before she sins it, and supplies her with an excuse preparatory to her need of it. Criseyde cannot help being faithless to her lover. The act was decreed by "destinee," and neither her sweetness, her integrity, nor her charm can alter one whit the inevitability of her doom.

This device was as reasonable to a medieval audience as the ghost in *Hamlet* was to an Elizabethan one, and through it Chaucer succeeded in saving both his plot and his heroine's character. Even from the modern point of view Chaucer's device is effective. As a result of his use of the stars it is not Criseyde's fall that lingers in the reader's mind but Criseyde herself. It is not her sin the reader remembers, but her happiness:

> The play, the laughter, men were wont to finde
> In her . . .

her love of fun, her gentleness, her youth, and all the engaging inconsistencies in her personality that go to make up a real woman.

Nor is the sense of unity in the poem lost, for in spite of its bitter ending the total effect of *Troilus and Criseyde* is undeniably one of happiness. The quality of happiness, like the quality of humor, was one that Chaucer was never able to keep out of his poetry.

Above all, however, the total effect of the poem is one of reality, and it must have had a startling effect upon the first medieval audience to which it was read. What would today be called a lack of surface realism in the poem—such as the fact that ancient Troy is obviously medieval London, with armored knights and stubborn burgesses convening in a real Westminster parliament—would only serve to make the events of the poem more inescapably real to Chaucer's contemporaries.

These contemporaries of his had been brought up on routine, highly conventionalized French romances, and they had nothing to prepare them for so real and brilliant an evocation of human passion. The men and women in the French love stories were hardly more than personified abstractions of romance, gentility and courtly love, while Chaucer's people, still real after the passage of six hundred years, must have seemed so close to the members of a medieval audience that they could almost have heard them breathe.

Especially would this have been true in regard to the younger members of the audience, who lacked the instinctive conservatism of their elders and whose emotions were close to the surface where the subject of love was concerned. And these are the people, the "younge, fresshe folkes, he or she," to whom Chaucer addresses his epilogue.

The epilogue is a curious production, reflecting so many moods in its author that it seems safe to assume it was not written all at one time. It opens in Chaucer's best court manner with an apology to the ladies for having told a story about a woman's unfaithfulness. He beseeches

> every lady bryght of hue
> And every gentil woman, what she be,
> That al be that Criseyde was untrue,
> That for that guilt she be not wroth with me.

He calls to mind all the women that have been betrayed by false lovers and with a typically Chaucerian twist suggests that his audience beware of the male sex.[8]

[8] Chaucer's courtesy towards the ladies here was probably inspired in part by his dislike of the unpleasant tone of Boccaccio's epilogue. Boccaccio's advice to the young is delivered entirely to young men. "A young woman is fickle and desirous of many lovers. And many women also . . . turn up their noses and go about with a disdainful air . . . Choice should not be made in haste . . . because age lesseneth worth." *Et cetera.*

Then Chaucer continues with his famous farewell:

Go, litel book, go, litel myn tragedye. . . .

He says that *Troilus and Criseyde* makes no pretense of competing with the great masters of storytelling, and he hopes that in spite of the uncertainties of the English tongue it will not suffer too much from having its language or its meter misunderstood.

This might have been the end, and perhaps it was in the first version of *Troilus and Criseyde*. But Chaucer had run a distinct risk in writing a love poem with such realism. He not only stirred the young people of his audience in a way they could not have been stirred by the conventional French romances, but in evoking human passion so realistically he found himself in conflict with the teachings of his religion.

Such a conflict was inevitable. A pretty little *jeu d'esprit* like *The Parliament of Birds* might glorify the delights of human love and yet be dismissed merely as a gay bit of foolishness. But *Troilus and Criseyde* was from beginning to end a direct denial of the set of values which medieval Christianity promulgated, incorporating this denial in a work of such solidity and force that it could not be ignored.

Chaucer as a Christian would never have agreed to such a denial. It was Chaucer as a creative artist who could not avoid it, since he was attempting to show human life as it actually is lived. Again, therefore, there is the spectacle of Chaucer being pulled in two directions at once and able to go with a whole heart in neither.

The result, in this instance, is ten additional stanzas in which Chaucer sets out to destroy the emotions he himself has created in the reader. He has Troilus slain in battle, and his spirit, freed from the bonds of earth, rises to the eighth sphere. From this vantage point Troilus looks down with supreme contempt upon "this litel spot of earthe." His only emotion is to "despise this wrecched world" and all that it contains, and especially does he despise the "blinde lust" that once bound him to Criseyde.

Having removed the whole emotional foundation upon which he built his great poem, Chaucer then proceeds to stamp upon the ruins. He demolishes even the harmless fiction of heathen gods through which he has tried to give a little local color to his tale of Troy. The religious observances of the main characters are nothing but "cursed olde rites," and Jove and Mars and Apollo are no more than "rascaille." As for love, it is nothing but lust— "this wrecched worldes appetite"—and may all young people turn themselves from such vanity and occupy their minds only with the love of Christ.

Once again Chaucer the medieval Christian has overtaken Chaucer the artist, the delighted realist who valued the whole world and everything in it. It is a repetition of the mood that briefly marred the unity of *The Parliament of Birds*, except that in *Troilus and Criseyde* the shock is of course much greater. It is impossible for the startled reader to agree to the proposition that human love is unimportant when Chaucer has throughout the whole length of his poem devoted his subtle, glowing art to making it seem important.

Chaucer never tried it again. He never again undertook to write a love story about real human beings, and *Troilus and Criseyde* remains an isolated masterpiece—a pre-Renaissance evocation of a Renaissance theme. But if Chaucer felt himself obliged, as a Christian, to repudiate his great achievement, as an artist he apparently had no regrets. For he put his retraction in a postscript and did not alter any of the stanzas themselves. His denial of the poem leaves the poem itself untouched, and Pandarus and Criseyde are free to move and breathe in a world that no reader can believe is false and wretched. If it had been, Geoffrey Chaucer could never have loved it so.

CHAPTER XII

HE DATE of *Troilus and Criseyde* is not known, but it is probable that Chaucer did not finish writing it before 1382—the year that Anne of Bohemia was crowned Queen of England. There is a line in the description of Criseyde that can only be interpreted as a compliment to the new queen.

> Right as oure firste letter is now an A,
> In beauty first so stood she. . . .

The combination of "our" and "now" implies more than a routine reference to the first letter of the alphabet.

Geoffrey Chaucer had been very fortunate in the women of the court with whom he had previously come into contact, like Queen Philippa and her daughter-in-law Blanche, and he was equally fortunate in having the privilege of knowing the new Queen Anne.

Anne was the daughter of the late Emperor Charles IV, reverently known to the Bohemians as the "Father of his Country." Charles was a man of intelligence and common sense who had given his country, in the words of a contemporary chronicler, "such peace as had not been in the memory of man." As the founder of the University of Prague he saw to it that his daughter was well educated, but the marriage commissioners chose her for Richard largely because of the nobility of her birth and the gentleness of her disposition. The report does not mention her appearance but it is doubtful if she was strikingly beautiful; the house of Luxemburg was not noted for its looks.

It was a highly successful match. The lonely, passionate young King loved Anne with a singleness of heart that kept him devotedly at her side through the twelve years of their marriage, and she gave the unstable Richard a steadfast happiness that he lost forever when she died. Her political influence was always on the side of moderation and there is no chronicler, of whatever political affiliation, who fails to express his admiration for a "noble and a gracious lady."

The only criticisms ever made of Anne of Bohemia were the kind that any young girl who was also a foreigner would have to expect. It was said that she encouraged the extreme fashions of padded shoulders and pointed toes that had swept over England and that her Bohemian entourage spent too much money. It was also said that both Anne and Richard were too fond of gaiety. But they were only fifteen years old apiece when they married each other, and they shared a normal delight in dances and games and parties.

Chaucer dedicated his next poem to Anne of Bohemia. It was called *The Legend of Good Women,* and John Lydgate says that it was written at her request.

It is not at all unlikely that Chaucer wrote *The Legend of Good Women* at the Queen's suggestion. The poem is a perfect court product, graceful and civilized, written to be read by women. Its charm is the charm of unreality, of a convention tossed about lightly by an expert to amuse a cultivated taste. It is so French in its tone and so alien to the realism towards which Chaucer was moving that it is easy to believe it was written to order.

The Legend of Good Women has neither the psychological reality of *Troilus and Criseyde,* which preceded it, nor the universal reality of *The Canterbury Tales,* which came after it. In fact it lacks reality of any kind, and if Chaucer himself did not specifically state that it was written after the *Troilus* any reader might be forgiven for dating it earlier. It is excellently done, but done in a manner that Chaucer was outgrowing, and it is not surprising he never finished it.

The Legend of Good Women is based upon what might be called a family joke, the family being the court circle and the joke being Geoffrey Chaucer's attitude towards the subject of love. In writing *Troilus and Criseyde* Geoffrey has done a wicked thing. He has portrayed a faithless woman and thus has committed heresy against the laws of love. He must therefore repent, and his repentance shall take the form of writing a series of stories of

186

"good" women, women who have been faithful in their love. Geoffrey shall write, in fact, the tale of love's martyrs.

Chaucer encountered no clash here with his religious sense, for there was nothing for it to clash against. He might as well have apologized for a soap bubble. When he set himself to describe how real people fall in love, he was acutely aware that he had to ask forgiveness for his sin. But here he is playing no more than an amusing game, and neither he nor the court circle took it more seriously than it was intended.

It was a game of which the aristocrats knew all the rules. Outsiders were not admitted, and in a sense this works to the disadvantage of the poem. For the reader of today is an outsider and he feels shut out because he does not know the rules of the game.

Careful research has shed a little light on one or two of these rules. It is known for instance that there was a literary cult of the daisy (called in French the marguerite) that had largely supplanted in literary circles the earlier cult of the rose as the one true flower of love. It is also known that a game was played in both the French and English courts of dividing lovers into two sects, or orders: that of the Flower and that of the Leaf.[1]

Yet it is impossible to reconstruct just the sort of smile that would pass around the circle of Chaucer's listeners when he pauses in his reverence for the daisy to say that he never meant to praise the flower more than the leaf. It is a lost world today, a world as charming and as unreal as that which was once inhabited by Marie Antoinette and her shepherdesses. Chaucer knew it well, as intimately as Shakespeare knew the Forest of Arden. The strange thing is that he, like Shakespeare, knew so many other kinds of worlds and moved in them all with equal freedom.

Yet even in this charming and conventionalized little fairyland Chaucer keeps his contact with the real earth. Among the best loved lines in all his poetry are those in which he describes his excitement in the spring, when he puts away his books and goes to visit the flowers that are coming up in the meadows.

[1] According to Eustache Deschamps, that prince of journalists, the leader of the cult of the Flower in England was Philippa of Lancaster, the daughter of John of Gaunt.

Of all the floures in the mede
Then love I most these floures white and red,
Such as men callen daysyes in our toun.

Chaucer's flower may be the conventionalized and literary French marguerite, but it is also a real English daisy.

Chaucer makes his readers see so clearly, and with such affection, the small red and white flowers growing low in the grass, that it comes as a distinct shock when he begins to refer to his daisy in the terms that a lover would use in describing his mistress. He calls the flower his sovereign lady, his guide, the mistress of his wit and his "earthly god." The daisy is clearness and light in a world of darkness, which is precisely the phrase that Boccaccio used to describe his emotion towards Maria d'Aquino.

The shock that this gives a modern reader is no fault of Chaucer's. He was writing for a special group of readers who were intimately acquainted with the game he was playing. It is his modern readers who are outside the closed circle. Anne of Bohemia and Philippa of Lancaster may walk inside it along with him, but the best we can do is to peer over the fence.

Chaucer's springtime is the same sort of blend of reality and conventionality as his daisy. The birds that sing on the trees are unmistakably English, but they do not behave in a way that would please an ornithologist. They are as versed in the ways of courtly love as were the falcons in Chaucer's *Parliament of Birds*.

This engaging mixture of fact and fantasy continues when Geoffrey finally leaves his worship of the daisy because it is night. He returns home and falls asleep on "a litel herber that I have" which has been newly turfed and strewn with flowers in honor of the spring.[2]

Chaucer dreams that his flower comes to life as a beautiful woman whom the god of Love is leading across the fields. She is

[2] If this could be accepted as an autobiographical reference it would be helpful in dating the poem. Chaucer's garden at Aldgate was probably not large enough to accommodate an arbor, and since Chaucer gave up Aldgate in 1386 the *Legend* could safely be placed after that date. But the poem as a whole is so conventional and so literary that it is not entirely safe to take any of its data as autobiographical.

188

clothed all in green, with a crown of petals upon her golden hair. The poet composes a poem in her honor, one of the loveliest that Chaucer ever wrote. It is the exquisite ballade,

"Hide, Absalom, thy gilte tresses clear . . ."

and is composed with all the grace that his years of experience in French verse forms had given him.

The god of Love and his queen come to a halt by Geoffrey, who is kneeling humbly in the grass. The god fixes him with a stern eye and remarks that he would prefer to have a worm next the daisy, which is his own flower, than to have Geoffrey. For Geoffrey is a heretic where the court of love is concerned. First he translated *The Romance of the Rose*, which is full of insults to women (the god is referring to the Jean de Meun section, of course) and then he wrote the story of *Troilus and Criseyde* which records a woman's unfaithfulness.

The queen requests her lord not to be like a tyrant of Lombardy and jump to conclusions. Possibly Geoffrey wrote these two wicked books in "innocence" and did not quite realize what he was doing. In any case, the man has been as respectful to love as his feeble wit will permit.

He made the book that hight the Hous of Fame
And eek the Deeth of Blanche the Duchesse
And the Parlement of Foules, as I guesse . . .
And many a hymne for your holydays,
That highten balades, roundels, virelayes.

Because of all this she imposes upon Geoffrey a relatively light penance. He is to spend the rest of his life composing "a glorious legende of goode women," recording all the faithful women who died as martyrs to love. In each case he will carefully point out that it was the man who was untrue and thus he will make amends for his sins.

The god of Love then introduces the lady to Geoffrey. She is Alcestis, the lady of Greek legend who died to save her husband and thus became a symbol of faithfulness; and Geoffrey recognizes her at once as his daisy and the queen of his heart.

189

There have been many attempts to identify Alcestis with Anne of Bohemia. But the identification is not very satisfactory, since the queen of Love specifically makes mention of the queen of England.

> "And when this book is made, give it the queen,
> On my behalf, at Eltham or at Sheene."

It has also been suggested that Alcestis may be intended to represent Anne's mother-in-law, the beautiful Joan of Kent. But it is risky to attempt any identification with real people six hundred years after the event unless, as in the case of the Duchess Blanche, it is Chaucer himself who makes the identification. Otherwise, there is not enough information to go on. Anyone who attempts to enter the intimate, casual, courtly circle for whom *The Legend of Good Women* was written must remember that he is a guest from another century and not go too far in his efforts to make himself feel at home.

The god of Love brings the prologue to a close by giving Geoffrey some exact instructions as to how he shall proceed with his task.

> "At Cleopatre I will that thou beginne,
> And so forth, and my love so shal thou winne."

Then the god of Love and his lady leave for paradise, and Geoffrey obediently settles down to his task by beginning with the tale of Cleopatra.

The fact that Cleopatra heads a list of "good women" shows how necessary it is to read *The Legend of Good Women* in the same mood in which it was written. Cleopatra was faithful to Antony and therefore she was a martyr in the religion of love, and she went to Paradise because it was part of the code of courtly love that no true lover could go to hell.

This conception of heaven and hell was not precisely the Christian one, and yet it accommodated itself quite comfortably to the Christian religion. There is an excellent example of this sort of accommodation in the speech Alcestis makes, for when she lists

Chaucer's works of "holyness," as she calls them, she does not stop with his love poems.

> "He hath in prose translated Boece,
> And of the Wrecched Engendring of Mankinde,
> As men may in pope Innocent y-fynde;
> And made the life also of Seynt Cecile." [3]

All these were serious devotional works. Boethius ranked as a Christian martyr, and Pope Innocent's extremely gloomy tract on the viciousness and corruption of mankind is Christianity at its most unrelenting and severe. The life of Saint Cecilia is a typical medieval saint's legend, and it is curious to find three devout works of this kind in the list that Alcestis offers the god of Love to persuade him to forgive Geoffrey for writing *Troilus and Criseyde*.

This typically medieval mixture of the sacred and the profane occurs also in the course of the legends themselves. When Chaucer describes Dido he says that she was so good and so beautiful a lady that if God Himself were to choose someone to love,

> "Whom should he loven but this lady sweet? [4]

This may come as a shock to the modern reader, but it would not be a shock to a medieval one. He had seen God many a time, along with Adam and Herod and Noah and the rest, and while he knew that the miracle plays were not quite real and only approximated these holy characters, he was also convinced that God was only a short distance upwards, residing with all His court about Him in the sky.

[3] Chaucer's translation of Pope Innocent's treatise is not extant, and the loss is a small one. The life of Saint Cecilia later made its appearance in *The Canterbury Tales*.

[4] There is an exact echo of the same note in John Skelton, who was writing poetry about a hundred years later. In describing the Lady Isabel Pennell he says,

> It were a heavenly health,
> It were an endless wealth,
> A life for God himself . . .
> to hear her sing.

Skelton, incidentally, was a great admirer of Chaucer's. While most of his contemporaries were criticizing what they called the old poet's incorrect meters, Skelton found him "pleasant, easy and plain."

The medieval habit of speaking of holy things as a man might speak of his neighbor is excellently illustrated by the Knight de la Tour Landry. That conservative fourteenth-century gentleman was trying to explain the Virgin Birth to his daughters and he put it as follows: "God wished to be born in wedlock, to comply with current legal requirements and to avoid gossip." A God capable of making business-like arrangements of this kind is exactly the sort of God who might well fall in love with Dido. This was not the God of the great men of the century like Bradwardine or Wyclif, but it was the God who made the common people happy. Like the devil, or like the Greek and Roman deities, He was human enough to be understood.

It would not be safe to say that this was Chaucer's God. A mind as subtle and as complex as Chaucer's would not be content with so simple-minded a religion. But Chaucer was capable of a number of points of view, some of them simultaneous, and one of these was a point of view so innocent that it dealt with a world that might have been made of painted cardboard. He expected his audience to follow him into this world and they evidently did, or he would never have dared to write with a freedom that otherwise would have been irreverent.

It seemed equally natural to his medieval audience that the naval battle described in the legend of Cleopatra could have taken place in the English Channel. It did not surprise a fourteenth-century audience to learn that the Egyptian ships were equipped with all the naval devices mentioned by Froissart, any more than it surprised an Elizabethan audience to see Cleopatra appear in a ruff and a farthingale. After all, Chaucer and Shakespeare were not writing for Egyptians. They made the ancient stories contemporary to their own generation and at least avoided a later tendency to make the classical characters look like plaster abstractions posing on a pillar.

Ovid had done the same thing when he made his ancient Greek heroines behave like women he had met in Rome, and many of Chaucer's best stories in the *Legend* come from Ovid.

Working with Ovid was always a pleasure to Chaucer, and he shared with the Roman a profound interest in women. Nevertheless, the farther Chaucer progressed with *The Legend of Good Women* the more bored he became. All his stories had the same plot—the faithfulness of a woman to a man who is not faithful—and it was a plot that eventually began to pall.

Chaucer was not Gower. Gower retold these same stories of Thisbe and Philomela and Phyllis neatly and vividly and had no difficulty in keeping his interest in them to the end of his poem. But Chaucer was not a talented rhymer; he was a creative genius and he became increasingly restless under the plan he had imposed upon himself. He had already learned in *Troilus and Criseyde* that his forte was real people and not an interminable series of woeful Anelidas mourning the unfaithfulness of a series of false Arcites.

Chaucer knew that if he followed the scheme with which he began he would have "many a story for to make," and that he would never be finished unless he condensed them. But this condensation meant the elimination of all the small, vivid, realistic details of which he was now a master. If he had had space for a few of them, he might conceivably have succeeded in making some of his heroines come alive; for while the structure of the tales is excellent there is not room in them for the heroines to breathe. The three women who possess signs of individual life are Dido, Lucrece and Ariadne, and it is perhaps not entirely a coincidence that the stories about these three are the longest in the *Legend*.

Chaucer grew increasingly desperate as he struggled with his noble ladies, seeing a lifetime ahead of dealing with nothing but unrelieved feminine virtue. By the time he reaches the legend of Philomela he is frankly complaining aloud:

> But, shortly in this story for to pass,
> For I am weary of hym for to telle. . . .

In the next legend, that of Phyllis, he is prepared to admit that he has lost all interest in his project.

> For I am agroted [surfeited] herebyforn
> To wryte of them that ben in love forsworn.

193

He intended to "haste me in my legende," but for all his hurrying Chaucer did not manage to outpace his own increasing boredom. The next legend, that of Hypermnestra, he never finished, and he failed to reach the legend of Alcestis that the god of Love had enjoined him with special strictness to relate. Later on Chaucer revised his prologue, but he never worked up enough interest in the legends themselves to do any more with them.[5]

The chief literary interest in the legends is the light, intimate tone that Chaucer maintains with his audience. It is Chaucer and the ladies in league against the men. Men are indeed wicked creatures, faithless, wanton and unreliable, and probably no man is really trustworthy except, of course, Geoffrey himself.

> Be ware, ye women, of your subtyl foe . . .
> And trusteth, as in love, no man but me.

The joke here is that Chaucer deliberately reversed the usual medieval convention, popularized by Jean de Meun and carried on by every poet since. He twists back upon the men all the epithets and accusations that were usually applied to women, and it is easy to see how effective this kind of game would be in a mixed audience.[6]

With the exception of this good-natured teasing there is not much in the legends that could be called distinctively Chaucerian in the sense that the word can be applied to the prologue. But in one sense the prologue and the legends combine to testify to a new and important step in the development of Chaucer's art.

The meter of *The Legend of Good Women* is entirely new. It is the five-stress rhyming couplet and Chaucer was the first to use it.

Chaucer evolved this verse form by combining the rhyming couplet of *The Book of the Duchess* with the five-stress line of *Troilus and Criseyde*—a device that seems obvious enough once a

[5] Both versions of the prologue are in existence, and, for convenience, lines from both versions have been used in this discussion.

[6] It was probably a mixed audience because Chaucer himself mentions the possibility that there may be a man faithless in love somewhere "in this hous."

194

poet had actually accomplished it. The result was what is called the heroic couplet, which proved to be one of the most useful verse forms in English literature.

Chaucer was a brilliant and tireless experimenter even when he was working on a poem as French and as conventional as *The Legend of Good Women*. He was not interested in meter for its own sake, as were Machaut or Deschamps. He was interested in meter because he was a careful, intelligent craftsman and wanted tools he could trust.

Chaucer knew he had an excellent tool in his new couplet, and in time he found a subject that was worthy of it. When it came it was neither a court joke nor a record of the woes of the ladies of antiquity. It concerned a mixed group of men and women who set out from a London suburb to ride to Canterbury one morning in April.

The Canterbury Tales was no accident. Chaucer had spent a lifetime preparing for it, and he held securely in his head all the various skills that were necessary to produce his great work. For Chaucer had been under the best of disciplines from the beginning of his career as a poet—the discipline of loving his art.

CHAPTER XIII

HE LADY to whom *The Legend of Good Women* was addressed had arrived in England in December, 1381. John of Gaunt took her to Leeds Castle over the holidays and in January she married King Richard at Westminster. The Londoners gave her a cordial welcome, the goldsmiths' guild thriftily using again the tower they had built for Richard's coronation.

Anne arrived in England at an unsettled moment; the sudden storm that capsized her ship just after she had quitted it was as nothing to a different kind of storm that had swept over England a few months before her arrival. The Archbishop of Canterbury had lost his life in the course of it, and the reason for the delay in Anne's wedding was that no one could decide whether the Archbishop-elect or the Bishop of London should have the privilege of performing the ceremony.

The name of this storm was the Peasants' Revolt, and it shook the whole London area in a way that even the plague years had failed to do. One may become resigned to the wrath of God but not to the madness of men. Froissart, in fact, actually calls it the pestilence, although most contemporary accounts call it "the hurling time."

The conflagration that overran southeastern England in the early summer of 1381 was caused by thirty years of unpopular labor legislation that could not be enforced and by new ideas on the equality of man that the upper classes were not able to check. But the actual spark that lit the bonfire was the ancient source of contention—taxes.

Parliament had exhausted every other way of raising money to finance the war with France and had finally decided that a poll tax was the only fair solution. A census was ordered so that the tax could be levied on all alike, and the immediate drop in the population of England was remarkable. In some villages hardly a man could be found who possessed a taxable aunt or sister-in-law. Even

London, the wealthiest city in the kingdom, sent in returns so obviously faked that the aldermen were obliged to institute a house-to-house recount to correct the rolls.

The poll tax was universally hated, and when the harried government officials attempted to collect it by force all the laboring unrest that had been slowly gathering since the year of the great plague came suddenly to a head.

The governing classes had been amply warned what to expect, for throughout the opening week of June reports had been coming in steadily of riots in Essex and Kent. But the King's official found such reports incredible, and were startled to the point of hysteria when the rebels suddenly turned up from two directions on the twelfth of June and encamped outside the walls of London. If Chaucer was at home that Wednesday evening he could have seen thousands of Essex peasants camping in the fields by Mile End due east of Aldgate.

The government officials responded to the emergency by hurrying into the Tower of London for refuge. The actual responsibility for making decisions rested with the Chancellor, who at once tried to hand over his seals of office to someone else.[1] The only individual who seems to have retained a degree of self control was the Mayor, Chaucer's friend Walworth. But the drawbridge over the Thames was lowered against Walworth's orders by an alderman who sympathized with the rebels, and the men of Essex and Kent streamed in to take possession of the city.

The peasants were not an undisciplined mob. Their password was "King Richard and the true commons," and their intention was to obtain charters of freedom for themselves and to punish the wicked government officials who had been misleading the King. When they went out to burn the beautiful palace of the Savoy to avenge themselves upon John of Gaunt (who was luckily not in London at the time) they made so strict a law against looting that they executed one of their own number who broke it. They also burned the Temple, because it was the headquarters of all the lawyers in England, and destroyed the records; and they

---

[1] The Chancellor was Simon of Sudbury, Archbishop of Canterbury, a gentle prelate but no warrior.

burned the Fleet and Newgate prisons after releasing the prisoners. From some parts of town on Thursday night it must have looked as though the whole city was aflame.

By Friday the revolt was getting out of hand. While King Richard was at a conference with its leaders, the mob invaded the Tower of London in a gay mood, shaking hands with the soldiery and trying to persuade the Princess of Wales to give them a kiss. Then they found the Chancellor in the chapel of the White Tower, where he and the Treasurer had spent the morning preparing for death. As the two highest officials in England they were responsible for the poll tax and the mob dragged them out and struck off their heads on Tower Hill.

From one murder it was easy to go to others, and the mob was augmented by Londoners, drunk with excitement, who saw an opportunity to pay off old scores. Among those who died that day were a great many Flemings, who were unpopular because it was believed they took trade away from the local weavers. They were hunted through the streets and thirty-four were trapped and murdered in the parish church of Chaucer's boyhood.

The anxious government officials in the Tower kept on making placating gestures in the direction of the rebels, but the average middle-class Londoner had by this time grown furious over the way property rights were being disregarded by a looting mob. On Saturday there was another conference between the King and the rebels, and Walworth, Brembre and Philpot accompanied Richard with coat-of-mail under their gowns. A short time later Walworth was back in town with the news that he had struck down Wat Tyler, the leader of the rebels, and that if the citizens of London would follow him he could rescue the King.[2]

In less than an hour Walworth had a force of several thousand armed Londoners behind him, and before evening the Peasants'

[2] Meanwhile Richard had been behaving like the gallant son of a gallant father. When Tyler was struck down his followers automatically raised their bows, and the unarmed fifteen-year-old boy set his horse at a canter towards the armed lines. "Sirs, will you shoot your king?" The gesture was successful and Richard kept them engaged in conversation until Walworth returned.

Revolt was over as far as London was concerned. Leaderless and confused, the movement petered out all over England, to be followed by years of special judicial commissions seeking to determine who had started it.

No one knew precisely what had caused so untoward an event as a rising of the peasants, but the general conclusion reached by thoughtful men was that it was God's judgment upon England for her sins.

John Gower wrote a long poem, called *Vox Clamantis,* in which he interpreted the rising as a warning from on high.[3] Everyone had been misbehaving lately—lords, clerics, lawyers, merchants and peasants alike—and this was the inevitable result. Gower was a Kentish landowner, and his shocked surprise over the whole event was probably characteristic of the average, conservative holder of property. Every chronicler gives horrified details of the revolt, but Gower's Latin poem is the most vivid picture that exists of an individual's reaction to it.

It seemed to Gower that the Tower of London was like a ship, aboard which everyone, himself included, huddled in terror while a great storm raged outside. Neither the captain nor the sailors had any idea what to do, and it was not until William the Mayor took matters into his own hands that the storm finally abated.

As to what caused the storm, it is Gower's theory that God's curse has descended upon the peasants and turned them into beasts. They are asses who decide they want to be horses and career bloodstained over the fields where they refuse to do any more work. They are oxen whose only thought is murder. They are swine possessed of the devil. They have armed themselves with poles and rusty sickles and mattocks and the branches of trees, and they have names like Wat and Bet and Gib and Hick and Jack.

Gower was an expert poet but he lacked the imagination that might have made him a great one. It was impossible for him to realize that anyone with a name like Hick or Bet or Gib might be

[3] This was exactly the same way that another poet, the author of *Piers Plowman,* interpreted another catastrophe, the Great Wind that had leveled so many buildings in the London area in 1362.

a real person, with the same hopes and fears that members of his own class possessed.

In this, Gower was the exact opposite of his friend Geoffrey Chaucer. Chaucer was almost incapable of picturing human beings as composing a class or group; he thought of them first as individuals. When Gower thought of the labor problem, Chaucer thought of a miller with a quick temper and a wart on his nose. When Gower thought of religious abuses, Chaucer thought of a pardoner with a love song running through his head and a glassful of "pigges bones" that he passed off as holy relics.

Chaucer would not have made a successful reformer. To be a reformer requires the ability to look at one's subject in a broad and general way and not permit one's attention to be attracted to the oddities and inconsistencies of individual human beings. What Chaucer thought of the Peasants' Revolt as it swept in under his gateway will never be known, but at least it is safe to say that his reaction was certainly not Gower's.

Many people felt that the social unrest which produced the Peasants' Revolt had been caused by the religious unrest that was sweeping England at the same time. This was called Lollardy, and many of the chroniclers were firmly of the opinion that men like Wat Tyler and John Ball got their radical ideas on human freedom from those "erroneous dogges," the Lollards.

The leader of the Lollard movement was John Wyclif, the last man in England who might have been expected to turn into a religious radical. Wyclif was an Oxford schoolman, the most eminent doctor of theology of his day, the King's chaplain, and a leader in the party of John of Gaunt.[4]

When Wyclif first began to constitute himself a critic of the Church, he did it in a thoroughly orthodox way. Everyone criticized the Church, layman and cleric alike. John Gower spent much of his time in the *Miroir de l'Omme* denouncing the sins of the Church with such thoroughness that not a stone in that great edifice remained uncriticized, and John Bromyard indicts the

[4] Twenty years after Wyclif's death many of his friends at Oxford were still convinced that he had been an orthodox theologian. "God defend that our prelates should have condemned so good a man for a heretic."

whole hierarchy, from the Pope down, with such thoroughness that it is hard to believe that the great Dominican preacher was also the conservative Chancellor of Cambridge University.

These men, like Chaucer's good friend Ralph Strode, were sure that the Church could be reformed without altering its existing structure. Wyclif became increasingly sure that it could not. The tall, thin, bearded Yorkshireman eventually found that he could not agree with the Church's claim to full authority over the conscience of the individual. Wyclif took the Bible for his authority instead, and sent his russet-clad, ardent followers out over England to spread a doctrine that was quite as upsetting as any of John Ball's. For Wyclif's was as fundamental a denial of the authority of the ecclesiastics as John Ball's was of the authority of the landowners.

The task of the Lollard preachers was made easier by the fact that there were now two Popes ruling in Christendom, who hurled insults at each other across the Alps with the same freedom that Wyclif insulted both of them.[5] The split in the Papacy made it a hard period for devout Christians, and as a matter of fact no man could call himself a simple Christian any longer; he was now either a Clementist or an Urbanist, depending on whether his country's sympathies rested with Avignon or with Rome. The height of absurdity was finally reached when the military young Bishop of Norwich organized a crusade against France and offered religious dispensations to anyone who would give a financial contribution, exactly as though he were conducting a campaign against the heathen Turks.

In the torn and broken ground of the Great Schism it is no wonder that the seed of Lollardy flourished. The movement acquired such momentum that one especially anguished chronicler insisted that out of every three people one met two of them were sure to be Lollards.

Among the distinguished people who were at least mildly interested in the new movement was the Queen of England. It was

[5] Wyclif called the Pope everything from "a simple idiot" to "the head vicar of the fiend." Wyclif had a real talent for invective, and a quick temper that he himself regretted.

probably through Anne's Bohemian courtiers that Wyclif's pamphlets made their way to Bohemia and lit a searing flame there when John Huss died as the first martyr of the Reformation. Anne had especial reason to be sympathetic to Wyclif's project of having the Bible translated into the vernacular, for her own psalter was written in Latin, German and Bohemian.[6]

Anne's mother-in-law, the Princess of Wales, was also interested in the Lollard movement. When Wyclif was put on trial for heresy, Joan sent an order to the Lambeth Council that he was not to be harmed; and among the members of her immediate household were several of the "Lollard Knights."

The Lollard Knights, who were nearly all friends of Chaucer, are reminiscent of the London triumvirate of Brembre, Walworth and Philpot in the way their names interlock in contemporary documents through a series of public and private relationships.

One of the Lollard Knights was Chaucer's old friend, Sir Richard Stury, who had served with him on the diplomatic mission to France in the days of Edward the Third. Another was Stury's close friend, Sir Lewis Clifford, who had been sent with Joan's message to the Lambeth Council. Clifford was on such intimate terms with Chaucer that it has been suggested that Lewis Chaucer was named for him.

Clifford was about ten years older than Chaucer and deeply interested in poetry; he was even a valued member of the brilliant literary circle that surrounded the Duke of Orleans in France. Also interested in poetry was his friend, Sir John Clanvowe, who was fifteen years younger. Clanvowe's name is associated with a charming poem named *The Cuckoo and the Nightingale*, which is so typically in the Chaucerian manner that it was believed for a long time that Chaucer himself had written it. Clanvowe's closest friend was another Lollard Knight of his own age named Sir Wil-

---

[6] Parliament was less liberal than the Queen. Six years after Wyclif's death it tried to check the growing interest in the Bible by ordering all translations to be confiscated. The bill was blocked by John of Gaunt, loyal to the end to his heretical associate. "Let us not be the dregs of all nations, seeing that others are . . . translating the Word of God into their own language."

liam Neville, and when Clanvowe died at the opening of the following decade Neville refused food and died two days later.

The Lollard Knights were evidently not looked upon as heretics in court circles, for the most devout Christians named them as the executors of their wills. The Duchess of York, for instance, appointed Clifford and Stury as her executors, and Sir Guichard d'Angle named Clifford, Neville and Clanvowe.[7]

This does not fit the frenzied contention of the monkish chroniclers that the Lollard Knights were the kind of men who took the Holy Sacrament home and ate it with their oysters, for the Duchess of York would not have left the arrangement of the masses for her soul to an infidel. In anything to do with Wyclif or his followers the chroniclers are more passionate than reliable, and they make statements more suitable to a pamphlet in a political campaign than to sober history. In any case, the word "Lollard" was as vague a term in the eighties as the word "radical" is today, and no two people meant exactly the same thing by it.[8]

Even the arch-heretic, Wyclif, apparently did not realize how deep he was digging. He did not think he was disturbing the Church by taking its foundation stone away; he thought he was merely reforming it. But the foundation stone of the Church was its unquestioned, absolute authority, and when Wyclif struck at this he was unwittingly striking at the whole basis of medieval existence.

The Middle Ages operated according to a rigid pattern of order and control in which the individual was invariably subordinated to

[7] Sir Guichard's fourth executor was not a Lollard. But Sir William Beauchamp belonged to the same court circles and was also a good friend of Chaucer's. Chaucer went surety for Beauchamp in 1378 when he was appointed to the custody of Pembroke Castle, and Beauchamp signed his name to the Cecily Chaumpaigne deed as one of Chaucer's witnesses. Neville and Clanvowe signed this Chaumpaigne deed also.

[8] Chaucer makes this point clearly in a piece of incidental byplay in *The Canterbury Tales*. The Parson gently reproves the Host for swearing, and because the Lollards opposed the use of oaths one of the other pilgrims is immediately convinced the Parson is a Lollard. He hurriedly embarks upon a story of his own to prevent the Parson from indulging in any more subversive activities.

the group. Medieval life was like a great tree in which every man had his exact place in the branches, the serf obeying his lord, the apprentice his master and the Christian the Pope. The root of the tree was authority, whether political, economic or social, and when the root of the tree was attacked the whole intricate structure began to tremble.

The conservative business men of England were shocked by the Lollard movement yet in their own way they were contributing just as effectively to the destruction of the Middle Ages. For individual competition had reared its head, and the business men themselves were destroying the patterned regimentation of the guilds.

A London merchant like Gilbert Maghfeld, for instance, fitted nowhere into the guild system. Instead of settling down as a specialist in some subdivision of manufacture, with every aspect of his business under· strict communal control, Maghfeld was an individualist. He was a free-lance broker in commodities that ranged from hats to pearls and from ginger to coal. He then reinvested his accumulated capital by going into the loan business and numbered among his clients not only writers like Chaucer and Gower but also architects, merchants, abbots and even the City of London.

The Church disapproved strenuously of loaning money on interest, but there was nothing it could do to check the practice. To the Church an interest-bearing loan was usury, and since fourteenth-century business men were devout sons of the Church they had to go through extraordinary convolutions in order to continue in business. The usual practice was to make the loan free for about a week; then interest was charged, not on the money but as a fine for failing to return it. St. Thomas Aquinas knew what he was about when he condemned all commerce as evil. For commerce begets individual initiative, and individual initiative did not fit into the tight, orderly pattern of medieval life.

It was not only a business man like Maghfeld, a preacher like Wyclif or a reformer like John Ball who heralded the growth of the new doctrine of individualism. Geoffrey Chaucer was doing the same thing when he thought out his plan for *The Canterbury Tales* and decided, most unmedievally, to portray his pilgrims not as samples of the various social orders but as real human beings. The day of the pattern was ending and Chaucer was one of those who helped it to end.

The period of change had its painful moments, and there were aspects of it that made a conservative like John Gower feel that the world was coming to an end. But the growing pains that England experienced as she emerged from the Middle Ages were as nothing to the kind of agony that shook the Continent in the fourteenth century.

England had her Peasants' Revolt, but it was a mild and almost a respectable affair compared with the animal-like passion that characterized the rising of the Jacquerie in France. The English laboring class had acquired certain rights and was in a hurry to acquire more, but the French peasants had been treated like beasts and they murdered like beasts.

London had its emotional moments when the guild system began to break up under the stress of new business methods, but it was never subjected to the savage class wars that racked Flanders until the streets of the cities were red with blood. A few trade unions were organized among the London apprentices and forcibly broken up by their employers, to the accompaniment of a certain amount of hard feeling on both sides; but in Flanders the exploited workers, the "blue nails," fought the capitalists who ruled the clothing industry with a hatred that tore the industry apart until it was ruined.

England had its heretics; but no Lollard was burned in Chaucer's lifetime and Wyclif died peacefully in bed. In Europe, on the other hand, the Inquisition raged like a plague, nearly depopulating whole villages in its earnest attempt to stamp out heresy in men's minds by destroying their bodies.[9]

[9] The result was that there was much more heresy and sorcery on the Continent than there was in England. In 1372 a lone sorcerer was arrested in Southwark, with a dead man's head and a book of magic in his trunk. He was taken before a royal magistrate who told him not to do it again and ordered the contents of the trunk burned at their owner's expense. On the Continent he would have been brought before the Inquisition, tortured until he had involved someone else, and then executed.

As a nation, the English do not go to extremes. England had always been less medieval in its point of view than any other nation in Europe, because its people clung almost by instinct to a sense of personal rights. Even in his most communal moments the average Englishman still thought of himself as an individual, and the change from the old to the new was therefore much less violent than on the Continent.

This easygoing and individualistic attitude on the part of the English was accurately reflected in their courts of law. Like every other nation in Christendom, the English had royal law and church law. But they also had a more informal kind of justice that was administered neither from the king's bench nor from the ecclesiastical courts. It was administered instead by groups of men inside each county who were known as the justices of the peace.

It is a pleasure to report that Geoffrey Chaucer served as a justice of the peace. He was himself so characteristically English that it is fitting he should have been appointed to serve in so characteristically English an activity. Fourteenth-century France, for instance, could never have produced either a poet like Chaucer or an office like the one to which he was appointed in the autumn of 1385.

The justices of the peace all came from the landowning classes, but they seem on the whole to have been an approachable and democratic group of men. The fact that they were local residents gave them a more sympathetic and informed approach to local problems than could be achieved by the royal justices in their stately progresses through the realm; and the fact that most of them were amateurs in law rather than professional legal practitioners kept them from the stylized rigidity of the law courts at Westminster, where a trained lawyer could be understood by no one except his equally learned opponent.

Chaucer and his fellow justices for the County of Kent held their sessions four times a year, moving about from village to village to listen to the cases and deliver their verdicts. They probably held sessions in whatever hall was available, that of the lord's castle if the village was a small one or the local guild hall or shire hall if the meetings took place in a town. The cases were put before them by a presenting jury, which was made up of local inhabitants and had the function of a modern grand jury. Any Englishman except a monk could serve on a jury, except that in cases involving Lollards there was a minimum property requirement. The indictments that have survived from the fourteenth century show that the justices of the peace let each man tell his story comfortably and in his own words. No one was expected to be unduly formal or legal, and for a law court the atmosphere must have been fairly pleasant.

The cases that Chaucer and his associates listened to covered the whole range of human misdeeds, from murder to assaulting a tax collector and from arson to playing "penny-prick" in a tavern. The business of the justices, in fact, was literally to conserve the peace. When they took their oath of office they affirmed that they would loyally serve "the King and his people," and the fact that they served the people as well as the King is indicated by the devoted interest that the House of Commons took in the institution. Some justices were lazy and failed to attend their sessions, and some justices were dishonest and took bribes; but most of them were loyal to their oath and helped the experiment of decentralized county justice to succeed in England where it would have failed anywhere else in Christendom.

It seems safe to assume that Chaucer made a good justice of the peace. He had a sympathetic interest in people and in the springs of their actions, and since he was not as stiffly conservative as Gower he would have no difficulty in remembering that he was dealing with real human beings instead of the stereotyped representatives of the lower classes.

In return the common people of Kent gave Chaucer a gift of their own. He already knew the court circles of Westminster and the business circles of London, but now he entered intimately into the lives of villagers as well.

These men and women might seem unimportant folk to other people but they were not unimportant to Chaucer. He watched them with the same delighted and uncritical affection he accorded everyone else, and he fitted them into an accurate memory that was already well stored with places and people from all over England. Millers and carpenters and village parsons took their place inside Chaucer's head along with knights and abbots and sailors and merchants, living in democratic amity side by side, and in the end they all emerged and took the road together for Canterbury one April morning.

CHAPTER XIV

CHAUCER was living in the County of Kent when he became a justice of the peace in the autumn of 1385, and he probably owned land there also. He was still the Comptroller of the Customs, but he had taken a month's leave of absence from office work the previous November and in February he was given a permanent deputy to take over his work on the Wool Quay.

Chaucer was appointed a justice of the peace in mid-term to fill out the period of service of Thomas Shardelowe, who had just died. Shardelowe had been the steward of all the King's lands in Kent, and the official who succeeded him in this office was not resident in Kent and therefore not eligible to the position of justice. The post went to Geoffrey Chaucer, who served out Shardelowe's term and was recommissioned the following June for a full term of his own.

Chaucer served with a distinguished group of men, for Kent was an important county. The personnel of the commission was supposed to consist of "one lord, and with him three or four of the most worthy in the county, with some learned in law." The justices who worked with Chaucer during his term of service included several members of the landed nobility and five sergeants-at-law.[1]

The "one lord" was Sir Simon Burley, the King's close friend who had carried him at the coronation. He had been made Constable of Dover Castle and Warden of the Cinque Ports as a reward for negotiating Richard's marriage with Anne, and he was therefore the chief executive in Kent. He was also a major Kentish landowner, for he had been collecting estates at the rate of several

[1] The rank of sergeant-at-law was the highest a lawyer could achieve. There were only about twenty of these men in England at the time, and they were not obliged to uncover their heads even in the presence of royalty.

a year, but he was so constantly at court that his local duties were performed by a deputy. This was Hugh Fastolf, and it is Fastolf's name that appears on the list of justices of the peace. Chaucer probably knew Fastolf well, for he was a prominent London merchant who belonged to the same faction as Walworth and Brembre (Philpot had just died) and he was also an official in the customs service.

Most of the justices in Kent belonged to the King's party. The lists of candidates were drawn up by the Chancellor and the Treasurer and agreed upon at a meeting of the royal council, in spite of the steady petitioning of the House of Commons for a more democratic form of procedure. There was also, of course, a certain amount of jockeying for position and the application of subterranean political pressure; but the same thing applies in practice to more democratic methods of appointment, and the method seems to have resulted in a fairly good group of men.

English politics were in a tangled state, as usual. There were three major factions the year Chaucer became a justice of the peace, one headed by the King, one headed by John of Gaunt and one headed by Thomas, Duke of Gloucester.[2]

The King's leading minister was a competent bureaucrat named Michael de la Pole, who had made a fortune in wool and was one of the first laymen rich enough to be able to afford the dignities that went with the office of Chancellor. The court party held London in its pocket as long as Brembre controlled the city elections, but it was not popular with the country as a whole. Especially disliked were two of Richard's closest friends, hot-tempered, extravagant Sir Simon Burley and the headstrong Earl of Oxford, Robert de Vere. De Vere was about the same age as the young King and Queen, with social tastes very similar to theirs, and in Richard's adoring opinion he could do no wrong.[3]

[2] Richard's third uncle, Edmund, Duke of York, was a mild-mannered gentleman who took no real interest in politics.

[3] Richard did not even object when de Vere divorced his wife to marry a landless Bohemian girl in the Queen's service, although de Vere's own mother, the dowager countess of Oxford, was so furious she took her former daughter-in-law into her own home.

Opposing the court party was the baronial party. This was headed by the King's uncle, Thomas, the Duke of Gloucester, who was about thirty at the time and admired by the common people as the Prince of Wales had been before him. The Duke possessed a brutal drive and an ambition unusual even in a Plantagenet, and the King hated him. Only the previous year Richard had publicly requested his uncle's chief ally, the Earl of Arundel, to go to the devil.

About midway between these two factions stood John of Gaunt, who was not on especially good terms with either one. Behind him was ranged the tremendous Lancastrian retinue, which was more of a feudal household than a political party and which was strong enough to maintain a balance between the King and the Duke of Gloucester.

In the summer of 1386 John of Gaunt and his retinue left England. The Duke of Lancaster was still pursuing the golden dream of becoming King of Castile, and he had organized a large military expedition to obtain the throne for himself and Constance. It was also a religious crusade, for the reigning King of Castile was a supporter of Pope Clement and Pope Urban therefore promised remission of sins to whoever went with Gaunt on the Spanish campaign. The Duke sailed in June, after having been formally presented with a gold crown by his nephew Richard, and with him went the one great force in England that stood for compromise.[4]

In the autumn of this same year, three months after Gaunt set sail for Spain, Geoffrey Chaucer made what was apparently his sole excursion into politics. He went up from Kent as a member of Parliament and served in one of the most stormy sessions of that century.

Chaucer probably owed this post to the fact that he was a king's esquire, acquiring the office in much the same way as that of justice

De Vere's wife was the granddaughter of Edward III; but she was a Clementist, and Pope Urban was quite willing to give de Vere a dispensation so that he could divorce her.

[4] The Princess of Wales had done her share in keeping the peace, but she had died the previous year. Geoffrey and Philippa Chaucer wore black to her funeral.

of the peace. Elections in the fourteenth century were not contested. They were voted upon in county court, which theoretically consisted of the whole body of freehold tenants but actually consisted only of those sufficiently politically minded to attend. In general the leading landowners were free to make their own choice, and the leading landowners of Kent, with the exception of the Archbishop of Canterbury, belonged to the King's party.

It was important to the King to get as many members of his own party as he could into the forthcoming session of Parliament, for it did not promise to be an easy one. It was being called to raise money for the war with France, and the war with France was going very badly. In fact, at the moment France was preparing to invade England.

It was common knowledge that young King Charles was preparing a fleet on the other side of the Channel that threatened to surpass anything previously attempted in warfare. The French preparations were even more elaborate than the English ones had been at the time of Chaucer's first military service. All summer long the Frenchmen had been making biscuits to pack into barrels and grinding egg yolks to powder, to be stored along with pigs and bandages and kitchenware in the great fleet of ships that lined the French coast. In Brittany the Constable was constructing an entirely new invention, a portable fort that could be shipped in sections and reassembled by a crew of carpenters as soon as the doomed shore of England was reached.

Eustache Deschamps was wild with excitement. He left home loaded down with a tent and other martial equipment, leaving instructions to his wife to pray for him, and arrived on the coast to write verses telling the English exactly what was going to happen to them. They were going to be destroyed so completely that men of later days, contemplating the ruins, could only murmur incredulously, "In olden days, this was England." [5]

The English received regular reports on the extent of the French preparations, since Sir Simon Burley was Constable of

[5] There was every excuse for Deschamps. Six years earlier the English had pillaged and burned his country house, and Deschamps had deeply loved his little home in spite of its windy location.

Dover Castle and the fishermen of Dover fraternized freely with the enemy. But there was not much the English government could do except to plan a scorched earth policy in the southeastern counties. Watchers paced along every coastal hill on planks raised on casks of sand, and the tension was higher than at any time since the Peasants' Revolt.

When Chaucer arrived in London in September to be ready for the session of Parliament that was opening on the first of October, he found the city in a highly nervous state. The Londoners had reason to be frightened, for only a few years earlier the French had burned Gravesend, a few miles down the Thames from their beloved city. The citizens ran about putting up guns and pulling down houses in the suburbs outside the walls, and the chroniclers unite in scorn over what they call their timidity. But the chroniclers were secure in the knowledge that the invasion never took place, a piece of information which the men and women of London lacked at the time.[6]

The state of confusion in London was aggravated by the presence of a large body of militia who had been quartered there and who had not been paid, and the unrest all over the city was naturally a great help to the baronial party of the Duke of Gloucester. Everything that went wrong with the country was the fault of the current administration, and now that Gaunt was abroad the opposition was free to point this out.

Chaucer made the journey up to London, so the sheriff's writ informed him, to take part in discussions over the defense of the realm. His fellow member from Kent was William Betenham of Betenham House, Cranbrook, and they were called knights of the shire to distinguish them from the burgesses that were sent to Parliament by the towns. Neither of them was actually a knight,

[6] The threat of invasion lifted with dramatic suddenness, for in the middle of November the English heard that the French fleet was being broken up. One of the French King's uncles (like Richard, he had three of them) had deliberately delayed his arrival until it was too late to sail. The mound of stores that had been collected on each lord's ship were sold at a fraction of their original cost, and a piece of the great portable fort was washed ashore in the Thames to be brought in triumph into London.

but knighthood in any case was growing to be a barren honor. [7]

Parliament assembled at Westminster, which was its usual but not its invariable place of meeting. Westminster had such a large staff of government workers lodging there that the members of Parliament had to be accommodated in London, the members of the House of Lords staying in their town residences and the members of the House of Commons staying either with friends or at one of the local inns. They commuted daily to Westminster by way of the Thames, and costs were kept down by a strict government rule that no boatman should charge more than twopence for the trip.

The opening of Parliament was not the stately occasion it later became. It was a comparatively new experiment in government, and was not taken as seriously, even by the members themselves, as it might have been. A system of roll call had been in use for nearly a decade, but many members were absent and many more were late.

Parliament convened in the Palace of Westminster on Monday, the first of October, at about eight o'clock in the morning. It met in the Painted Chamber, a long, narrow room whose walls were decorated with scenes from English and Jewish history. [8] The King was seated in the front of the room with his two archbishops on either side of him. The secular and the ecclesiastical lords were seated facing each other on either side of the archbishops, while Chaucer and his fellow members of the House of Commons stood in the back of the hall facing the King.

The room must have looked as gay as a flower garden, with so many brightly costumed men under its painted walls, but there was nothing gay about the proceedings. The peevishness displayed by the feathered members of Chaucer's *Parliament of Birds* was as nothing to the bad temper generated in Westminster before the month of October was over.

It was the unhappy duty of Michael de la Pole, as Chancellor, to open the proceedings by asking for money. The request was not

[7] Chaucer's son Thomas paid actual cash to avoid having a knighthood thrust upon him, for the feudal dues made the position an expensive one.

[8] One side showed the career of Edward the Confessor and the other that of Judas Maccabeus, whom Chaucer calls "Goddes knyght."

214

well received. The average Englishman felt that money had already been poured into the royal treasury from a tax-ridden populace, and that it was the fault of the King's bureaucratic advisers that better use had not been made of it. When the Chancellor added that Richard was planning to invade the Continent with the extra money no one believed him, and the Lords and Commons retired to their private deliberations in a state of dissatisfaction that accurately echoed the sentiments of the whole country.

The Commons had existed as a separate body for so short a time that there was no special room set aside in Westminster Palace for its meeting place. Chaucer and his associates were obliged to go through the palace yard and beyond the wall to meet in Westminster Abbey. The monks of the Abbey lent their chapter house to the Commons when Parliament was in session; but the arrangement was not convenient for the monks and it was even less convenient for the members of the House of Commons.

The acoustics of the chapter house were poor, and the speeches of the members had to be delivered from a lectern in the middle of the room so that they could be heard. A clerk was on hand to copy out the proceedings, and any member could have a copy of his speech to take home with him at the standard rate of ten lines for a penny.

In theory the function of the House of Commons was to assent to whatever the King and the House of Lords planned to do. Actually, however, the Commons was feeling its first stirrings of power and was just beginning that wonderful political development that in the end made the people the rulers of England.

The Commons did not permit itself to become a battleground of parties. Its members took an oath to stand together as a body and elected a speaker to represent them in the discussions that would begin as soon as they rejoined the House of Lords.

The men who met with Chaucer in the Abbey chapter house belonged mostly to the country gentry, for, with the exception of London, the towns were not especially well represented.[9] The men

[9] The chief reason why the burgesses failed to appear was that their home areas had failed to vote them in. It cost a borough two shillings a day in wages and expense money to send a representative to Parliament and many towns thought this was a complete waste of money.

from the southeastern counties, like Kent, were less opposed to war taxation than the others, because they were nearer the actual point of invasion. But the majority were sure of two things: that taxes were too high and that the country was being mismanaged.

On the fifteenth of the month Chaucer was briefly interrupted in his duties as a member of Parliament. He went to the refectory in the Abbey to give his deposition in a trial that was being conducted there by the Court of Chivalry. Every man of consequence in England served as a witness on the case for one side or the other.

The case was that of Scrope *versus* Grosvenor. It had started when Sir Richard Scrope, a former Chancellor and the brother-in-law of the present one, was on his way to the Scottish wars the preceding year. He discovered that a certain Sir Robert Grosvenor was using the Scrope family arms of *Azure, a bend Or* (a diagonal gold stripe against a blue background). He at once brought suit, for the distinctions of heraldry were still a serious business in the fourteenth century. The privileges symbolized by a man's coat of arms were the basis of his position in the feudal world.

Chaucer testified for Sir Richard Scrope. Four days later three of Chaucer's friends, Sir Lewis Clifford, Sir John Clanvowe and Sir William Neville, did the same. Clifford, who later was appointed one of the commissioners to hear the appeal, was inclined to show his irritation over the cumbrous affair of giving testimony, and so was Neville. But Chaucer, who was the last of nineteen witnesses on the day he appeared, showed a good temper that was only matched by the vivid explicitness of his testimony.

Chaucer testified that he had first seen the Scrope arms twenty-seven years earlier, when he was bearing arms for the first time in Edward the Third's campaign in France. Since then he had seen the arms many times on banners and glass and paintings and vestments, always as the property of the Scrope family. But one day he was in London, walking down Friday Street, and he stopped a passer-by to inquire why the arms of the Scrope family had been painted on a new sign which was hanging outside an inn. He was told, "They are not hung out, Sir, for the arms of Scrope. They are painted and put there by a knight of the County of Chester, called Sir Robert Grosvenor." This, said Chaucer, was the first he had ever heard of Sir Robert.

The only part of Chaucer's deposition that is not specific is the part that concerns himself. Sir John Clanvowe testified that he was thirty-five and Sir William Neville that he was thirty-six, but their friend Chaucer merely said vaguely that he was forty years old and upwards. It would have been a thoughtful gesture on his part towards subsequent biographers if he had been as interested in establishing his own age as he was in establishing the right of Sir Richard Scrope to his own coat of arms.[10]

The nervous irritability shown in the testimony of members of the court party like Clifford and Neville was perhaps a reflection of the growing strength of the opposition party as it was manifesting itself in Parliament. King Richard himself showed no skill in statecraft as the tide began to turn against him, and when the Chancellor was impeached the King's only answer was to go and sulk in his manor at Eltham.

Parliament immediately went on strike. The whole body agreed it would transact no business and vote no money until the King returned and removed the Chancellor and Treasurer from office. Richard suggested as an alternative that forty members of the House of Commons should come to Eltham, and it shows the overstrained nerves of all concerned that the rumor at once arose that the King was plotting with Brembre to have the innocent forty murdered. The impasse was finally ended by the Duke of Gloucester, who went down to Eltham and bluntly threatened his nephew with deposition unless he behaved. Richard finally consented to a committee of inquiry and Parliament adjourned, having been in session the better part of two months.[11]

One of the first things that Gloucester's committee of inquiry

[10] Scrope finally won the case after six years of litigation. Grosvenor was assessed the costs, but Scrope, like the gentleman he was, had the charge lifted. The two men then had a public reconciliation after Grosvenor had explained earnestly that his attacks in court on the Scrope family and its antiquity had not been his own idea but that of his lawyers.

[11] Chaucer was paid for sixty-one days' service, which included his journey to and from London. The County of Kent paid him £24 9s, which would be about eighteen hundred dollars in modern money.

investigated was the wool tax. This was natural, since the collection of the wool customs had been for so long in the hands of Brembre and his associates, and since part of the revenues of the Dukedom of Gloucester were derived from it.

On the fourth of December Chaucer left his position as Comptroller of the Customs. He had not been personally connected with the office for nearly two years, the work having been done by a deputy, and he may either have been deprived of his office because he belonged to the King's party or have quitted it voluntarily because he disliked the association with Gloucester. Gloucester at any rate did not succeed in removing all the men of the opposition, for the Comptroller who replaced Chaucer in the petty customs had been Chaucer's own choice as a deputy at an earlier date. Whatever political repercussions there may have been in the customhouse, Chaucer had evidently decided that there was very little to keep him in London. Nearly two months earlier he had given up his lease on the house over Aldgate to Richard Forester; and in May of the following year he was still living in Kent, for he served on a judicial commission headed by Sir William Rickhill to investigate the abduction of a Kentish heiress.

Meanwhile a Council of Reform had been set up to run the country. It was composed mostly of moderates like Sir Richard Scrope and the King's uncle, Edmund of York, and was designed to operate for only one year. King Richard would have been wise to let the year run its course. Instead, with the impulse to firmness that almost invariably visited him at the wrong moment, Richard decided to fight and toured the country for reinforcements.

It was conceivably on the King's business that Chaucer went to Calais in July, but since he was given a year's leave it is more likely that he went for personal reasons. Chaucer must have been a privileged individual in Calais, for his friend, Sir William Beauchamp, was captain of the town, and another friend of his, Sir Philip de la Vache, was captain of the castle.[12] Calais was a very English town, for it had been King Edward's policy to remove its

[12] Sir Philip was Lewis Clifford's son-in-law, for he had married Elizabeth Clifford in 1380. The most popular ballade Chaucer ever wrote was addressed to Sir Philip de la Vache.

French inhabitants and subsidize English shopkeepers and house-holders to settle there instead. Most of these had been men from Kent, and, like any southeastern town in England, Calais was under the jurisdiction of the Archbishop of Canterbury. A Kentish landowner like Chaucer must have felt very much at home in Calais.

It is possible that Philippa Chaucer was living with her sister Katherine in Lincolnshire when Chaucer went abroad. Five years earlier Katherine Swynford had retired to the northern estates that she had received through her husband and through John of Gaunt, and Philippa Chaucer certainly spent at least part of her time there. In February of 1386 Chaucer's wife had been inducted into the extremely aristocratic fellowship of Lincoln Cathedral.[13] Inducted with her were John of Gaunt's son, Henry of Derby, and Katherine's son, Sir Thomas Swynford. Also inducted was their mutual son, John Beaufort, and various members of Gaunt's household. Philippa Chaucer was the only woman to take part in the ceremony.

Chaucer did not stay long in Calais. He was back in England by November and his return can be best accounted for by the death of his wife. He had collected her pension for her in June before he left, but in November he collected only his own.

Chaucer returned to England to find more than his personal life in dislocation and confusion. The country was on the brink of civil war, thanks to Richard's inability to take defeat gracefully, and it was not until the combined forces of Gloucester and Arundel were drawn up grimly at Waltham that he finally capitulated.

Richard spent a miserable Christmas in the Tower of London, watching Gloucester avenge himself on the King's friends. It was done with a show of legality, but the Parliament that Gloucester summoned in February was packed with his supporters and it was not unjustly called the Merciless Parliament. Robert de Vere had escaped to France and Michael de la Pole was given merely a

[13] John of Gaunt entered the fellow-ship of Lincoln Cathedral when he was three years old, along with King Edward and the Prince of Wales. King Richard and Queen Anne took their oath of fidelity to the church and chapter the year after Philippa Chaucer's induction.

heavy sentence of imprisonment. But Sir Simon Burley was beheaded, and only the fact that he was a Knight of the Garter saved him from a more brutal method of execution.[14]

Sir Nicholas Brembre, Chaucer's former colleague in the Customs, was hanged. The charges against him were a pointless jumble, including the accusation that he was plotting to have London named New Troy, and it took a special petition from his ancient enemies, the clothing guilds, to give his murder even the color of legality.

Among the lesser victims who were killed by the Merciless Parliament was a subordinate of Brembre's named Thomas Usk. Usk had begun his political career as private secretary to John of Northampton—Brembre's leading opponent in the clothing trade —and then had betrayed him. Brembre rewarded him with the post of under-sheriff only six months before Gloucester's Parliament destroyed them both.

Usk's relationship to Geoffrey Chaucer is rather curious. Usk was something of a literary man and as an apology for his career he wrote a prose treatise, *The Testament of Love*. He modeled it on *The Consolation of Philosophy*, for he rather optimistically found in Boethius' career a parallel to his own. Then he included in it a rather florid tribute to Chaucer, that "noble philosophical poete," with especial praise for *Troilus and Criseyde*. Possibly Usk sent a copy of *The Testament of Love* to Chaucer, since Chaucer had made a translation of Boethius, and possibly Chaucer let it remain among his own papers; for *The Testament of Love* was attributed to Chaucer's authorship for centuries in spite of the fact that Chaucer would not have been likely to include a tribute to himself in his own work. All the earlier *Lives* of Chaucer are marred by the fact that they are based on Usk's pathetic little prose *apologia*.

Usk wrote *The Testament of Love* as one whose soul had at last

[14] John of Gaunt's son Henry was one of the five Lords Appellant who ran Parliament, but he fought in vain to save Burley's life. Queen Anne went on her knees before Gloucester when she asked him to spare Richard's closest friend, but Gloucester told her merely that she would do better to keep her prayers for herself.

220

risen above politics, and he met the day of his death in the same spirit. From the Tower to Tyburn he recited penitential psalms and even managed to deliver the whole of the Athanasian Creed. His beheading was mismanaged by a clumsy executioner, and his head was then exposed on Newgate to gaze down upon the house of his parents and his beloved "citee of London, that to me is so dere and sweet."

There is not much record of Chaucer's activities during the bloody spring of 1388. It is possible that he found himself short of money, for in May he surrendered his annuity to one John Scalby; but the sale of annuities was common, and it is possible that Chaucer wanted money for some private reason of his own.

In April there was a warrant issued for his arrest by John Churchman, the builder of the customhouse, who claimed that Chaucer owed him three guineas. Before June was over two more warrants had been issued, and the sheriffs certified that they had searched all over London, Surrey and Kent, as instructed, and could neither find Geoffrey Chaucer nor any detachable goods of his. This might lead to the assumption that Chaucer, as a King's man, had fled to parts unknown, if on the thirteenth of May he had not peacefully drawn his pension at the Exchequer in person. The most probable reason why the sheriffs certified they could not find Chaucer was that one of the sheriffs was Hugh Fastolf, Chaucer's old friend and his former fellow justice of the peace.

In the autumn of this year John of Gaunt returned to England. He had brought the war of the Spanish succession to a successful conclusion by marrying his daughter Katherine to Henry of Castile, and his arrival in England had a dampening effect upon his brother, the Duke of Gloucester.

The following spring Richard decided that the time had come to assert himself. He staged his little drama at nine o'clock on a May morning when the council was in session. The King suddenly appeared in the doorway in full regalia, with two pages carrying his ermine mantle and a throng of men-at-arms in the passage outside.

Richard's sense of drama was that of a born actor, and he probably looked every inch a king as he stood there. It was easy to forget that his shoulders were narrow and sloping under the royal mantle, that his kingly beard was hardly more than a fringe of down on his chin, and that he stuttered when he talked. He asked his council how old he was, and its members had to admit he was twenty-three and old enough to rule.

Richard managed his return to power with intelligent moderation and gave no outward show of any desire to avenge his friends. His new Chancellor and Treasurer were men who belonged neither to his party nor that of Gloucester, but who had been trusted court officials in his grandfather Edward's reign.

The next nine years were so quiet that the chroniclers found themselves with almost nothing to write about. They no longer had a Peasants' Revolt to describe, or a Merciless Parliament, and they were reduced to recording a plague of gnats at Eltham, or the weather and social events.

CHAPTER XV

Two months after King Richard returned to power, Geoffrey Chaucer was given a new government position. On the twelfth of July, 1389, he became the Clerk of the King's Works.

The Office of the Works was the organization responsible for the maintenance and repair of royal buildings like the Palace of Westminster and the Tower of London. It also had jurisdiction over the royal castle at Berkhampstead, a lodge in the New Forest, the mews for the King's falcons at Charing Cross, and eight royal manors.

King Richard was even more interested in architecture than his grandfather had been, and during his reign the size of the Office of Works had been increasing. The large staff of permanent officers included some of the famous craftsmen in England.[1] A few of these officers, like the chief smith and the sergeant plumber, had their workshops in the Tower of London, but the greater part of the organization was located in the Palace of Westminster.

Geoffrey Chaucer had charge of the financial side of the Office of Works. He kept the accounts, distributed the money that was received from the Exchequer, and had general supervision of the building operations.

Chaucer had his Comptroller, William Hannay, who performed the same service for him that Chaucer had performed for Philpot, Walworth and Brembre in the London customhouse. Hannay had been removed from office by the Merciless Parliament a short time before, because the Parliament was pledged to a program of economy and had found a man who would do the work for sixpence

---

[1] The master mason, for instance, was Henry Yevele, who had nearly as long and as influential a career as Sir Christopher Wren's. Yevele had been working as a master mason for the Prince of Wales when Chaucer was still a page, and he served the kings of England for forty years after that as a distinguished architect and builder.

less a day; but Hannay was reinstated in his position of Comptroller after Richard returned to power.[2]

One of Chaucer's first acts after he came to his new post was to appoint four purveyors. The purveyors were the men responsible for selecting the building materials and hiring the workmen for a given piece of work. As government officials they had the power, through the sheriffs, of taking workmen away from any kind of private building enterprise except church building and of paying them a fixed government wage that was usually less than the one stipulated by the local guilds. In the earlier part of the century, the Clerk of the Works had filled the office of purveyor himself. But now that the organization had grown more complex the Clerk of the Works was merely the general supervisor and had a deputy under him in each district. Thomas Segham, for instance, was Chaucer's purveyor for the castle at Berkhampstead, and Peter Cook for the manor at Eltham.

When Chaucer took office he was given a list by his predecessor of the stock that belonged to the Office of the Works. The list is still extant, written in that curious mixture of English and Latin that was apparently the interdepartmental business language of the government offices. It includes useful items, like an iron ladle for melting lead in the plumbery, but much of it consists of odds and ends that apparently had been collecting for decades: broken andirons, bells, decrepit sieves, the remnants of a chariot, broken handmills and other bits of junk that no careful householder would like to throw away.

Among the items included in the list from the Tower of London is a "fryingpanne." The tower was undoubtedly a building of many uses, since it served as a government mint, an arsenal, an arms factory, a prison, a treasury, a royal residence and a zoo, but just why the Office of Works cherished a fryingpan there is not altogether clear. Chaucer, at any rate, left this valuable article un-

[2] It is difficult to credit the Merciless Parliament with a really profound desire for economy when it dismissed William Hannay. It had just voted its five leaders a bonus of twenty thousand pounds (about one and a half million dollars in modern money) as a reward for saving the country from the rapacity of Richard's friends.

disturbed. He received it from his predecessor, Roger Elmham, and passed it on to his successor, John Gedney, and on both these lists the fryingpan has come down triumphantly to posterity.

Chaucer's position as Clerk of the Works required an expert knowledge of bookkeeping. It also needed a high degree of executive ability to handle all the building operations that came under Chaucer's jurisdiction, from major construction works involving huge sums of money to minor repairs of park fences and fish ponds. Chaucer had the responsibility of meeting a large pay roll and he was responsible for a multiplicity of financial details that ranged from buying hinges to adjusting the freight on huge consignments of stone. In return Chaucer received a salary of two shillings a day (about three thousand dollars a year), a generous allowance for food and traveling expenses, and the use of a house rent-free in the outer ward of the Palace of Westminster near that of the master carpenter.

The large sums of money that Chaucer handled came to him direct from the Exchequer, exclusive of seventeen shillings and fourpence that he realized from the sale of timber after a high wind blew down some of the royal oaks at Eltham. The office of the Exchequer was in the same building as the Office of Works, but Chaucer had as much difficulty as anyone else in getting money out of it. When he ended his two-year period of service he found that he had paid out over twenty pounds more than he had received, and it was nearly two years later that the Exchequer finally succeeded in paying him back what he had advanced out of his own purse.[3] This involuntary loan on Chaucer's part does not include the large sum of £66 13s 4d which he formally "lent" the Exchequer shortly before he left his office. This would be about five thousand dollars in modern money, and was nearly the equivalent of Chaucer's whole salary during his period in office.[4]

[3] The Exchequer paid Chaucer back in three installments and when it was all over he was still 12s 5½d short.

[4] It was no new thing for the Office of the Works to have trouble in getting money from the Exchequer. As Clerk of the Works, Chaucer paid Henry Yevele arrears in his salary that had been owing him for over a decade.

In addition to his regular duties as Clerk of the Works, Chaucer was given a special commission to oversee the repairs that were scheduled for St. George's Chapel at Windsor. This was the chapel in which the Knights of the Garter did reverence to their patron saint, and it had highly decorated walls, a great alabaster table before the high altar, and two volumes of French romances chained within the chapel. King Edward had finished what he called this "chapel of convenient beauty" only forty years earlier, and it was already in such a state, according to the commission appointing Chaucer to his task, that it would fall to the ground unless it was speedily and effectually repaired. Perhaps the language of the commission is exaggerated. On the other hand, Chaucer's expense accounts as Clerk of the Works show that he paid out a hundred pounds to repair the Wool Wharf and the customhouse that John Churchman had built there less than a decade earlier. A hundred pounds is a large sum (its modern equivalent would be about seventy-five hundred dollars) and the Exchequer would never have agreed to such an expenditure unless it had been needed.

Chaucer had another commission which concerned maintenance and repairs, although it had nothing to do with his position as Clerk of the Works. His old friend, Sir Richard Stury, was appointed to head a commission to make a survey of the drainage system of the Thames in the London area, and Chaucer was made one of his fellow commissioners. He and his colleagues were responsible for inspecting the walls, bridges, sewers, ditches, and so on, between Greenwich and Woolwich, with power to sit as justices for the purpose of the commission and to compel the neighboring landowners to make whatever repairs might be considered necessary. The question of drainage was an important one in a densely populated area like London, and the local authorities gave it more serious attention than they are sometimes credited with doing.

During this same year of 1390, Chaucer was busy in May and in October putting up scaffoldings for two sets of tournaments that were held at Smithfield. The second of these two tournaments was one of the gayest social events of the decade, for Richard was trying to outdo in splendor a series of festivities that had just taken place in France.

When tournaments were first invented they were not the elaborate and formal sporting events they later became. They differed very little from actual warfare, and the one idea was to win as quickly as possible.[5] But in the twelfth century, tournaments went the way of literature; they were taken over by the ladies and became courtly, stylized and romantic. Each knight was supposed to be fighting for the love of some fair lady, as well as experiencing the delights of competition and gratifying his male wish to show off. By the time Chaucer was putting up scaffoldings, the contestants fought in special jousting armor, with gilded helmets and embroidered surcoats, and victory was gained on a technical system of points. It was true that the young Earl of Pembroke had died in a tournament held the previous year, but this was considered the same kind of tragic accident as a modern death on a footfall field.

A tournament was a combination sporting and social event in which everyone participated. All London could watch the initial procession as it wound its way from the Tower through the broad street of Cheap, the musicians coming first and the squires following. Sixty high born ladies, gorgeously attired and mounted on palfreys, led the sixty knightly contestants with chains of silver through the city gates and out to Smithfield, where the King and Queen and other aristocratic spectators were waiting for them, seated on Chaucer's scaffoldings.

The scaffoldings had to be portable, because Smithfield was a horse and cattle market in its everyday existence. They had to be sturdy, for they stood six days' use and the weight of a great many excited people.[6] They also had to be handsomely painted and

[5] It was not considered unchivalrous in the Count of Flanders to arrive at a tournament accompanied by foot soldiers who were armed with hooks so that they could drag the opposing knights from their horses.

[6] Sixty years earlier there had been a near-tragedy in this connection. The scaffolding from which Queen Philippa and her ladies were viewing a tournament collapsed, and all the ladies fell through upon the knights beneath. With characteristic gentleness Queen Philippa forgave the carpenters and interceded for them with King Edward.

decorated and comfortable to sit upon, since they were used by royalty.

The festivities lasted nearly a week, and gave a great deal of work to a great many people.[7] Chaucer, like all the members of the King's household, wore the badge of the white hart, the first time that this particular emblem had ever been used, and it must have been a busy season for him. The jousting alternated with dancing in the evening, with Queen Anne keeping open house in her lodgings at the Bishop of London's palace, and John of Gaunt giving a special dinner to the foreign knights and their ladies at the end of the week. There were a great many of these foreign knights engaged in the tournament, for there was a lull in the hostilities abroad and they had nothing else to do with their time.

About three weeks before this tournament opened, Chaucer was involved in an unpleasant experience in connection with his duties as Clerk of the Works. He was obliged to carry around large sums of government money to meet the pay roll requirements, and he inevitably became a target for thieves. When he was riding through Kent on the third of September he was robbed in a locality bearing the sinister name of the Foul Oak. Three days later he was robbed twice, once at Westminster and once at the village of Hatcham in Surrey, and at that time lost not only the money he was carrying but his horse and his gear.

The second series of robberies was the work of an organized gang whose members also operated as horse thieves. They were captured while pursuing their calling elsewhere and one of their number, Richard Brerelay, tried to save himself by turning state's evidence. His judicial fate was a typically medieval one. He was freed as far as the courts were concerned, but was defeated in "trial by battle" with one of the men he had accused. Brerelay was therefore hanged, for it was assumed that the saints would not have permitted him to lose the duel if he had been speaking the truth. Another of the men who robbed Chaucer was William Huntingfeld, who escaped hanging by another twist of medieval law. Huntingfeld could read and therefore claimed he was a clerk

[7] A similar tournament in France required the services of two hundred water carriers just to keep the field free from dust.

and entitled to "benefit of clergy." This put his case before the ecclesiastical court instead of the civil one, and saved Huntingfeld from execution.

The Exchequer gave Chaucer a writ in January, absolving him from the necessity of rendering account for the twenty pounds in government money of which he had been robbed, but the case involved Chaucer in frequent visits to the Westminster law courts until the following June. In June, Chaucer's association with Westminster ended, for he gave up his position as Clerk of the Works.

It is probable Chaucer gave it up voluntarily. Even without the risk of robbery and the extra duties in which he had become involved, a high position in the Office of Works was a hard position for a man no longer young. It was well paid, but it certainly could have given him no extra time for writing.

Chaucer left on the seventeenth of June, after having served the King as his building superintendent for just under two years. He left his file of sixteen vouchers with the clerks of the Exchequer, and he turned over to the new Clerk of the Works the large pile of stone he had collected from Reigate and Stapleton to repair St. George's Chapel and which was now stored, ready for use, in the great hall at Windsor. Chaucer was responsible no longer for seeing that the gay little chapel did not fall to the ground or for getting from the Exchequer the wages due the gardener at the manor of Sheen.

Chaucer was given a new salaried position so promptly that it must have been waiting for him. Before the twenty-third of the month he had been appointed deputy forester for the forest of North Petherton in Somerset. Seven years later, in 1398, Chaucer's appointment was renewed, and he probably held the position until he leased the little house near Westminster Abbey the year before he died.

The forestership of North Petherton was an hereditary office which belonged to the owner of the North Petherton estates.[8] The actual owner at this time was the third Earl of March, but he was in his minority and the custodian of the land was Sir Peter Courte-

[8] This accounts for the fact that in the days of Edward the First the forester of North Petherton was a woman.

nay. Two years after he had appointed Chaucer as his deputy Courtenay leased the North Petherton property outright and it remained in his possession throughout the whole of the decade.

Courtenay was probably well acquainted with Chaucer already, for he had had more than one opportunity to meet the Clerk of the Works. Courtenay was Master of the King's Falcons when Chaucer had jurisdiction over the building that housed the falcons at Charing Cross, and as Constable of Windsor Castle he was making building repairs at Windsor when Chaucer was in the same locality collecting stone for St. George's Chapel.

Courtenay was a Knight of the Garter, a member of the select military club that included so many of Chaucer's friends. He had been variously Lord Chamberlain, Governor of Calais and King's Standard Bearer, and was so gallant and reckless a fighter that Richard had been obliged to put him under the restraint of the Earl Marshal to prevent his risking his neck unnecessarily on the Continent.

As Courtenay's deputy for the North Petherton forest, Chaucer was no more a forester in the commonly accepted sense of the word than was Courtenay himself. There were two foot-foresters at North Petherton to tour the woods in person and see to it that the various forest laws relating to the conservation of timber and the protection of game were being obeyed. Chaucer's was an executive position, concerning itself with the administration of the property. All writs connected with the administration of North Petherton were addressed to him, and he probably had to know a certain amount about that complicated subject, medieval law.

For a man of Chaucer's experience the duties in connection with the North Petherton estate would not have been especially onerous and he evidently did not spend all his time in Somerset. He was still active in Kent, for his name appears on a board of Greenwich freeholders in 1396. The Archbishop of York was conveying a large block of Kentish real estate to the King's Butler, and Chaucer's name appears as that of one of the witnesses. Along with three other local landowners Chaucer was appointed by the new owner of the property to act as his attorney and take possession of the land.

230

It once was believed that Chaucer became very poor in this last decade of his life, but there is no actual evidence of this. The kind of man who could advance the Exchequer the equivalent of his own salary for two years in a single sum out of his own purse is not the kind of man who can be called poverty-stricken. In 1394 the King gave him a new annuity of forty marks to replace the one Chaucer had sold the previous decade, and while his salary as deputy forester is unknown it must have been a fairly good one for the North Petherton property was a valuable piece of land.[9]

What gave rise to the legend of Chaucer's poverty in the nineties was his persistent struggle with the Exchequer to get the payments due him. He was constantly borrowing small sums on account, not because he had to have them but because there was no other way of getting actual cash out of the slowest of all the Westminster offices. Chaucer had been doing that for a long time; in the early eighties, for instance, during what is conceded to have been a period of considerable prosperity with him, he borrowed from the Exchequer the extremely small sum of six shillings and eightpence. It seems safe to conclude that both in the eighties and the nineties it was the finances of the Exchequer that were in a difficult state rather than those of Chaucer.

The secure position that Chaucer had attained at Court can be illustrated by what happened when a suit was brought against him in 1398. It was brought by Isabella Bukholt against Chaucer and one John Goodale of Milleford jointly, demanding a payment of fourteen pounds from Chaucer and twelve from Goodale. Isabella was the administratrix of the estate of Walter Bukholt, who had been a purveyor in the Office of the Works. He had evidently not

[9] Courtenay's successor to the control of the North Petherton forest was obliged to pay ten pounds more a year for the privilege of administering the property.

This successor was Thomas Chaucer, most of whose prosperous public career belongs to the fifteenth century. His marriage, however, belongs to the century under consideration, and it was a brilliant one. He married Maude Burghersh, the niece and ward of Lady Joan Mohun. Lady Joan was a very prominent member of John of Gaunt's household. She was the *magistra* of Gaunt's Spanish daughter, Katherine, and donned the blue robes of the Order of the Garter even before Katherine Swynford did.

been a permanent official but one of those hired as needed, and the suit brought by his widow probably had something to do with his payments.

The protection which Chaucer was given during the course of the suit is reminiscent of the protection he had already received during the Churchman suit against him in the eighties, except that in the Bukholt case the King himself interfered. He gave his esquire letters stating that he had been ordained "to do and dispatch very many arduous and urgent affairs" and in order that Geoffrey Chaucer may not be impeded in these urgent affairs he and his goods are to be taken under the royal protection.

When the case was called to court Chaucer and his fellow defendant failed to appear, and the court naturally could not recognize the King's order since it was not presented. Therefore it ordered Chaucer's arrest. The sheriff, oddly enough, had no idea where to find him, although Chaucer was not only in the same building as the Court of Common Pleas but practically next door. The King had promised him a grant of wine, and it was necessary for Chaucer to appear at Westminster in person in order to get the spoken promise translated into a documentary form.

The secure position that Chaucer had achieved as a public official is paralleled by the secure position he had achieved as a writer. It was at about this period that Eustache Deschamps wrote a ballade in his honor, sending it across the Channel by the hand of a mutual friend, Sir Lewis Clifford.[10]

Deschamps also sent, by courtesy of Clifford, some of his own poems to Chaucer. He thought of Chaucer primarily as a translator, because of the Englishman's monumental version of *The Romance of the Rose,* and he hoped that the

Great translator, noble Geoffrey Chaucer

[10] Clifford also makes his appearance in one of Deschamps' ballades, in an echo of what was evidently a private joke in French court circles. Deschamps asks a question concerning love which it would take an expert to answer, and then travels around looking for experts. He asks a long list of Frenchmen, from the Duke of Orleans to the Marshal of France, but always returns in his ballade refrain to the one supreme expert of them all, Sir Lewis Clifford.

might like to render a few of his own pieces into English. Deschamps is very coy about this, for a grown man and an established writer. His little works are hardly more than schoolboy productions, and he himself would be a nettle in Chaucer's garden of poetry; but he hopes very much that he will be transplanted there, and that in return Chaucer will send to France some of his own poems to slake Deschamps' feverish thirst for the water of the Muses that flows from Mount Helicon.

Deschamps did not always write this way. He was merely trying to do honor to Chaucer in this particular instance by summoning up all the rhetorical flourishes he had acquired in his long career as a poet. According to this rhetorical code, Deschamps could not call England merely England. He called it the Isle of the Giants, or the home of the men of Brutus, or the land of the Lady Angela which thus became Angle-land. He evokes a whole battery of the ancients, from Socrates to Ovid, to compare with noble Geoffrey Chaucer in wisdom, in personal uprightness, in poetic accomplishments and in grasp of practical affairs.

This ornate pseudo-classicism is not Deschamps' natural style. It was merely the one that descended upon the poets of the period when they wished to show off, and Chaucer had been poking gentle fun at it ever since *Troilus and Criseyde.*

Chaucer may have been sufficiently moved by Deschamps' grandiloquent ballade to transplant samples of the Frenchman's work into his own garden of poetry, but, if so, there is no record of it now. He did, however, translate some of the work of Sir Oton de Graunson, a French poet who was a contemporary of Deschamps.

Chaucer may have known de Graunson personally, for he was a popular and brilliant figure at both the English and the French courts. He had once been in the service of John of Gaunt, and King Richard gave him a large pension for services rendered. Froissart and Deschamps were proud to count him as their friend, for he was the very pattern of a chivalric knight.[11]

[11] He was killed in a duel which he fought to establish his innocence in the death of his sovereign. It was in part the scandal caused by the death of so prominent and well-liked a man that gave the coup de grâce to the elementary medieval legal procedure of trial by battle.

De Graunson was very popular as a poet, and his work was known as far away as Portugal and Prussia. His writings dealt exclusively with courtly love. This is a subject that can become painfully monotonous in the hands of lesser writers, as any reader of minor Elizabethan and Jacobean love lyrics can testify, but it suited the taste of the fourteenth century. Chaucer made a free translation of three of de Graunson's love poems, combining them in the ballade that is now called *The Complaint of Venus,* and ended with a graceful apology for the shortcomings of the English language as a medium for the intricate workmanship

> Of Graunson, flower of them that make in Fraunce.

Not only did literary compliments pass back and forth across the Channel, but they also bloomed in England between Chaucer and his literary associates. One of the chief of these associates was John Gower, who at the beginning of the decade had just finished his last major poem.

This was called *Confessio Amantis,* or *The Lover's Confession,* and contains a pretty little compliment of seventeen lines from the author to his friend Chaucer. Like everyone else, Gower thought of Chaucer as a love poet, for all his major works to date had dealt with the same subject, and in his poem Gower records a message that Madame Venus gave him to hand on to her chief poet and disciple. It is the conviction of Madame Venus that Chaucer ought to crown his career by writing a final "testament of love," since of all poets he is the one who is most certainly love's "owne clerk."

When Gower rewrote the *Confessio Amantis* at the end of the decade, he omitted these seventeen lines. Events had made them out of date, for by 1399 Chaucer was well advanced upon the crowning work of his career and it was *The Canterbury Tales* that was being delightedly passed around from hand to hand. The new poem was certainly not a "testament of love," and Gower's lines ceased to be complimentary and merely looked foolish. Therefore he omitted them, adjusting his lines to changing conditions in the same way that he omitted his original dedication to King Richard and expanded instead a complimentary reference to Henry of Derby, who was by then the new King of England.

Nevertheless, in one sense the whole of the *Confessio Amantis* is a compliment to Chaucer. For it is written in English, the first time that Gower ventured to use his mother tongue, and it was almost certainly Chaucer's success in using the vernacular that nerved Gower to go and do likewise.

It is worth noting, however, that Gower chose at the height of his career the meter that Chaucer had abandoned towards the beginning of his. The *Confessio Amantis* is in the four-stress meter that Chaucer used in *The Book of the Duchess* but had already outgrown when he wrote *The Parliament of Birds*. It is a smooth meter but a flimsy one, only too likely to degenerate into doggerel unless its pretty, tripping cadences are handled with a firm hand.

Gower was an expert poet, and he handles the octosyllabic meter well. His was a minor talent that was happily adjusted to its own limits and never tried to go beyond them. Gower is never clumsy, never makes mistakes, never permits himself errors in taste; and if Addison had been familiar with his work he would doubtless have bestowed upon him the praise that he felt called upon to withhold from Chaucer.[12]

In his own generation John Gower ranked as the most important poet in England. His *Confessio Amantis* was instantly successful, and it was apparently the first production in the English vernacular which men of other nations thought worth translating into their own. A Portuguese version was made almost at once, to be followed a short time later by a Spanish one, and Gower's name must have been known all over Europe. In England he was considered Chaucer's equal for many centuries after, and both men would have been surprised at the difference in their relative positions today.

Chaucer apparently found his most ardent personal admirers

---

[12] Addison said of Chaucer:
In vain he jests in his unpolish'd strain
And tries to make his Readers laugh in vain.

But, as Pope remarked in one of his rare moments of charity, Addison was very young at the time.

among the younger generation—the new poets who were just beginning to try the experiment of writing in English. It would be pleasant to report that Chaucer's influence upon these young men was a beneficial one, but it was not. Poets like John Lydgate had a deep admiration for Chaucer; but they remained impervious to everything he could have given them that was of value and instead copied from him a kind of writing that only a skillful poet may risk with impunity.

For instance, the freedom that Chaucer brought into English versification degenerates with Lydgate into mere sloppiness, for Lydgate lacked Chaucer's strict early self-training, his private integrity and his respect for discipline. Chaucer's assured use of words of French origin degenerated among his fifteenth-century admirers into the dreadful literary style known as "aureate." It is also known, most unfairly, as Chaucerian, but Lydgate himself had moments of suspecting that he and his fellow writers were not succeeding in reproducing exactly the tone of their master.

> We may essay for to countrefete
> His gaye style but it wyl not be.

This state of affairs was no fault of Chaucer's, for he made every effort to pass on to his young disciples the art of poetry as he himself had learned it. He gave them the full benefit of a long career of trial and error with a generous selflessness that was evidently characteristic of him.

Lydgate describes how bitterly he missed, after Chaucer's death, the "supporte" he used to receive from him and the helping hand that used to

> amende and correcte
> The wronge traces of my rude penne.

Lydgate testifies also to the extreme gentleness with which Chaucer criticized even bad poetry.

> Hym liste not pinche nor gruche at euery blot . . .
> Suffering goodly of his gentilnes
> Ful many thing embracid with rudeness

236

To every "maker" Chaucer gave the respect due to any member of so great a craft, and he never used his own brilliance to quench the glowworm flicker of a hopeful amateur. Because of his own devotion to the art of poetry he respected all poets, and however bad their work may have been, he "said alwey the best" when they brought it to him for criticism.

Another English writer who has left written testimony of Chaucer's efforts to help the younger poets of his day is Thomas Hoccleve. Hoccleve was doing office work in Westminster in the nineties, for he was attached to the Office of the Privy Seal. He hated office work in the days of his "skittish youth" when Chaucer first became interested in him, but apparently not on account of any divine poetic fire that was burning within him. By his own penitent account Hoccleve was a lazy young man who disliked getting up in the morning and would have liked to spend his day boating on the Thames or treating pretty girls at Paul's Head Tavern; and he says that Chaucer was not able to do very much for him.

> My dere maister—god his soule quyte!—
>   And father, Chaucer, fayn would have me taught;
>   But I was dull, and lerned lite or naught.

It is not clear whether Lydgate knew Chaucer personally or only by correspondence. But Hoccleve knew him personally, and a real devotion breathes through every reference he makes to his "maister deere and father reverent."

Posterity owes a debt of gratitude to both Lydgate and Hoccleve in their efforts to preserve some record of their master for posterity. When Lydgate wrote his *Fall of Princes,* he included in it a list of all the poems Chaucer ever wrote as far as his disciple knew them. Lydgate was obviously not writing from first-hand knowledge in every case, but the list makes a useful check upon the information that can be gathered from other sources. Hoccleve was even more conscious of the rights of posterity. He was aware that there was no portrait of Chaucer extant, and in a poem he called *The Regiment of Princes* he set himself to remedy this defect.[13]

Hoccleve commissioned a painter to make a miniature portrait of Chaucer in the margin of one page of *The Regiment of Princes,* explaining his reasons in the text adjoining.

> To putte other men in remembraunce
> Of his persone, I have heere his lyknesse.

Chaucer is drawn in the right hand margin with his finger pointing to the word "likeness," and since the portrait was commissioned and approved by one who knew him well it is reasonable to assume that it is as good a likeness as a medieval draughtsman could achieve.

The portrait that Hoccleve commissioned is one that many reproductions have made familiar, and it is extant in more than one manuscript copy. It shows a rather portly man (a point that might have been guessed independently from Chaucer's rude references to his own shape) with a heavy English nose and dark, hooded eyes. He wears his grey hair rather short, showing his ears, and his mustache and small forked beard are in the current fashion. He is dressed in a black hood and gown, rather conservatively cut for a period in which clothes were either very short and tight or very long and full, and the only touch of color about his person are the red strings of his pen case. It is unwise to examine the portrait for indications of character, since the fullness of the lips or the deep lines between the nose and mouth may not be characteristic so much of Chaucer as of the individual idiosyncrasies of that particular illustrator. Medieval drawing was not very realistic, for the art of perspective was still unknown and the work was stylized rather than accurate; but the portrait is good enough so that

---

[13] Posterity owes an incidental debt of gratitude to Hoccleve and Lydgate also. A book which contains Lydgate's *Story of Thebes* and Hoccleve's *Regiment of Princes* was backed with a fragment of parchment which turned out to be a page torn from the account books of Elizabeth of Ulster. Without this particular book no one would ever have known that Chaucer had been a page in her service.

any of Hoccleve's readers could recognize Chaucer if he passed by on the street.[14]

There is another portrait of Chaucer that dates from the fifteenth century also, painted by the artist who illustrated the beautiful Ellesmere copy of *The Canterbury Tales*. He inserted in the margins of the manuscript a series of little colored drawings showing all the pilgrims who made up that immortal company. There is the Miller with his bagpipes, the Monk with his hunting dogs and the Wife of Bath with her large shady hat; and since Chaucer lists himself as one of the company of pilgrims, he rides along with his pen case, as brightly colored and detailed a little figure as any of the rest.

Chaucer's appearance is not dissimilar to the Hoccleve portrait, but there is something especially engaging in seeing him riding along on horseback among the characters of his own imagination. It is pleasant to know his appearance through the devotion of Hoccleve, but it is pleasanter still to see him in the company of the Miller and the Wife of Bath.

[14] In judging medieval artists it is only fair to remember that most of their work has disappeared. What remains is mostly book illustrating, an art which naturally tended towards stylization.

The danger of generalizing on the subject can be illustrated by the Tickhill Psalter, which contains some little sketches of plants and flowers done by a contemporary hand. In their delicate realism and the quality of their line they look like the work of some French botanist of the eighteenth century, and no one at first glance would call them medieval.

CHAPTER XVI

N<small>O ONE</small> knows when Chaucer began to write *The Canterbury Tales*, much less when the idea of writing it first came to him. Perhaps he thought of it suddenly one day when he was among the crowd of travelers that used the busy road between London and Canterbury. Perhaps he himself went on a pilgrimage to the most famous shrine in England. Or perhaps the idea of writing a collection of stories told by pilgrims had been in his mind for several years before he put it down on paper, in the same way that Milton knew he was going to compose an epic long before he sat down to write *Paradise Lost*.

Whenever the idea for *The Canterbury Tales* came to Chaucer, it came obviously as a product of his full maturity as an artist. It snapped the last link between his particular brand of genius and the pretty conventionalities of the Garden of the Rose, and Geoffrey Chaucer emerged at last as the first great English realist.

For many years Chaucer had been meeting people of all classes and all types, and he had been watching them with so fascinated and affectionate an interest that he knew them better than they knew themselves. He knew the furniture in their houses and the cut of their clothes, the turn of their speech and the very color of their minds. He knew them all—the rowdy ones and the quiet ones, the dignified professional men and the drunks, the girls with plucked eyebrows and the cackling old men with thin necks, the knaves, the fools and the innocent. He knew and loved them for the one quality they all had in common, the fact that they were alive.

Chaucer had already shown in *Troilus and Criseyde* what he could do as a creative artist with the men and women he had met at court. Inside the artificial pattern of courtly love he could create gentle, gracious women, and inside the equally artificial pattern of feudal chivalry he could create delightful, intelligent men. Chaucer knew the aristocracy of his period as accurately as

Jane Austen knew the county gentry of hers, so accurately in fact that he could reproduce the exact tone of voice in which they teased each other.

But the great Londoner knew that court life was not the whole of England, and that outside that delicate barrier most of the life of England rolled along its rowdy, lively way. He knew that London was full of all sorts of people, not only in the shops and the churches but in the bedrooms, the taverns and the gutters. So was every town in the realm, from Oxford to Bath, and every little village from Holderness to Trumpington. Each human being was different, from the shape of his nose to the twist of his mind, but all of them were wonderful. These were the common people that Froissart pitied and that Gower harangued but that Chaucer loved.

No hint of this had ever appeared before in Chaucer's work, except possibly for the brief excursion he made into the point of view of the duck, the goose and the cuckoo in *The Parliament of Birds*. Yet the attitude must always have been an integral part of Chaucer himself, for so mighty a tree needs a deep root. There is a lifetime of observation packed into *The Canterbury Tales*, and never was a work of art more unmistakably the product of the whole man.

The peculiar merit of the structure of *The Canterbury Tales* was that it gave Chaucer an opportunity to use everything he possessed. Once the original idea was conceived of an assorted group of people going on a journey together and each one expected to tell a story, the possibilities were endless. Everything Chaucer knew about people could be included in it, for the design was elastic enough to include a thick-necked miller and a refined prioress and a middle-class doctor and a rowdy cook and an embroidered squire and a fat cloth-maker. Everything that Chaucer knew about poetry could go into it also, for every mood could be represented from romance to farce and every kind of versification from rime royal to doggerel iambics.

No one knows where Chaucer got the original idea for his *Canterbury Tales*. It was evidently not from his reading, for nothing like it had ever been done before. There had, of course, been many

241

collections of tales set within a framework, as Chaucer set his own *Legend of Good Women.* Boccaccio had the idea of retelling stories told by a group of men and women, and another Italian writer, Sercambi, used a pilgrimage as a basis for a similar collection of tales; but in Sercambi's *Novelle* one narrator tells all the stories, and in the *Decameron* the highborn youths and maidens who tell the stories are so little characterized that they might as well all have been the same person.[1] Chaucer's idea was precisely the contrary. Each of his storytellers is a living human being, a distinct and highly opinionated pilgrim. Each man and woman tells a story in his or her own way and sometimes the story is the least of it, submerged in the private tiffs or the sudden loquaciousness that make up the irrepressible personalities of Chaucer's pilgrims.

It is as difficult to find a source for *The Canterbury Tales* as it is to find a source for Chaucer's original decision to base his whole literary career on the vernacular. The source was evidently within himself, born of his own independent way of thinking. Books were a great help to Chaucer and he acknowledged their help eagerly, sometimes giving his fellow authors more credit than they deserved. Books, however, did not help him here. The idea for *The Canterbury Tales* was entirely his own, and not only had nothing like it ever been done before but nothing like it was ever done again.

Chaucer never finished the poem; his magnificent plan was still much more in his head than it was on paper when he had to leave it. He had planned to write a hundred and twenty tales, and he only completed twenty-one. Some of the characterizations are complete but some are hardly more than sketched in, and the tales are not in order. *The Canterbury Tales* as it stands now is only a collection of fragments. The fragments have been tentatively arranged in some sort of order by later editors, all of whom naturally disagree with each other, but nothing definitive can be done with the series of unfinished sketches that survived into the

---

[1] In any case, there is no evidence whatever that Chaucer had read either Sercambi's *Novelle* or Boccaccio's *Decameron.*

fifteenth century as Chaucer's legacy.[2] Yet for all that, Chaucer completed enough of *The Canterbury Tales* to make it one of the literary masterpieces of the world, and he visualized his characters so clearly that after the dust of six centuries they are still as real and as familiar as the day they met each other at the Tabard Inn.

So real, in fact, are the twenty-nine pilgrims who rode with Chaucer to Canterbury that it has been suggested that the poet was describing actual contemporaries of his. It has been suggested that the Shipman may be identified as John Piers, the Sergeant-at-law as Thomas Pynchbek, the Canon as William Shuchirch, and so on. It is an interesting occupation to search for the prototypes of Chaucer's pilgrims in the record books of fourteenth-century England, but at the same time it is risky to assume that because Chaucer probably knew William Shuchirch of the King's Chapel at Windsor, and because Shuchirch dabbled in alchemy (as many intellectuals did) that Shuchirch must therefore be the model for the sweaty quack whose own servant sets out to expose him.[3]

Some of his pilgrims Chaucer certainly drew from life in the sense that some real human being started the picture forming in his mind that eventually emerged as an independent artistic creation. No artist works in a vacuum, and no doubt somewhere in Elizabethan England walked the man who first made Shakespeare think of Falstaff. But this is not to say that Chaucer was consciously picking out real people from among his acquaintances, with real names and addresses, and that he expected his readers to identify them as such. He knew that the Miller had a wart on his nose and that the Monk's sleeves were trimmed with fur at the wrist and that the Reeve had a grey horse named Scot and that the Ship-

[2] The order followed in the discussion of the *Tales* in this book is that of the Cambridge Edition edited by F. N. Robinson.

[3] The one character who might most safely be identified with a real Englishman is the Host, Harry Bailly. There was a real Harry Bailly who was an innkeeper in Southwark, although whether he kept the Tabard Inn is not known. The name of the wife is not the same, and if Chaucer really intended his henpecked, hard-swearing, hot-tempered Host to be identified by his readers with a real man the original would have had every right to sue the poet for libel.

man's boat was called the *Magdalen*, in exactly the same way that he knew at the beginning of his career that the pillowcases on an imaginary bed were made of Brittany linen.

Francis Beaumont, the father of the dramatist, made a just remark when he said of Chaucer,

> One gift he hath above all other authors, and
> that is by the excellence of his descriptions
> to possess his readers with a stronger
> imagination of seeing that done before their
> eyes, which they read, than any other that ever
> writ in any tongue.

The attempt to provide Chaucer's pilgrims with names and addresses is as good a tribute as Beaumont's to this particular gift of Chaucer's, but it is not well to let even the finest of tributes get out of hand.

The wish to connect Chaucer's creative imagination with actual people is natural enough, as it is natural to want to connect *The Parliament of Birds* with actual court events. It is natural, but it is unwise. The truth is that we know so little about fourteenth-century personalities and events and Chaucer knew so much about them that it is unsafe to make assumptions of this kind unless Chaucer himself gives the lead.

For instance, even the greatest scholar of the Middle Ages does not know the answer to so simple a question as this: Could a social group as mixed as Chaucer's really have gone on a pilgrimage together, or would a well-born lady like the Prioress have objected to riding behind the bagpipes of so rowdy a commoner as the Miller? We do not know, yet it is a question that any of Chaucer's contemporaries could have answered at once. If we know so little of the feel of the period that we cannot even answer a question like this, it is perhaps unwise to attempt to prove something that even Chaucer's contemporaries probably did not know.[4]

[4] Charlotte Brontë's contemporaries, for instance, were convinced that the hero of *Jane Eyre* was a thinly disguised portrait of Thackeray. They were further convinced that the author chose to remain anonymous because she was the former governess of Thackeray's children, and they succeeded in building up a thoroughly probable edifice of conjecture whose only fault was that it was untrue.

At any rate, whether Chaucer's pilgrims actually once walked the streets in the towns to which he assigned them or whether it was the poet himself who gave them a local habitation and a name, the important fact remains that they are alive now. They have walked out of England and into immortality because they were born of a universal rather than a contemporary truth, and they are citizens now of a more enduring town than either London or Bath. Although they are deeply rooted in their own generation, down to the most minute details of their dress and appearance, there is no antiquarian quaintness about them because Chaucer did not stop with the cut of their shoes or the manner of their speech. He knew them in their hearts.

The characters whom Chaucer had time to develop fully, like the Pardoner and the Prioress and the Wife of Bath, take on a depth of reality that no other writer in England but Shakespeare ever surpassed. Chaucer is of course no Shakespeare, but in this respect he came nearer him than any other poet, and even the best of later novelists and dramatists are usually not a match for him here.

It can be put down to inspiration that Chaucer hit upon an idea for a major poem that would make use of his profound knowledge of character, but the fact that he could make full use of the idea after it came to him must be attributed to a lifetime of disciplined respect for the art of poetry. Since the early days of his 'prentice devotion to the easy rhythms of Machaut, Chaucer had been testing, experimenting, rejecting and testing again, and the tools that he had patiently forged for himself now lay ready to his hand when he needed them.

Chaucer knew at once the meter that was right for his new venture. It was the one he had tried out for the first time in *The Legend of Good Women,* and for all its novelty and its strangeness he knew that it was suited to his purpose. Chaucer introduced other meters for variety from time to time, but in the Prologue, in the links between the tales and in most of the tales themselves he uses the heroic couplet. To realize the valuable support that Chaucer the craftsman gave Chaucer the artist, it is only necessary to imagine *The Canterbury Tales* written in the flimsy four-stress line with which Chaucer began his career and Gower climaxed his.

Chaucer's inspired wisdom in choosing the five-stress iambic line for *The Canterbury Tales* is of course obvious, but there is one aspect of his use of it that has not received quite the attention it deserves. This is the way in which Chaucer manages to suggest the rhythms of ordinary speech in what is, after all, a stylized verse form.

It is something of an achievement to have a common man swear in iambic pentameter and still make the line sound exactly like a common man swearing. Shakespeare could have done it, but there was nothing Shakespeare could not do. The Nurse's reminiscences in the first act of *Romeo and Juliet* carry exactly the tone of ordinary speech into iambic pentameter that Chaucer achieved two hundred years earlier. Yet even Shakespeare preferred to have only his well-born characters speak in verse and to let his constables and porters and gravediggers speak in prose.

Chaucer, as a poet, is a little outside the normal traditions of English verse. He shows only occasionally the lyric line that sings even in minor English versifiers and is so characteristic of English poets as a whole. He does not possess the mighty sweep of Marlowe, the sharp elegance of Pope, or the sensuous approach to beauty that belonged to Keats. Browning, perhaps, comes nearest to him. Yet even Browning could not have set down in iambic pentameter the exact tone of voice of a miller plaintively discussing his own drunkenness, or have kept out of it the various mannerisms that were peculiar to Browning's own style of writing.

Chaucer, as has been said before, had a plain style. Even when his verse forms are at their most intricate, his actual style is very close to the ground. He is one of the easiest of poets to read because he is the most natural, and this naturalness is not so much the result of simplicity as of an art so practiced it conceals itself.

This style of Chaucer's was an ideal medium for recording the conversations of Pandarus and Criseyde, for the advantage of naturalness is that it is at home anywhere. In *The Canterbury Tales* it is equally suited to the courteous comments of a gentleman like the Knight and the vulgar bleatings of the Reeve, the friendly good humor of the Franklin and the wonderful inelegance of the Wife of Bath. For Chaucer's style is like smooth water, reflecting the coloring of the objects around it with such clarity that the medium itself is almost forgotten.

The poem opens in April. It is the season when the birds start to sing and the world turns green, and everyone suddenly wants to go traveling. The tourist impulse was frowned upon in the Middle Ages if one took to the road merely for one's own amusement, but it was very respectable if one ended with a visit to the shrine of a saint. Theoretically this was done in a spirit of humble devotion; the pilgrim journeyed on foot, clad in a grey cloak, with a scrip and a pilgrim staff to proclaim his intentions. In actual practice, however, a pilgrimage worked out quite differently, and in the fourteenth century a trip of this kind was much more likely to be one of cheerful sightseeing than of devout meditation.

England was full of shrines, from one end of the realm to the other, but the most popular of all these holy attractions was the shrine of the murdered Archbishop of Canterbury, Thomas à Becket. Relics of the twelfth-century saint were scattered everywhere (Bury had his boots and Verona one of his teeth) but it was in the great cathedral at Canterbury that he had worked and died, and the blood of his martyrdom was still visible before the altar. There were monks to guide each new band of pilgrims, to show them the banners and the painted glass and the holy shrine in Trinity Chapel which probably had more jeweled wealth loaded into a single spot than anywhere else in England. The street that led to the cathedral was called Mercery Lane, and it was lined with shops where the pilgrims could buy souvenirs to take home with them.

The road through London was the natural thoroughfare for pilgrims from the north of England. They could pause to visit St. Paul's churchyard, where Thomas à Becket's father and mother were buried, and pray for a moment in the beautiful little two-story chapel on London Bridge that was also dedicated to London's most famous citizen. Then the average pilgrim would spend the night at Southwark, just on the other side of the bridge, so that he could avoid the early morning traffic into the city when he set out for Canterbury.

On this particular evening in April, twenty-nine people were

247

lodged at the Tabard Inn in Southwark on their way to Canterbury the next morning, and Chaucer says that he spoke with them all.

While this is unquestionably what Geoffrey Chaucer himself would have done, it is not the real Chaucer who makes his appearance in *The Canterbury Tales*. It is "Geoffrey," the same fat, well-meaning, not very intelligent individual who was so thoroughly lectured by the Eagle in *The House of Fame*. Geoffrey has become, if anything, slightly more feeble-minded with the passage of the years, for he is the only one among the pilgrims who is incapable of offering a presentable tale in rhyme. He does his best, but his best is so dreadful that the Host is obliged to stop him in the middle of it because the pilgrims can stand no more; and therefore Geoffrey, who is certainly Chaucer's favorite butt, is reduced to telling "a litel thyng in prose."

Chaucer does not draw Geoffrey's portrait in the Prologue; but he makes up for this omission by the vividness and accuracy with which he supplies the portraits of everyone else.

To realize the exact extent of Chaucer's achievement in the Prologue to *The Canterbury Tales*, it is necessary to remember that the Middle Ages was not a time of portraits. It was a time of patterns, of allegories, of reducing the specific to the general and then drawing a moral from it. An occasional poet had shown his ability to draw a picture in sharp, factual and occasionally comic detail (the tavern scene in *Piers Plowman*, for example) and some of the London preachers were in the habit of enlivening their sermons with anecdotes that they brightened with local color and a few highly realistic touches. But this was no more than a continuation of what Jean de Meun had done in his section of *The Romance of the Rose*, or what scores of anonymous writers had done in those rowdy, middle-class short stories in verse that are called *fabliaux*.

What Chaucer was doing was entirely different. As a major creative artist he had set himself to draw, with serious, factual, Holbein-like exactness, the portraits of twenty-nine people. He did not set out to be moral. He did not even set out to be entertaining. He merely set out to be accurate, so that each of the twenty-nine would be as vivid to the reader as he was to Chaucer himself.

This was the man who had been brought up on the precepts of the rhetoricians, and who had been told over and over again that this was the sort of thing no poet should permit himself. A poet was supposed to deal with types, not with individuals. If necessary he could memorize the models that the books of rhetoric offered so that he would not stray off into personal vagaries.

Chaucer threw the whole book of rules overboard in his Prologue. He even refused to obey the regulation, almost sacred by this time, which prescribed that a description should begin in an orderly manner and work from one end of the man or woman described to the other. When Chaucer describes his Miller, for instance, he leaps, with the appearance of doing it almost at random, from his prowess as a wrestler, to his red beard, to the tuft of bristles on his nose, to his sword, to the size of his mouth, to his business methods, to his hood, to his bagpipes. This is not done at random, of course. It is done deliberately, to give an effect of such reality that a man and not a pattern stands in front of the reader. Chaucer's method was unmedieval and so was his purpose. The two combine to make the Prologue to *The Canterbury Tales* unlike anything that had ever been written before in Christendom.

Chaucer begins with a Knight. Chaucer's Knight was everything that a knight should be and usually was not—honorable, courteous to all classes, gallant in war and very conscientious about the religious significance of a pilgrimage. He may have been Chaucer's answer to the rising tide of criticism from men like Gower and Deschamps as to the worthlessness of the current crop of knights, and he may also have been a composite portrait of some of Chaucer's own friends. Nevertheless the Knight is not a type but a real individual. Chaucer knows exactly how many battles he fought and where, what kind of horse he rode, and even the way the metal on his coat of mail has marked his tunic underneath.

The Knight's son, the Squire, was also everything that he should be. A proper courtly lover, he had fought for his lady's smile in Flanders and Picardy, and he knew how to sing and dance and joust and write love lyrics as any well-educated young gentleman should. He was dressed in the latest fashion, his locks were so neatly curled they might have been laid in a press, and he reminded Chaucer of a field full of daisies.

These two aristocrats had an efficient servant along with them. He was clad in green, with his dagger well-sharpened and his arrows tipped with peacock feathers. He does not open his mouth in any of the subsequent conversations, but Chaucer is of the opinion he was a forester because there is a silver image of St. Christopher, the patron saint of foresters, hanging upon his breast.

Next comes Chaucer's famous Prioress. Hers is so delicate, subtle and affectionate a portrait that it deserves special mention. Like Flaubert's portrait of the old serving woman in *A Simple Heart,* it is a superlative example of how the very soul of a woman may be built up through a series of skillfully chosen objective details. Flaubert, however, could not have smiled in print if his life depended upon it, while Chaucer cannot prevent himself from teasing the Prioress a little even while he loves her.

Madame Eglantine was a perfect lady, and well she knew it in her gently complacent way. She spoke French very well, although not, it is true, with a Parisian accent. Her wimple was just so, her nose was elegantly formed, and her table manners were charming. She kept several little dogs, whom she spoiled by giving them the kind of food that puppies are not supposed to eat, and she had so tender a heart that she wept if she looked at a dead mouse caught in a trap.

Chaucer teases his Prioress in a way that would not be immediately apparent except to a contemporary. He describes her in exactly the phraseology that would be suitable if he were presenting the heroine of a courtly romance. Madame Eglantine had the small, soft, red mouth that was fashionable in contemporary fiction, a straight nose, blue eyes, and the high forehead that was considered so desirable by the ladies of the period that they plucked back the hairline to achieve it. Moreover Chaucer lifts his apparently respectful description of her table manners, bodily and with full knowledge that his readers would recognize the source, from a particularly unecclesiastical section of *The Romance of the Rose.*

250

Any English reader of Chaucer's day would realize instantly what Chaucer was doing here, just as he would know that the Prioress' wimple should have been arranged to hide her high forehead and that she was not supposed to keep lap dogs in the convent. But he would also know, as Chaucer knew very well, that the church and the world can lodge comfortably side by side in one innocent woman's heart, and that when the Prioress glanced down at the gold brooch on her rosary, with its motto "Love Conquers All," she would not think of the connotation that would occur at once to the unregenerate reader.

Chaucer's portrait of the Monk is very much less gentle and somewhat less subtle, but there is the same skill in the handling of objective detail in order to arouse a specific emotional response in the reader. The Monk was one of those full-feeding sportsmen that occur in every age, and he had no intention of letting the fact that he was in holy orders interfere with his fondness for hunting or for roast goose. Chaucer agrees with bland politeness that of course St. Augustine was wrong; quite the best thing any monk can do is to keep a pack of greyhounds and a stable full of horses, and to ride about the country with his bridle bells jingling, his bald head shining, and a gold love knot under his fat chin.

Equally courteous are Chaucer's remarks about the Friar. For the Friar was a fine figure of a man, with his thick white neck and his easy manners, and it was quite natural that he should have more acquaintances among the tavern keepers of a town than among the sick and the poor. For what kind of "avaunce" could a man get by making the acquaintance of a leper? His tippet was stuck full of knives and pins, which he used to establish intimate relations with the young ladies of the town, and he lisped a little because he thought it sounded fetching. He had a remarkable talent for extracting money from the unwilling, his eyes twinkled like the stars on a frosty night, and his name was Huberd.

Next came the Merchant, a member of a class that Chaucer had reason to know intimately. He had a forked beard and a high saddle, a beaver hat and a pair of excellently fitting boots. His soul was chiefly occupied with pride over his business successes and worry over the lack of security of Channel shipping, and Chaucer was not really very fond of him.

Chaucer was very fond, however, of the Clerk. The Clerk spent all his money on books and Chaucer's heart went out to him. With his shabby coat and thin horse he was the kind of man who never gets on in the world and enrages more successful people by not minding. The Clerk's own idea of success was to have twenty books at the head of his bed where he could reach them easily. Chaucer said of him,

> Gladly would he lerne and gladly teche,

which is the handsomest compliment that one lover of books could give to another.

Next came a Man of Law, a class that Chaucer knew as well as he knew merchants. This particular individual was a sergeant-at-law, and had identified himself so thoroughly with his profession that he had lost some of his interest as a human being. He was a distinguished lawyer but there was nothing inside. However, he was adept in real estate deals and could quote every legal decision that had been handed down since William the Conqueror.

A much more affectionate portrait is that of the Franklin. The Franklin was a freeholder, a member of the county gentry of the kind that Chaucer encountered so frequently in Kent. A solid sort of Englishman, he had presided many times over local meetings of the justices of the peace and had represented his county frequently in Parliament as a knight of the shire. The Franklin was not a profound man, but he was good company and very fond of guests. He was also very fond of eating—in fact, he was an expert on the subject of food—and his beard was as white as a daisy flower.

There were five guild members from various London professions, new enough to wealth so that their outfits had been freshly bought. They were all rich enough to be aldermen and their wives were all hoping they would be elected; for, as Chaucer says, it is delightful to be called "madame" and to be given precedence at the guild festivities.

The five guildsmen brought along a Cook with them. He was

not a private cook but the proprietor of a cook-shop, which was a combination restaurant and delicatessen. The Cook was skilled in his profession, in spite of the insults he had to endure on the subject from his fellow pilgrims, and he knew all there was to know about the mashed and heavily spiced foods that were popular in a period of no forks and little refrigeration. He was a little too fond of London ale, and it was perhaps on that account that he had a bad ulcer on his shin.

There was also a Shipman, riding uncomfortably upon that alien method of travel, a horse. The Merchant must have eyed him a little thoughtfully, for the Shipman was not above stealing part of the wine cargoes that he was supposed to ship across the Channel. He lived somewhere near Dartmouth, which Chaucer knew by personal experience was notable for its pirates, and after a naval battle he left the defeated side to walk home by water. Apart from his elastic morals he was a good mariner, for he knew even the little-known waterways of Spain. He had a fine coat of tan and wore his dagger on a string around his neck.

Another very successful professional was the Doctor. The practice of medicine was a lucrative one in fourteenth-century England, and the plague had made Chaucer's Doctor a rich man. He deserved to be, for he was a very learned one; the range of books he had read covered the Greeks, the brilliantly experimental Arabian doctors who had worked in Spain, and such contemporary Oxford practitioners as John of Gatesden. He was of course well grounded in astrology, for no reputable physician would have thought of trying to cure a fever unless he knew at what hour it had begun and how it coincided with the constellation of the patient.[5] The Doctor was very fond of gold, but this, says Chaucer,

[5] Astrology was considered one of the most respectable of sciences by the learned men of Chaucer's day, although it was still a controversial subject and a few men like Petrarch followed the old-fashioned conservatism of St. Augustine in condemning it. It remained respectable throughout the Renaissance, and Galileo cast horoscopes at the court of the Medici. As long as the Ptolemaic system of astronomy was followed astrology could not be disproved, but it collapsed automatically with the arrival of the Copernican theory and survived after that only as a popular superstition.

was of course because gold has such excellent medicinal properties.

The next pilgrim was the Wife of Bath, that lusty realist beside whom only Falstaff and Sancho Panza are worthy to walk. It is not until the lady swings into action that her remarkable qualities become evident, but even the brief portrait in the Prologue makes it clear that here is no ordinary woman.

Everyone knows her red face and her broad hat, her scarlet stockings and the outer riding skirt that she wears wrapped around her broad hips. She was already an old hand at pilgrimages, for she liked "felaweships" and gadding about and had taken three times the long trip to Jerusalem. The Wife of Bath had gone through five husbands, not counting "oother compaignye" in her youth, and she had a high opinion of her gifts as a weaver and her social standing in the suburb of Bath where she lived. It was an unwise woman who tried to precede her when the offerings were made in church on Sunday. She was a little deaf (a fact that may have had something to do with her unparalleled gifts as a monologist) and there were gaps between her teeth.

After her came a Plowman and his brother, a Parson. They were both very good men, and it is sad that they should be so much less interesting. The Plowman was everything he ought to be; he loved his neighbors and paid his taxes and worked hard, and some of Chaucer's fellow landowners in Kent probably read the description with the same sort of disbelief that a modern capitalist might give to a similar portrait of a modern workman.

The Parson is a more interesting man than his brother, for Chaucer describes him in greater detail. He was well-educated, as a peasant could be in the Middle Ages if he wanted to, but his learning had not made him restless. He labored through the thunder and the rain from one end of his large parish to the other, and never thought of the easy money that could be made by going up to London and establishing himself in a chantry to pray for some dead merchant's soul. He preferred to give money to his parishioners instead of taking it away from them and refused even to "cursen for his tithes." [6] He was in sharp contrast to

---

[6] Cursing as a way of collecting money was considered perfectly proper. The King once had to restrain a London parson from ex-

254

the Friar, whose courtesy towards the rich was a wonder to behold, in that he would "snybben" a wealthy man without hesitation if he thought he deserved a reproof. The Parson was a most uncommon ecclesiastic, gentle to the poor and austere only with the rich, and if there had been a few more like him in England Wyclif's doctrines would never have made the headway they did. The man even believed in example as well as precept.

> Christes lore and his apostles twelve
> He taught, but first he followed it hymselve.

The rest of the company consisted of five extremely low-class individuals, with Chaucer himself bringing up the rear.

The first of these is the Miller, upon whom Chaucer lavishes a minutely realistic description worthy of a Flemish portrait painter of the following century. The Miller was a heavy-set fellow, with thick shoulders and a head so hard he could break a door with it. He had a red, spade-shaped beard, and the tuft of hairs that stood up from a wart on his nose were as red as the bristles in a sow's ear. He had wide black nostrils, and was both an accomplished stealer of corn and a teller of dirty stories. He wore a white coat and a blue hood, and led the pilgrims out of town by blowing on his bagpipes.

The next of the five was the Manciple. He is chiefly interesting in showing that Chaucer was well acquainted with a minor official of the Inns of Court at Holborn. The Manciple was a purchasing agent, responsible for buying the provisions for the lawyers; and while they were a "heep of lerned men," Chaucer's Manciple was clever enough to make fools of them all.

Another agent was the Reeve. His function was that of general manager for a country estate, a business he managed so efficiently that no auditor could frighten him and he earned his lord's thanks by lending back to him his own money. He had trained in his

communicating all the Wardens of London Bridge (they had rented out some property on the Southwark side which the parson felt belonged to him) but the King interfered because the Church did not own this particular piece of land and not because it was wrong to use excommunication as a weapon in money matters.

255

youth to be a carpenter, and came from Norfolk just outside the town of Baldeswell. He wore his beard cropped as close as he could get it, with his head shorn like a priest's, and his legs were so thin that they showed no calf at all. He wore his long coat hitched up and held by a girdle and he kept always to the rear end of the procession.

The Reeve was a crook, but he was a man of high virtue in comparison to the Summoner and the Pardoner, the two individuals who complete the list. A man like the hunting Monk was not temperamentally suited to the religious life and the Friar was an oily rascal; but the Summoner and the Pardoner were the vicious dregs of an ecclesiastical system whose wealth and power attracted a crowd of hangers-on as sugar attracts flies.

Chaucer looked upon these two with the same fascinated interest that had observed the youthful picturesqueness of the Squire or the innocent worldliness of the Prioress. He watched everyone; he judged no one. It was literally true that nothing human was alien to him. If they were alive, that was enough for Chaucer.

The Summoner was a member of the group that made a living out of citing delinquents to appear before the papal court. He was indeed a "good felawe"—the kind who would lend out his girl for a twelvemonth in exchange for a quart of wine. His face was blotched with a skin disease, so that children were terrified of him, and he had scabby eyebrows and slits of eyes. His breath was always heavy with garlic and onions and he yelled like a madman when he was drunk. His head was decorated with a garland for the occasion and he carried a large cake as a shield. He also supplied the refrain in a trumpeting voice while his dear friend the Pardoner sang, "Come hither, love, to me."

The Pardoner had been sent out by a hospital near Charing Cross to raise money by selling papal indulgences.[7] He had flat yellow hair, as yellow as wax, which hung down in limp strips over his shoulders, and he wore no hood upon it because he believed this to be the latest fashion. He had staring eyes and a voice as thin as a goat's and because he was sexually abnormal he had

[7] Church councils were continually trying to suppress this practice but they never succeeded.

not been able to grow a beard. He was well supplied with the tools of his trade, for he had a glass full of "pigges bones," a piece of Saint Peter's sail, and a pillowcase which he said had belonged to Our Lady. With these appliances he could go into a church and raise more money in a day than the local parson collected in a month.

In introducing men of this kind into serious poetry, Chaucer was running directly counter to the whole spirit of his age. He had no moral purpose in describing the Pardoner, and no religious purpose. He describes the Pardoner merely because the man was like that, which was a Renaissance point of view and not a medieval one. The Middle Ages could never have understood why Rembrandt, for instance, chose to paint an old woman cutting her nails when he could have been making a picture of the Holy Family. Rembrandt was a man who loved this world, and so was Chaucer. But Chaucer lived in a period whose whole attention was focused in another direction, and he antedated by many years the shift of emphasis that came in with the Renaissance.

Chaucer had no intention of giving up his own vision of reality, but he was well aware that he had to apologize for it. Men like the Summoner and the Pardoner might be familiar figures in the brothels and taverns of London, but never before had a court poet mentioned them in so unequivocal a manner. It is not that the court circle of Richard and Anne was a particularly sheltered one. Chaucer had been able to use a kind of plain speaking in *Troilus and Criseyde* that any Victorian novelist would have given much to be permitted. But in *Troilus* he wrote of noble folk, such as the Summoner and the Pardoner obviously were not. Nor did Chaucer present his erring pilgrims as a moralist might, illustrating various aspects of sin so that his audience might draw the necessary moral. He suggested no moral. There was none to suggest. He merely described people as they were.

Chaucer apologized for this, but his apology is characteristic. He says that he is very sorry he is obliged to speak so "pleynly" in describing the appearance and conversation of some of his pilgrims. He hopes that this will not be set down to a lack of breeding on his part. But if you wish to repeat a story a man has just told you, you must use the words he used or else "telle his tale untrewe." To Chaucer, that one-time wanderer in the dream Garden of the *Rose,* such an alternative was impossible. He could not tell his tale untrue, or modify any of his characters to make them fit the literary prejudices of his audience.

Chaucer adds a further apology, not exactly heartfelt, in case he has failed to introduce his characters in the exact order which their social standings require.

> Also I pray yow to forgive it me
> If I have not set folk in hir degree
> Here in my tale, as that they sholde stand.
> My wit is short, ye may well understand.

There is no doubt that Chaucer found a most convenient literary refuge in his pet legend that he was short of wit. He could use it whenever he wanted to do something that he was not supposed to do. According to this convenient fiction he was merely a fat, well-intentioned man, not at all bright, who happened to be going on a pilgrimage in April, met a mixed group of people at an inn, and carefully set down on paper what each of them looked like and what they said. The Canterbury pilgrims were not his; he merely met them at an inn. *The Canterbury Tales* were not his; he merely overheard them.

There was probably no one in Chaucer's audience who actually believed this fiction, but it had the virtue of disarming criticism. No one can be severe with an author who starts out by cheerfully proclaiming himself to be a fool.

The device of disclaiming responsibility for both the pilgrims and the tales leaves Chaucer free to do what he likes with them. The Pardoner and the Reeve, the Miller and the Wife of Bath, are able to behave as a great realist wished them to, and to "speke hir wordes properly" in accordance with Chaucer's own standards rather than with the standards of his age.

CHAPTER XVII

HE OWNER of the Tabard Inn was greatly interested in the thirty people who had gathered together that April evening under his roof. The Host had not seen a livelier group that year, and it seemed to him that the pilgrims ought to derive some benefit from each other's company on the road to Canterbury. It would be a pity if they were all to be as "doumb as a stone."

The Host was an instinctive organizer. It was his idea that each member of the company should tell four stories, two on the way to Canterbury and two on the way back. The best storyteller could be given a dinner at the general expense when they all returned to the Tabard Inn, and the Host himself was willing to go along as master of ceremonies at his "owene cost." This was thoughtful of the Host, especially as he was thus guaranteeing that the whole company would stop at his inn when it returned.

The pilgrims set out the next morning in a mood that could hardly be called devout, and the Host settles down early to the question of storytelling. He decides who shall begin by drawing lots; but by an extraordinary piece of good luck the winning length is drawn by the Knight, who has the highest social position, and the amenities are thus preserved.

The Knight, naturally enough, chooses to tell a romance. For two centuries romances had been the most popular fiction of both sexes in the upper classes of England and France, and many were the lords and ladies who handed down illustrated romances to their descendants. The Knight's romance is an especially charming example of the species, and perfectly fitted to the man who tells it.

The tale is a judicious mixture of courtly love and knightly combat. Two young Theban knights named Palamon and Arcite are imprisoned in a tower by their conqueror, Duke Theseus. They see his sister Emily walking among the green leaves in a garden below and simultaneously fall in love with her. After a suitable period of woeful love-longing they fight for the love of the fair Emily in a wood, where Theseus finds them and puts their rivalry on an official basis by organizing a tournament in which they are the chief contestants. Arcite is the favorite of Mars, god of war, and therefore he wins the tournament. Palamon is the favorite of Venus, goddess of love, and therefore he wins the lady.

Chaucer did not find this tale in any French romance. He found it in Boccaccio's *Teseide*, where it is the thin thread that binds together the twelve books of Boccaccio's would-be epic. Chaucer had tried to use the *Teseide* once before and had only managed to produce the unsuccessful fragment called *Anelida and Arcite*. Now, however, Chaucer knew a great deal more about story construction, and he was able to retell Boccaccio's story much better than Boccaccio had told it and in one-fifth the space.[1]

Chaucer shortened the *Teseide* for the same reason that he lengthened *Il Filostrato*—because he was a wise artist. He saw the story of *Troilus and Criseyde* as one that concerned real people, and he lavished on it a series of small perceptive details that made them real and the poem consequently much longer. The tale of Palamon and Arcite, on the other hand, was that of conventionalized, brightly colored little figures taking part in a courtly dance of love and combat. Chaucer's problem as an artist was to leave the steps of the dancers free by cutting away the load of extraneous detail Boccaccio had added to the story under the impression that he was thus producing an epic.

Chaucer begins the tale by condensing the first book and a half of the *Teseide* into a dozen lines, remarking that the "remanent of the tale is long ynough" without describing the battle of the Amazons or the wedding of Theseus with their queen. In fact, Chaucer mentions the need of brevity and of excluding extraneous detail so often that he ends by making a joke of it; he describes Arcite's funeral by the device of announcing firmly that he will not describe it. He will not describe how the fire was built, first

[1] It is not known how soon after *Troilus and Criseyde* Chaucer wrote the Knight's Tale. Some version of it antedates *The Legend of Good Women*, for Alcestis mentions the tale of Palamon and Arcite while she is defending Chaucer against the charge of having made light of love.

with straw and then with dry sticks split in three and then with green wood and then with cloth of gold and then with garlands of flowers. He will not describe how the half-gods of the woods, nymphs and fauns and hamadryads, ran out of the trees in fear when their homes were cut down to add to the fire. He will not describe this and this and this, and continues with his protestations until Arcite's funeral is fully described. It is described because the details lend color and richness to the story, but Chaucer, being Chaucer, could not at the same time resist a mild dig at his own anxiety to condense.

The tournament scene is another example of Chaucer's colorful use of detail, and it is of particular interest to modern readers because the Clerk of the Works knew so exactly what he was talking about. He knew how the seats had to be slanted so that the spectators could see over each other's heads, and he knew how much money the artist who decorated the lists spent on his paints. He knew how the armorers ran about with files and hammers and the way the knights glittered with goldsmiths' work and embroidery as they stood about waiting to be laced up. He knew the free speculation that went on in the audience, with judgments based on a black beard or a grim expression or the weight of a battle-axe. In fact, Chaucer knew all about the day of the "grete fight": the procession through the city streets, the scramble for places, the herald on the scaffold going "Oo," the unhorsed knight rolling under foot like a ball, the pause for refreshments during the afternoon, and the dances given afterwards for the foreign knights. This is not one of those conventionalized descriptions of a tournament such as appear and reappear in the romances. It is Chaucer's re-creation of a scene he knew well.

It was of course true that the tale of Palamon and Arcite was supposed to take place in ancient Athens rather than in medieval London, and Chaucer was aware that it would involve a little explaining when he gave a Greek knight a Prussian shield. But Chaucer says he refuses to believe that things were so very different in Greece, for "ther is no newe gise that is nat old." His was the same attitude towards history that led Shakespeare to introduce clocks into ancient Rome; and while Petrarch would not

261

have approved of it (Petrarch had a well-developed historical sense) it is interesting to know that Chaucer did not do it by accident.

In any case, Chaucer's audience was accustomed to seeing even Biblical figures in medieval hoods, and, as the Host remarked reasonably, a man must adapt himself to his auditors.

> "Whereas a man may have no audience
> Naught helpeth it to tellen his sentence."

Chaucer's ability to adapt himself to the point of view of his audience can be illustrated by his treatment of the heathen gods that operate in Boccaccio's epic. They are an important part of the story of Palamon and Arcite, but no fourteenth-century Christian audience could be expected to believe in them. Therefore Chaucer makes a slight but brilliant shift; he changes Mars and Venus, the heathen deities, into Mars and Venus, the planets. They are personified, of course, but they are nevertheless stars, exerting their potent force upon the characters by operating within the intricate astrological pattern whose details were familiar to every well-educated member of Chaucer's audience.[2] When Chaucer describes the victorious Arcite being thrown from his horse by the intervention of Saturn, no member of his audience would picture an actual heathen deity. They would visualize the planet Saturn bending its dark influences upon a doomed man.

The question of fate was of considerable interest to Chaucer, and he gives Theseus a speech that is an excellent restatement of Boethius' views on the subject. But Chaucer never felt called upon to maintain a consistent sobriety of mood, and when the subject of fate is discussed by the Duke's garrulous old father the effect is rather different. According to Egeus, there was never a man who died who did not live in some degree, and there was never a man

---

[2] Chaucer never permitted himself to get into any arguments on the still controversial subject of astrology, and he was one of the few medieval writers capable of using it successfully in poetry. There is, for instance, the pleasant little *jeu d'esprit*, *The Complaint of Mars*, in which Chaucer takes a love story by Ovid and translates it into astrological terms.

lived who did not some time die. This was a truly remarkable piece of wisdom, and must have comforted the populace greatly for the death of Arcite.

Chaucer cannot resist the impulse to be frivolous even on the subject of courtly love. He describes the unstable emotional state of Arcite earlier in the poem as being "now up, now down, as bucket in a welle," and when Duke Theseus finds the two rivals battling in the wood he considers it a huge joke. The "beste game of alle" to the Duke is that his sister Emily, for whom the two young men are striving so mightily with their swords, knows no more about their deathless love-longings than might a cuckoo or a hare; for they have failed to inform her.

The same lack of gravity in the presence of serious subjects is evident when Chaucer is describing the death of Arcite. He had been wounded when his horse stumbled under the influence of Saturn, and Chaucer describes with almost medical interest what had happened to his lungs and why a laxative would not work. He then remarks suddenly that if nature refuses to co-operate in healing a sick man,

> Farewell, phisik! go bear the man to church,

which is as flip a way of introducing a man to his own funeral as might be imagined. As to where Arcite's soul went after it left his body, Chaucer has no idea. He never went to that particular locality himself and he fails to find it listed in the "registre."

Chaucer's occasional irreverence does not seem in the least out of place against a tapestried background of temples and jewels and knights. The tale of young love on a May morning is not made less charming but only more entertaining by the touches of humor, the occasional moments of realism, and the streaks of medical and astrological lore with which it is interlaced. The Knight's Tale is a successful work of art, skillfully balanced and proportioned, and it is a long way both from the ponderous bulk of the *Teseide* and from Chaucer's original unsuccessful experimentation with Boccaccio's epic.

All the pilgrims agree that the Knight's Tale is a "noble storie," and the next in social rank, the Monk, is now asked to tell a tale.

This suggestion of the Host's evokes a yell of protest from the Miller. The Miller is drunk already and finding some difficulty in sitting his horse, but he has a "noble tale" of his own that he is convinced should follow the Knight's.

The Host points out to dear Brother Robin that better men than he are present and should come first, but dear Brother Robin announces that he will not stay with the pilgrim band unless he is allowed to do what he likes. The Host finally gives a permission that is something less than courtly:

> "Tell on, a devil way!
> Thou art a fool; thy wit is overcome."

The Miller remarks with dignity that he is quite aware he is drunk; he can tell by the sound of his own voice. Therefore the company can lay it to Southwark ale if there is anything wrong with his story.

The Miller announces that his tale will be of a carpenter who was made a cuckold by a clerk, and this preliminary synopsis brings forth an impassioned protest from the Reeve. The Reeve had once been a carpenter, but he feels that his objections are based on the highest moral grounds. It is wrong, says the Reeve loftily, to defame honest men and their wives with "drunken harlotrie," and the Miller can just as well choose another subject. The Miller refuses to choose another subject and embarks upon his tale in his great bull's voice because no one is able to stop him.

The Miller's idea of a noble story is exactly what might be expected of him. It is a rowdy piece of horseplay which depends for its humor on the stock subject that is still the basis of nearly every burlesque skit today. To the Miller's simple mind any joke based on an intimate physical function was automatically uproarious, and it would not occur to him that anyone might object to it.

> "Why artow angry with my tale now?"

Chaucer, however, was not the Miller. He knew that there were sections of his audience who might object strenuously to this kind of plain speaking and that an apology was again in order.

Chaucer's apology repeats and reinforces the position he took in the Prologue. The Miller tells his tale "in his manere" because there is no other way he can tell it, and if Chaucer omitted some of it he would be falsifying his material.

> For I must reherce
> Their tales alle, be they bettre or werse,
> Or elles falsen some of my mateere.

As Chaucer points out, anyone who does not wish to read the Miller's Tale is quite free to turn over the leaf and choose another story. There are plenty of tales in the book that are told by virtuous characters and deal with holy things. The author is not to blame if the reader chooses the wrong tale, for he had already clearly stated that the Miller was a dissolute character and so was the Reeve. Men of that kind would inevitably choose "harlotrie" for their tales. Moreover, Chaucer adds pleadingly, there is no reason to take too seriously what is only a joke after all.[3]

The Miller's Tale is really two dirty stories, held together by the thinnest of connectives. From the narrative point of view it is not one of Chaucer's most distinguished contributions to the art of storytelling, but from the point of view of portraiture it is a masterpiece.

An excellent example of Chaucer's achievement in this field is his portrait of the carpenter's wife. On its surface it follows the pattern supplied by the rhetoricians, and it is very similar in its design to those interminable portraits of noble dames, complete with golden hair, blue eyes, small noses and straight backs, that clutter up so much of the poetry of the period. But Chaucer uses the pattern here, not to give an idealized picture of a story-book heroine but to give a realistic picture of a small-town flirt.

---

[3] Chaucer found a certain support for this point of view in Jean de Meun, who put the whole question down to one of manners rather than of morals.

If noble dames of France use not
These words, the reason is, I wot,
Simply because the usance they
Have lost in this our squeamish day.

For if the fashion was, no sin
Or harm fair dames would find
    therein.

Jean saw no reason why a writer should not give "each created thing its proper name," and in this he must have been a great comfort to Chaucer.

Chaucer knows his heroine from her plucked eyebrows to the laces on her shoes. He knows what the silk embroidery looked like on her collar, and how low her dress fastened in front, and he knows her neatness and liveliness and the way her purse was decorated. He calls her a pet and a doll and a piggie's eye, and records with delight that she was softer than sheep's wool and prettier than a pear tree in bloom. He is charmed with her, from the ribbons on her cap to the gores in her apron, and considers her so "gay a popelote" that the reader forgets, under Chaucer's brilliant and affectionate guidance, that she is only a common little flirt of a kind that could be duplicated by the dozen in any town in any century.

Chaucer can do the same thing with a small-town dandy like her admirer Absalom. Absalom is a type that is almost painfully familiar, from his extraordinary hair-cut to his advanced taste in shoes, but Chaucer's matchless combination of accuracy and affection makes him immortal. He knows the value Absalom puts on the straightness of the part in his hair and the way the hair sticks out like a fan on either side. He knows the kind of shoes Absalom wore, with the leather cut in imitation of the rose window in St. Paul's so that the full glory of his red stockings can show through. He knows about Absalom's garters, and his talents as a barber, and the "lovely look" he gives all the ladies, and the accomplished way he can dance in the local manner "with his legges casten to and fro." He knows exactly how he goes courting, beginning with the careful attention to his hair and the chewing of a bit of licorice to make him fragrant and irresistible. In fact he knows Absalom, that "joly lover" and typical small-town dandy, much better than Absalom knows himself.

That such an effect could be achieved by a medieval court poet passes the bounds of ordinary probability and becomes a sort of minor miracle. Everything in Chaucer's background and training was against this kind of realism, which had no precedent, no moral lesson attached, and was not even about picturesque or well-born people. Absalom and his Alison are silly, immoral little commoners, without nobility, without intelligence, and on the surface without interest. Yet no reader can resist either of them when Chaucer has finished their portraits.

266

Chaucer extends this same intimate knowledge to all the details of his story. He knows the carpenter's house from the hole that the cat uses to the red wool cover that the boarder has on his clothes press. He knows where the carpenter goes to work, and the position of the blacksmith's shop, and the exact height of the bedroom window.

The tone of the talk is incomparable, from the old carpenter's pathetic little platitudes to the skittish coquetry of his wife Alison. She is indeed a "gay gerl," and even her "Tehee" when she claps a window shut has the sound of a real voice in it. The whole story is alive with Chaucer's delighted appreciation of the reality of his characters, and what might have been only a commonplace piece of "harlotrie" becomes a masterpiece of Renaissance color.

The author wishes it to be understood that no one objected to the Miller's Tale, not even the Prioress apparently, and that the only one who was inclined to grumble over it was the Reeve. The fact that the carpenter was deceived seemed to the Reeve an insult to the profession, although as a matter of fact the carpenter is the only kindhearted and decent individual in the whole tale.

The Reeve says that he could tell a fine tale about a miller if he were not too old to indulge in ribaldry. He then lapses into maudlin self-pity on the subject of old men in general, condemned to hop desperately after the pipe that calls only to youth, and the Host asks him to please stop sermonizing since it is half-past seven and they are already at Greenwich. The Reeve decides that he will tell his story about a miller after all, and hopes, in an aside, that his fellow pilgrim of that profession will break his neck.

The Reeve's Tale is set at Trumpington, near Cambridge, where a miller named Simkin owns a mill near the bridge there. Simkin is several notches lower in the social scale than the characters in the Miller's Tale, with morals to match, and he is exceedingly proud of his wife's birth and breeding because she was the daughter of a country parson.[4]

[4] Parsons were not supposed to marry, but they showed much ingenuity in circumventing the ordinance. Unlike the monks they were celibates by ecclesiastical rather than divine ordinance, and therefore the marriage was not considered void unless it was brought up in ecclesiastical court during the lifetime of either party. Parsons also took the precaution of hav-

Simkin's wife, remarks Chaucer, was as respectable as ditch water; but she made a fine sight on holidays, dressed all in red, while her husband walked in front of her with stockings to match. They had a daughter with a flat nose; and Chaucer, who was deeply interested in such things because he was interested in everything, gives a lively and detailed picture of how the three of them looked in bed when they were drunk and snoring.

It is not necessary to trace the activities of this little family, and of the two equally immoral young men who rode out from Cambridge to have their corn ground, except to say that the two young men came from the north of England and that Chaucer took an unusual interest in reproducing their exact speech. It was of course an easy joke—one that would make a Londoner laugh with a comfortable sense of superiority—to have the young men say "God waat" instead of "God wot" and "Thou is a fonne" instead of "Thou art a fool." Nevertheless the joke is carried through with an accuracy and a consistency that show Chaucer to have been something of a philologist. He was deeply interested in the sounds of varying kinds of speech, and he had a much quicker ear for it than any man before Shakespeare.

Whatever the rest of the company may have thought of the Reeve's contribution, the Cook is delighted with it. He claws the Reeve on the back for joy over the complete filthiness of the tale and is then prepared to offer a gamesome little anecdote of his own.

The Host is evidently beginning to have his doubts over the rapid downhill course of the tone of the stories, and hopes that Roger's story will be better than Roger's wares. His cookshop in London has flies all over the place, the food is stale, and many a pilgrim has had a painful experience with his parsley. He then warns Roger against getting angry at what is only a joke, and the Cook hopes that he will remember his own advice; for the story he is about to tell concerns an innkeeper.

The Miller told of town life in Oxford. The Reeve told of vil-

ing the ceremony irregular at some point so that it could not be legally proved against them.

lage life in Trumpington. And now the Cook tells of city life in London.

The hero is an apprentice named Perkin Reveller. He is a disorderly youngster, black-haired and as cheerful as a goldfinch. He is an accomplished hopper at dances and an expert at dice, and he is never in the shop when there is a procession going by. Perkin is discharged by his employer and sends his bed and gear over to a friend of his "owene sort" to keep for him; and at this point the story breaks off.

Since Chaucer knew London so well, it is perhaps a pity he did not finish the tale. Or perhaps it is not. The story was obviously going to develop into the same sort of scurrilous anecdote as the Reeve's Tale, which the Cook had so much admired, and there is a limit to how much of this sort of thing can be read with pleasure by even the most sympathetic reader.

Chaucer had an excellent sense of proportion. He was aware that a broad streak of earthy realism gave his poem a solid basis in fact that could be achieved in precisely no other way, but he was also aware that the cheap jokes which served as his point of departure could make *The Canterbury Tales* not only boring but inaccurate if there were too many of them. The Reeve's sewer of a mind was real enough, but equally as real was the delightful, civilized wit of the Nun's Priest and the endearing innocence of the Prioress.

For all his originality Chaucer was not self-conscious in his use of realism. It was not realism Chaucer wanted so much as reality, and he was wise enough to know that a Miller, a Reeve and a Cook are not the whole of life or even the whole of a pilgrimage to Canterbury.

CHAPTER XVIII

HE FIRST four stories in *The Canterbury Tales* are in the order Chaucer wished them to be, but the rest of the poem is a series of fragments. These fragments may be fitted together in a general kind of way, but most of the pieces are missing and those that remain are frequently without narrative links.

Some of the stories exist in what is obviously a first draft. The Shipman's Tale, for instance, was originally written with a feminine narrator in mind, for at one point wives are spoken of as "we." Chaucer clearly wrote the story for the Wife of Bath, who was the only married woman in the company. Then he had a much better idea in regard to the Wife of Bath and transferred the tale to the Shipman, intending, of course, to fit the lines to a male character when he had time.

Another example of this sort of thing is the Second Nun's Tale. Chaucer evidently wrote this particular saint's legend some time earlier, for he lists it among his works of holiness in *The Legend of Good Women*. It fitted easily enough into the character of the Second Nun, who was a colorless woman at best, but Chaucer forgot to change the line in which the narrator refers to himself as a "son of Eve."

These are the sort of inconsistencies that Chaucer could very well have stopped to iron out as he went along; and no doubt he would have done so if his talents had been of a neat, domesticated kind like Gower's. But Chaucer's head was full of more interesting characters than the Shipman and the Second Nun, moving about in a half-formed state in his mind, and he could not afford the time at the moment to make lesser individuals convincing. No reader will find inconsistencies in the tales told by the Wife of Bath or the Pardoner or the Nun's Priest, but a poet with people like these in his head really needs a secretary to do the mechanical work of smoothing out the lesser characters and making them consistent.

270

Among these lesser characters is the Man of Law, whose introduction to his tale bears no relation to his tale at all. The Man of
Law announces that his story is going to be in prose and apparently
it is going to be about love. Then follow five stanzas in rime royal
on the subject of poverty, most of it a paraphrase of Pope Innocent's remarks on the subject in the dismal treatise that Chaucer
calls "The Wrecched Engendrynge of Mankind." The Man of
Law then continues with neither a prose love story nor an illustration of the sorrows of poverty, but with an account in rime royal
of the woes of a noble lady named Constance.

The story of Constance is a typically medieval production. The
characters are not individuals; they are allegorized types portraying virtue, endurance, wickedness and so on. The writing is sufficiently well done and certainly a vast improvement over the
Anglo-Norman chronicle that was Chaucer's source, but the story
as a whole is alien to Chaucer's particular brand of genius. Gower
told the same story in the *Confessio Amantis* and it was right for
him; it was never right for Chaucer. For all his skill as a writer he
could not make the story of Constance more than a routine production concerning the woes of a beautiful and innocent heroine
who is persecuted for many lengthy pages before she is finally
vindicated.[1]

The real interest of the Man of Law's contribution lies in the
prologue, where he gives his reasons for having decided to tell his
tale in prose. It seems that a certain writer named Geoffrey Chaucer has used up all the love stories that might be told in rhyme.
This Chaucer is no expert "on metres or on rhyming craftily" but
he has covered the whole field of love stories, from the tale of
Ceyx and Alcyone to that of all the noble wives in *The Legend
of Good Women*.

---

[1] The story was a popular one, for
the Middle Ages liked to have its
heroines suffer. So did the eighteenth
century, if the success of Richard-
son's *Pamela* is any indication. So
does the twentieth, judging by the
number of popular novelists who
make their living by following the
formula that is known technically as
getting the heroine behind the eight-
ball.

"And if he has not seyd them, leve brother,
In one book he has seyd hem in another."

This passage sounds as though it might be the echo of a joke current in London literary circles. Perhaps it was Gower who complained one day that Chaucer had used up all the good stories, for if Gower wrote the *Confessio Amantis* after Chaucer had written *The Legend of Good Women*, as he almost certainly did, he would have found himself in exactly the same position that the Man of Law complains about. The probability that it was Gower who started the joke is increased by the fact that Chaucer continues here with an amiable dig at his distinguished friend. He has the Man of Law remark primly that at any rate Chaucer has not gone in for really "horrible" stories, like the tale of Canace's incest or the crime of King Antiochus against his own daughter. These two stories had been told at some length by "moral Gower" in the *Confessio Amantis*. Chaucer had himself been scolded for his choice of subject matter, and he seized with delight on the opportunity to cluck his tongue in solemn reproof over the "cursed stories" of his equally sinful fellow poet.

Chaucer wrote an epilogue to the Man of Law's Tale, and it is one that could hardly be dispensed with since it contains the Lollard discussion that was set off by the Parson's dislike of oaths. But it ends in mid-air and Chaucer never incorporated this particular fragment into the structure of his *Tales* as a whole.

However, there is one group of stories which Chaucer apparently conceived of as a unit and finished very nearly to his own satisfaction. Except for occasional interruptions it deals with a discussion held by a highly opinionated little group of pilgrims on the subject of matrimony, and it is sometimes called the marriage group.

The marriage group gets off to an unsurpassable start, for it is the Wife of Bath who brings up the subject of matrimony.

The Wife of Bath had no intention of starting an argument. It was merely her idea to precede her tale with a few opening remarks as the Man of Law had done. But to say that she was a talkative woman would be putting it very mildly and before she finishes her preliminary comments on the subject of marriage they have run to more than eight hundred lines.

The Wife of Bath has so vast an enthusiasm for her subject, and knows so much about it, that she surges along like some great natural force and is quite unstoppable. Not that any of the pilgrims, much less the awed and delighted reader, would wish to stop her.

Once, it is true, the Wife of Bath checks herself, but that is only because, in the excitement of the moment, she has temporarily forgotten what she is talking about. Then she remembers that her current subject is the funeral of her fourth husband and the handsomely shaped legs of one of his pallbearers, and she continues on her way with a brief crow of triumph.

> "A ha! by God, I have my tale again."

The subject of the Wife of Bath's discourse concerns the "wo that is in mariage." This is not the woe experienced by the Wife of Bath, who had a most enjoyable time on the whole. It is the woe experienced by her five husbands.

The Wife of Bath considers marriage a very fine institution (her feeling remarks on the subject of virginity must be read to be appreciated) but she is sure that every marriage has one basic requirement: the wife must have the upper hand from the beginning. It is not that the Wife of Bath bears any ill will towards men. On the contrary, they are her hobby, her chief occupation, her passion and her delight. But as husbands they have much to learn, and Dame Alice is a self-constituted expert at the art of teaching them.

Three of her husbands were ideal material, for they were old and rich and amenable. She reduced each of them to the necessary state of subjection by her remarkable and inimitable methods, and she cannot resist a chortle of joy as she thinks back on what she put them through.

> "O Lord! the pain I dide them and the wo."

Her technique was a complicated one and had many interesting angles, but the main idea was to get a husband on the defensive and then keep him there. If a wife has been going out a little too much at night, she should instantly inquire what her husband means by making eyes at the female next door. The Wife of Bath not only knew from experience that this sort of thing keeps a husband under control but, as she adds charitably, it "tickleth it his herte" to be thought a devil with the women.

We will now, says the Wife of Bath, drawing breath after two hundred lines of advice on the art of handling men, consider my fourth husband. He, it seems, was not wholly satisfactory, for he had a paramour of his own. Dame Alice paid him back for this so thoroughly that it is her opinion that the man must have gone to heaven when he died because he had already undergone the whole period of his purgatory on earth. But she did not really like him and she buried him cheap.

Her fifth husband was a different matter. He was an Oxford clerk boarding with her dearest friend, and she met him while her current husband was in London during Lent. The Wife of Bath valued Lent to the full as a social season, for it was a time

> "to play
> And for to see, and eek for to be seen
> Of lusty folk."

She had been attending vigils and processions and preachings and miracle plays and weddings all over town in "my gaye scarlet," an occupation which did not prevent her giving some of her attention to the Oxford clerk, young Jankin. She had had an eye on him for some time, as a wise woman will keep her subsequent husband in view well before the actual funeral, and she got hold of him through the time-honored gambit of telling him provocatively that she had dreamed of him the night before.

Although the Wife of Bath was twice Jankin's age, it was her opinion that he got a good bargain. The only flaw in their marriage was that her husband was a learned man and had the irritating habit of being able to quote every author who disapproved of women from the days of St. Jerome onwards.

Jankin was one of those young men who think they know everything about women, and Dame Alison was not at all surprised that he was a student at Oxford. It is a strange thing, remarks the Wife of Bath in one of her sudden asides, but no clerk is capable of

274

speaking well of a woman unless he happens to be writing the life of some holy saint. "By God! if women hadde writen stories" about men, what couldn't they tell about those sons of Adam!

Jankin was especially irritating because he owned a large anthology on the subject of women, a "book of wikked wyves," which ranged from the misdeeds of Xanthippe to those of Livia with additional insults from the church fathers and other sources thrown in. Jankin used to sit by the fire every night and read aloud extracts from this book with rich enjoyment. He was especially fond of the tale of a man who had a tree in his garden upon which all his wives, one after the other, hanged themselves; whereupon a neighbor rushed over and begged for a cutting from the tree.

The Wife of Bath did not care to listen to stories of this kind, and since her husband was evidently resolved "to readen in this cursed book al night" she attempted to right matters by giving him a sudden blow that tipped him over into the fire. Jankin, being no gentleman, got up and hit his wife over the head, whereupon she made it clear that he had murdered her. The battle ended with a repentant Jankin burning his book and giving his wife full sovereignty, and from that time on there were no arguments in that particular Bath household.

This brief résumé of the Wife of Bath's prologue does little justice to an extraordinary characterization. One might as well try to re-create Falstaff by analyzing half a dozen of his jokes. It takes no account of the exact tone of the Wife of Bath's voice, her digressions, her comments, in fact the whole uncanny *tour de force* of self-revelation. Above all it does not take into account her huge zest for living, the quality that has endeared her to even her most embarrassed readers.

The Wife of Bath is without doubt the most outrageous woman who ever walked into immortality. By her own account she is coarse, sensual, dishonest, immoral and a scold. She is even more free in her language than the Miller and the Reeve, and there is nothing about her married life that she considers in the least deserving of reticence. But she is so frank in her enjoyment of her career that she is as irresistible as Falstaff, who was a coward, a cheat and a liar but who nevertheless had a wonderful time of it.

Chaucer has given the Wife of Bath his own irrepressible delight in living, and her whole discourse is one whoop of satisfaction over the fun she has had. Even when she stops to think of her vanished youth her tone is characteristic and not in the least mournful.

> "Lord Crist! when that it remembreth me
> Upon my youthe and on my jolitee,
> It tickleth me aboute myn herte roote . . .
> That I have had my world as in my tyme."

Her world had none of the gracious, intelligent aristocracy of Criseyde's or the holy innocence of the Prioress'. But it was her world and she loved it.

Chaucer's portrait of the Wife of Bath shows how perfectly he was able, in his full maturity as a writer, to combine the real world with the world of books. His lifetime of reading is echoed at every turn of Dame Alice's discourse, and the lady herself has a dozen literary ancestors. Chief among them are two women from Jean de Meun's section of *The Romance of the Rose*. Jean's sketches are lively and well-colored, and they almost certainly gave Chaucer's imagination its initial impetus. But the difference is the difference between a watercolor sketch and a real woman. The Wife of Bath is no flat creation on paper. She is a living, breathing woman and anyone who meets her can hear the tones of her voice and recognize the turns of her mind.

The prologue to the Wife of Bath's Tale represents Chaucer's final triumph as a master of objective portraiture. Even Criseyde he sometimes paused to explain, but Dame Alice rattles along as though no author at all intervened between herself and her audience. Every word she speaks during her flood of helpful advice about husbands gives her own character away, and it is only the Wife of Bath who does not know it.

Chaucer offers not a word of his own in regard to her temperament or her characteristics. He chooses a much more subtle and difficult way of painting a woman's portrait. The measure of his success is the unescapable reality of the woman herself, a reality that he was able to achieve out of what must have looked like a most unpromising source—the stale old medieval joke of the dominant wife.[2]

After the Wife of Bath has finished off her five husbands, she announces that she is now ready to begin her tale. The Friar laughs and remarks that he seldom heard a longer preamble, and the Summoner seizes the favorable opportunity to insult a competitor. (He and the Friar were rival practitioners in the art of raising money from the public.) The Summoner remarks to the world in general that flies and friars try to poke their way into every dish, and a lively squabble is only prevented from continuing by the Host. He requests Dame Alice to begin her tale, and she says she will be glad to if she has the worthy Friar's permission.

The Wife of Bath begins her tale graciously, but she has not forgiven Huberd the Friar for interrupting her. Her tale, she says, is of olden times, when King Arthur ruled the land and there were fairies everywhere. Now, of course, there are no more fairies. The holy prayers of friars have removed them all, for friars are as thick as sunbeams in the land and have done away with all pagan beings.

> "For there as wont to walken was an elf,
> There walketh now the lymtour himself." [3]

Women may now go safely up and down, for under every bush and tree there is only the limiter and he will do them no harm except to their honor.

Having thus triumphantly achieved the last word, the Wife of Bath continues with her tale. It is not so much a story as an *exemplum*, a kind of expanded anecdote much in vogue in the London pulpits to brighten up the sermons and drive home the

[2] How stale the joke had become can be illustrated by the work of Eustache Deschamps. About this time he wrote his *Miroir de Mariage*, and completed twelve thousand verses of a dismal anthology that contains all the old familiar charges against women and a few new ones he had unearthed. It is a sobering thought that Deschamps was working in the same soil that produced the Wife of Bath.

[3] Huberd was a limiter. The term applies to a friar who was licensed to beg within a specified area.

point the preacher wished to make. The text of the Wife of Bath is that women should have full sovereignty in marriage, and her delightful fairy tale is merely to illustrate the point. The Wife of Bath is incapable of keeping strictly to her subject, and the tale is full of side excursions and even a whole extra story from Ovid.[4] The main plot, however, is about a knight of King Arthur's court who finds himself married to an ugly old woman. She informs him that he can have her young and lovely and faithless, or old and ugly and true. The knight, with a sudden lucky inspiration, replies that he will do whatever she thinks best.

> "For as yow liketh, it suffiseth me."

To reward this correct view of marriage the wife promises to be both beautiful and virtuous, and with the sovereignty thus in the proper hands the two of them live a life of "parfit joye." And may Jesus Christ send every woman, ends the Wife of Bath as piously as any preacher, the gift of a young, lively and obedient husband.

The Friar does not like this ecclesiastical note. He gives it as his opinion that all this talk of sovereignty is well enough for the clergy but that a more frolicsome subject is better suited to a pilgrimage. He knows a tale which would be the very thing, and it happens to be about a summoner.

The hero of the Friar's Tale makes his living as a panderer, thus producing the sins from which he can derive a secondary profit by threatening to report them to the ecclesiastical court. In all England there is not a "slyer boy" than this summoner. But one day he goes to levy tribute on a harmless old country woman (her name is Mabel) and meets a bowman in a wood. When they introduce themselves to each other the summoner passes himself off as a bailiff; for of course, remarks the Friar, he cannot confess his real identity.

---

[4] "Will ye heere the tale?" It concerns the wife of King Midas and her agony when he came home with two asses' ears on his head. This agony was caused by the fact she was supposed to keep the occurrence a secret, and such self-restraint was impossible. Therefore, like a good wife, she rushed out to the nearest marsh and told her secret to the water. Then she sighed in perfect relief,

> "Now is myn herte al whole, now is it oute."

"He durste not, for verray filth and shame,
    Say that he was a somonour."

Then the summoner asks the name of his new friend and discovers
that he is a fiend from hell.

The summoner undertakes to help his friend with his collections. They pass a hay cart, deep in the mud, whose carter is con-
signing his three horses to the devil, and the summoner thinks he
sees a good opportunity for the fiend. But the fiend explains that
he cannot collect the three horses because a curse does not count
unless it comes from the heart; and it is quite true that as soon as
the cart jerks out of the mud the carter is crooning over his greys.

The case is different when the summoner tries to blackmail old
Mabel with a forged writ, threatening to take away her best pan
if she will not pay him twelvepence. Mabel's curse comes straight
from the heart and the fiend promptly goes off with the summoner, promising him a more intimate view of hell than even
Dante was given. And may all summoners, says the Friar in a
closing prayer, learn to repent before they are thus damned
eternally.

The Summoner does not take this story in the playful spirit
which the Host strove so often to inculcate. Shaking with anger he
stands up in his stirrups and gives a swift, vicious description of
exactly where it is the friars live in hell. Then he starts his own
story, which is about a friar in Yorkshire.

The story itself is worthless, but it gives Chaucer an opportunity to make a beautiful little sketch of a begging friar in action.
The friar goes from house to house with his skirts tucked up for
greater speed, while a friend follows behind to jot down names
and amounts and itemize the villagers' involuntary contributions.
If there is no money in the house the friar suggests an offering of
cakes, or a bit of cheese or bacon, or even an article of bedding.

"A dagon of your blanket, leve dame,
    Oure sister deere,—lo! here I write your name."

There is an opportunity for an incomparable bit of genre painting when the friar arrives at the house of his friend Thomas.

279

Thomas is bedridden, and he has already contributed so much money to the friars' building fund that he is inclined to be peevish. But the friar enters with great aplomb and shoves the cat off the bench so that he can sit down himself (Chaucer's way of saying that he chose the most comfortable seat in the room). His tone is the hearty one a man puts on in a sickroom and it becomes almost too hearty when Thomas' wife enters. He rather overdoes the holy salutation that is expected of him when he "kissed her swete and chirketh as a sparrow."

The wife is excellently done, harassed by the irritability of a sick man and very sorry for herself. Thomas grunts at night like a pig and whatever she does there is no pleasing him. Having a guest makes her think immediately of dinner, but the friar lives only on the Bible and does not think of food. He will have merely the liver from a capon, with perhaps a bit of her best white bread, with the head of a roast pig to follow.

The anecdote—it is hardly more than that—ends on the same kind of note as the stories told by the Miller and the Reeve, and perhaps the Host turns to the Clerk of Oxford for the next story because he hopes to raise the tone of the pilgrimage a little. The Clerk has been riding along as quiet as a girl, which makes the Host suspect he has been thinking of scholarly matters. He asks the Clerk almost piteously to tell his story in plain English if he can so "we may understonde what ye seye."

The Clerk has his own small account to settle with the Wife of Bath and has not forgotten it. But he has remained quiet up to this point with perfect good temper, and his quietness is in striking contrast to the loud-mouthed squabbling of the Friar and the Summoner. These two have been calling each other liars with more passion than force, but when the Clerk's own turn comes he calls the Wife of Bath a liar in so gentlemanly a way that she cannot answer him back. It was the Wife's contention, and one strongly expressed, that no clerk is capable of speaking well of women. The Clerk of Oxford therefore chooses for his tale the story of Griselda, the most noble and most patient wife that ever lived. Nor did he invent it; he heard it from another clerk.

This clerk told him the tale at Padua, and his name was Francis

Petrarch. Petrarch, however, told the tale in the "heigh style" of rhetoric, and since the Clerk has been asked by the Host to avoid complicated literary matters he will omit the geographical flourishes with which Petrarch began his tale.[5]

Like the Man of Law's Tale of Constance, the Clerk's Tale of Griselda is really an allegory. Griselda is not so much a real woman as a personified symbol of the Christian virtue of patience, and the indignities which her husband heaps upon her to test her patience are a lesson to all good Christians to show a similar patience under the scourging of God. This moral interpretation of the tale was really Petrarch's, for Boccaccio was openly furious with the husband and sympathetic with Griselda, but it was partly the allegorical treatment Petrarch gave it in his stately Latin that made the story so enormously popular. Chaucer was not familiar with Boccaccio's version, but his temperament was much closer to that of the author of the *Decameron* than it was to Petrarch's. It is curious to see how his slight changes in the story bring him closer to Boccaccio's original tale, and how the English and Italian storytellers join hands over the head of the Latin moralist.

The changes are slight, however, for Chaucer had in mind a direct translation from his original. He approached Petrarch's Latin prose with almost the respect he had shown for that of Boethius. He had a French translation of Petrarch to help him, for Chaucer was not one to venture into the intricacies of the Latin language unaided, and he followed the story carefully as it came to him through his two sources. Luckily his respect was not so profound that he felt he ought to keep the tale in prose, and he

[5] It used to be argued that this passage proved that Chaucer had visited Petrarch when he was in Italy in 1373, but if the passage proves anything at all it proves that Chaucer never met Petrarch.

The story of Griselda was not Petrarch's production, but Boccaccio's. It is the tenth tale on the tenth day of the *Decameron*. Petrarch did not like the *Decameron* as a whole but he liked the tenth tale, and he translated it into Latin to give it a wider audience. He meant this as an honor to Boccaccio, but the result was inevitable. All over Europe the authorship of the poem was attributed to the great poet laureate instead of to his obscure friend, and Chaucer is merely following current literary opinion when he gives his source as "Franceys Petrak."

turned Petrarch's rhetorical flourishes into faultlessly handled rime royal. The tale is a complete pleasure to read for its smoothness and its grace, but there is no doubt that the subject matter is not as moving to a modern reader as it would have been to a medieval one.

The chief charm of the tale of Griselda from the point of view of *The Canterbury Tales* is that it makes so perfect a missile for the Clerk to direct at the Wife of Bath. Not content with this, the Clerk directs an envoi to her, composed in her especial honor but directed through her to all women. The envoi is a marvel of prosody, perhaps the most metrically skillful ballade Chaucer ever wrote, but it is even more of a marvel as an example of the Insult Courteous. All that the Clerk is doing here is giving the Wife's advice on handling husbands back to her again, with grave politeness but with just enough overemphasis to make it clearly outrageous. It is the sort of underhanded and apparently guileless performance that a woman must expect from a man who reads too many books. There is nothing in the envoi of which Dame Alice can actually complain, for the Clerk is merely giving her back her own statements—helping her out, as it were. But it was probably some time before the Wife of Bath again went out of her way to bait a scholar.

Chaucer originally ended this section with a rather colorless comment from the Host. In his revision he expanded the Host's remark into a lively monologue, placed it elsewhere, and continued this section instead with some new developments on the subject of matrimony.

The Merchant now enters the arena. He picks up the Clerk's concluding phrase and uses it in earnest. To the Merchant there is nothing funny about the subject of marriage, and he is incapable of understanding that the Clerk was only teasing. The Merchant is two months married, and the bitterness of his opening comments is only matched by the bitterness of the story he tells.

The Merchant's Tale is a startling sort of narrative, the oddest and in some respects the most powerful thing that Chaucer ever wrote.

On the face of it the Merchant's Tale is merely a routine story of courtly love. It tells of a "noble knight" who married a fair maiden. She is adored by a lovesick squire, and the squire finally attains his goal. All the romantic background customary in such a plot is here, from the gay wedding in which Venus smiles down upon the company to the walled garden with its laurel and its well. It was so beautiful a garden, says Chaucer, that it might have come out of *The Romance of the Rose*.

But the picture that Chaucer has painted to fill this pretty decorated frame is one of such horrifying realism that even the Miller could not have approached such depths. The knight, the lady and the squire are cheap, vicious, degraded fools, and the fact that they move against a background of gentility and fine talk makes the total effect twice as unpleasant as it otherwise would have been.

The effect is deliberate. Never did Chaucer work with more clear, cold, deliberate art to achieve a special end, and from the technical point of view the story is as brilliant as anything he ever did.

Chaucer's special end was satire. It was not a satire on courtly love, for Chaucer was only using the romantic background to heighten the contrast. It was not a satire on women, for it is much easier to forgive May than it is to forgive her husband January. It was not a satire on old age, nor was it one on marriage. Chaucer was writing a satire on fools, and more especially on the kind of fool who thinks marriage is only an excuse for a long rein on lust.

January, the "noble knight," was an old man before a sudden spasm of legality hit him and he decided to enter into, the holy state of matrimony.

> Were it for holiness or for dotage
> I can nat seye.

His wedding night is as unpleasant a thing as exists in literature, which, considering the sole purpose for which he married, was only to be expected. But it is funny as well as painful when the knight sits up in bed the following morning. He carols a song in praise of love like any courtly young gentleman from Troilus to Romeo, in his nightshirt, unshaven, the slack skin shaking on his

283

old neck, and a nightcap topping the whole. God knows, remarks Chaucer, what May thought when she looked at him.

January has a walled garden which he keeps for the same purpose as his bedroom, and he invites May to enter it in a paraphrase of the *Song of Songs*. The lyric is beautiful in itself, but hideous in January's mouth. The same thing is true of May's speech that follows. She speaks nobly of her soul and her honor and her wifehood, but all the time she is making signs to the squire hidden in the bushes.

It is perhaps a pity that so skillful a use of the principle of contrast should have been put to so destructive a purpose. There was one sort of fool for whom even Chaucer's great heart had no pity; but the bitter, abrasive quality of the story is so alien to his usual habits of mind that it is easier to admire than to read it. It is wholly lacking in the delight in his subject that usually forms the basis of Chaucer's best work, and the invitation placed at the end,

> Now, goode men, I pray yow to be glad,

is only a part of the most unpleasant jest in *The Canterbury Tales*.

The Merchant's Tale holds about the same position in Chaucer's work that *Measure for Measure* does in Shakespeare's. Both are brilliant studies in disgust, a fact that does not necessarily mean that they were written in weariness of soul or exemplify any kind of a personal crisis. Chaucer and Shakespeare were both capable of understanding a number of points of view without personally sharing any of them, the exact contrary of a man like Swift who wrote his bitter satires from the depths of his shaken soul. Swift was not an objective artist; Chaucer was. The impersonal nature of his poetry is at its strongest in *The Canterbury Tales* and it is this quality, of course, that gives the characters and the stories their remarkable variety. The Merchant's Tale is perhaps the most unexpected example of variety in the lot, but in any view of the *Tales* as a whole it fits as naturally into the scheme of things as does the rowdiness of the Miller or the urbane courtesy of the Clerk of Oxford.

Another example of this variety of tone is the Squire's Tale, which follows the Merchant's. The Squire is a good young man, and when he is requested to "sey somewhat of love" he obliges with a tale of pure romance. It is a shining little tale of the kind that the Middle Ages loved. Its atmosphere is "of Fairye," and this particular fairyland is the enchanted ground made familiar to-day through the Arabian Nights.

The Squire tells of a great king of Tartary and of his lovely daughter, of a steed of brass and a magic ring and talking birds. The story rambles about pleasantly with Chaucer apparently improvising as he went along. (It is one of the few tales for which a source has not been found.) Chaucer never finished the Squire's Tale, but he evidently intended it to be a series of episodes designed to persuade the reader

> That never yet was heard so gret mervailles.

It is a colorful, amiable, not too clever little piece, and one that is very well suited to the character of the Squire.

There is one aspect of the tale, however, that is not at all suited to the man who tells it. The Squire was not a professional writer. He knew how to compose rhymes and turn out the love lyrics in which every man of the period was supposed to be proficient—

> He coulde songes make and wel endite . . .

but as an amateur he would have no deep interest in the rules of rhetoric. The attack on these rules in the Squire's Tale is made by a professional, and an annoyed one.

This seems to be the one case where Chaucer lost his temper. After he had outgrown his early reverence for the rhetoricians his attitude towards that school of writing was one of amused courtesy, with sometimes the courtesy uppermost and sometimes the amusement. But in the Squire's Tale he loses his usual detachment, and for once it is Chaucer speaking rather than one of his characters.

Chaucer no doubt had a good reason for losing his temper. Perhaps one of his friends had approached him, with that careful tact which is so hard to bear, and had pointed out how frequently

Chaucer had violated, in the Prologue especially, those sacred precepts on the art of writing that had been handed down from Geoffrey de Vinsauf and Matthew de Vendôme. This would be like telling El Greco that he had made a mistake in figure proportion, or Franz Hals that he had carelessly let his brush strokes show; and it would be useless to point out to this kind friend that the artist meant it to be that way.

It is not unlikely that Chaucer's portraits of the twenty-nine pilgrims had been under attack for their violation of the rules of rhetoric, for Chaucer begins the Squire's Tale by refusing to describe the princess of Tartary at all.

> I dare not undertake so heigh a thing.
> My Englissh eek is insufficient.

Such a task could only be undertaken by a "rethor excellent," who could settle down to "describen every part" with all the battery of similes and metaphors and colors of speech that he had at his command.[6]

A few lines farther on, Chaucer again refuses to supply a description, this time of a banquet, and gives his reasons. In the first place it would take all day, in the second place no man can "reporten al," and in the third place it would be a waste of time.

A few lines farther Chaucer balks at describing the speech given by a certain knight at the banquet. The knight spoke suitably for the occasion; but Chaucer is not going to try to "climben over so heigh a style" and will therefore paraphrase the knight's words in ordinary language.

Chaucer finds that his tale has involved him in a second banquet, and again he refuses to pad his tale with unnecessary descriptions.

> What needeth yow rehearsen hir array?
> Each man woot wel that a kynges feaste
> Hath plentee.

[6] It is an illustration of the octopus-like grip that the rhetoricians had achieved on every kind of writing that Chaucer is actually using a rhetorical device here when he refuses to use rhetoric. An author's refusal to describe a given thing comes under the technical heading of "*occupatio.*"

But Chaucer's longest and most explicit thrust at the contemporary school of fine writing occurs when the princess goes for a walk. Every story, according to Chaucer, has its point; but if a writer starts to string out his story instead of getting to his point he will lose his reader's interest,

> For fulsomnesse of his prolixitee.

By prolixity Chaucer did not of course mean the actual length of a story. He meant its long-windedness. A long description like the one he gave in the Miller's Tale of the carpenter's wife, with her plucked eyebrows and her low collar, is an integral part of the story and does not slow it up in the least. But the elaborate descriptions recommended by the books of rhetoric were not designed to make the characters come alive but only to show off the literary cleverness of the author; and with that sort of cleverness Chaucer had no sympathy.

Chaucer was usually sure enough of his ground and of himself to ignore without comment the strict rules on writing that bedeviled his generation, or else to make fun of them. But when he was writing the Squire's Tale something evidently occurred that made Chaucer wish to make his position in the matter of rhetoric unmistakably clear.

Chaucer had regained his usual detachment, however, when he sat down to the Franklin's Tale. It is that delightful gentleman himself, and not Chaucer, who begins by apologizing for the lack of rhetorical flourishes in his story.

> "I lerned nevere rethorik, certeyn;
> Thing that I speke, it moot be bare and pleyn."

The Franklin says he knows a little about colors, but only those that decorate the flowers of the field or are used in dyeing. He knows nothing at all about the colors of rhetoric.

There is no sting in this. It has the same pleasant dignity that is characteristic of the Franklin throughout, and characteristic also of his tale. It would be difficult to imagine a gentler or more courteous story of gentle and courteous people.

287

Like the Merchant's Tale, the Franklin's Tale is of a knight, a lady and a lovesick squire; and the parallelism is almost certainly deliberate. The knight and his lady love each other not only as husband and wife but as friends and as equals. When he leaves Brittany to go to the wars in England she is terrified for his safety, particularly by the black rocks that line the Brittany coast and make her think of shipwrecks.

> "Would God that alle these rockes blacke
> Were sunken into helle for his sake!
> These rockes slay myn herte for the feare."

A very handsome young squire has loved this lady for more than two years, and he plucks up courage to approach her now that her husband is away. She tells him with a smile that she will give him his desire on the day that all the rocks are cleared away on the Brittany coast—by which, of course, she meant never. But the squire journeys to Orleans, the home of scholars and magicians, and for a thousand pounds arranges to have the rocks disappear by magic.

The lady thinks she will kill herself but lacks the courage. Instead she tells her husband the whole story, and he keeps an unmoved countenance for her sake—"glad cheer, in friendly wyse." His heart is breaking, but he cannot ask his wife to go back on her word. Her pledge, her "trouthe," is as important a thing to him as his own.

> "Trouthe is the highest thyng that man may kepe."

The lady goes out to fulfil her promise. But the squire is also capable of setting certain things at a higher value than his own desires, and refuses to hold her to her bond. He takes his leave of

> "the truest and the beste wyf
> That ever yet I knew in al my lyf"

and goes to break the news to the magician that he cannot pay him the thousand pounds. He only has five hundred, but he hopes to be able to raise the whole amount within three years.

288

The magician inquires with some interest if he succeeded in getting the lady, and the squire tells him the truth.

> "Right as freely as he sent hir me,
> As freely sent I hir to hym again."

Thereupon the magician remarks that he is pleased with all three of them and does not want the thousand pounds anyway.

This is a charming story, and Chaucer tells it charmingly. It is made still more attractive by its position at the end of the marriage group, for it rounds out the whole subject under discussion and brings it to an adult, civilized conclusion.

It is for the benefit of the Wife of Bath that the Franklin introduces the question of which sex should have the sovereignty in marriage, and this answer is: neither one. What marriage needs for its success is not mastery, but love.

> "Love is a thyng as any spirit free.
> Women, of kynde [by nature], desiren libertee,
> And not to be constrayned as a thral;
> And so do men."

The best way to achieve liberty is to give it, and whoever loves someone should be willing to concede him the right to be free.

The Franklin glances with a smile at the Clerk of Oxford when he speaks of patience. For the patience that the Franklin recommends is not the somewhat feeble-minded fortitude of Griselda but the sympathetic realization that everyone makes mistakes sometimes.

> "For in this world, certein, ther no wight is
> That he ne doth and seith somtyme amiss."

A man may be sick or unhappy or drunk or under the influence of an unfavorable constellation, and it is unjust to hoard up his sins against him.

As for the Merchant, the whole story of the knight, the lady and the lovesick squire is directed against his tale of three similar characters. The Merchant devoted long passages of bitterly ironic praise to matrimony, and the Franklin retaliates with three quiet lines of personal experience:

> "Who koude telle, but he had wedded be,
> The joy, the ease, and the prosperitee
> That is betwixt an housbonde and his wyf?"

All that is needed to make a successful marriage is that the husband and the wife shall be loving and honorable people; for, as the Franklin makes clear in his tale, any marriage is exactly as good as the people in it.

The Franklin's Tale ends the marriage group, rounding out to a charming conclusion the one section of his great poem that Chaucer completed more or less to his final satisfaction. It finishes a section that is not only a masterpiece of comedy and portraiture but a series of subtle variations played on a single theme; and no reader can prevent himself from speculating wistfully upon what *The Canterbury Tales* might have been if Chaucer could have finished the whole of it.

CHAPTER XIX

HE NEXT individual who walks out of the pages of *The Canterbury Tales* and into real life is the Pardoner.

The Pardoner makes his appearance just after the Physician has finished his tale, which is the tragedy of a noble Roman maiden named Virginia. The whole Middle Ages had wept over the story (Jean de Meun, Boccaccio and Gower are only three of the poets who rewrote it) and the Host is prepared to weep over it also. Nothing will comfort him, in fact, but a drink of ale at the nearest tavern and a comic anecdote from the Pardoner.

The Pardoner is delighted to oblige; but the gentlefolk of the company have a dark suspicion that the Pardoner's idea of comedy will be something they do not wish to hear. They request "some moral thyng" instead, and the unruffled Pardoner agrees. He heads for the tavern however while he meditates on his lecture, on the basis that

"I moot thynke
Upon some honest thyng while that I drynke."

Chaucer paints the portrait of the Pardoner by reversing the method he used with the Wife of Bath. The Wife of Bath was not a clever woman. She chattered along with a happy disregard of everything but the subject in hand, and was quite unaware that she was revealing herself in the process.

The Pardoner, on the other hand, is perfectly aware that he is exposing himself to the assembled pilgrims. He even takes a certain twisted pleasure in the occupation. He knows he is a damned soul, and admits it with the sardonic detachment of a man who has ceased to care. He speaks of his profession as being "Christes holy werk" in about the same tone that the Merchant used when he said it was a "glorious thyng" for a lecherous old man to take a young wife. And the Pardoner's portrait of himself, standing in the pulpit and stretching out his neck east and west like a bird perched on a barn, has the same sort of bitter mockery that characterized the Merchant's picture of January caroling in bed under his nightcap.

The prologue to the Pardoner's Tale consists of an exposé of his methods of raising money, with especial emphasis on his skill in manipulating gullible villagers. He does not care in the least what the pilgrims think of him for it, and is quite willing to use his twisted, mocking wit upon himself. For instance, the pilgrims all know that he has a voice as thin as a goat's (Chaucer mentions it in the Prologue) and it is easy to picture the bitter grin with which the Pardoner accompanies the statement that his voice rings out from the pulpit "as round as gooth a belle." [1]

The Pardoner gives the pilgrims, as it were, a sample professional discourse. He describes how he offers his credentials,

> "Bulles of popes and of cardynales,
> Of patriarchs and bishoppes I shewe,"

intermixing them with a little Latin to show the villagers how very holy the business is. Then he brings forth his bits of bone and rag and gives a lecture on their wonderful properties as relics. By these methods he nets an average income of a hundred marks a year. The text of his sermon is the statement in the Bible, "The love of money is the root of all evil," and certainly no one is better fitted to discourse on the love of money than he.

The Pardoner's Tale, like that of the Wife of Bath, is an *exemplum*, an anecdote designed to illustrate a sermon. The Wife of Bath's subject was sovereignty in marriage; the Pardoner's is love of money. Both stories are perfectly fitted to the people who tell them and both are the product of Chaucer's wisest and most mature technique.

The Pardoner's Tale is about three revellers who were dicing

[1] This same self-mockery is evident when the Pardoner interrupts the Wife of Bath in her prologue. The Pardoner is incapable of marriage and everyone knows it, but he remarks that he is thinking of taking a wife and would like so obvious an expert on the subject to "teach us younge men of youre practike."

and drinking in a tavern in Flanders in a plague year. Mentioning the subject of drink sends the Pardoner off on an incidental lecture on the dangers of indulgence. "A lecherous thyng is wine," remarks the Pardoner meditatively, his own drink before him on the table as he talks. He shows a thorough knowledge of the cheap, strong Spanish wines that were currently sold in London, adds some further remarks on the evils of gambling and swearing, and then turns back to his waiting tale.

The Pardoner's Tale has sometimes been called the best short short story every written, and perhaps it is. Certainly it is a model of dramatic construction, as tight and accurate as de Maupassant at his best.

The story is this. The three revellers hear that a friend of theirs has been slain by a certain thief, and they go out to avenge themselves on this thief, whose name is Death. An old man directs them to Death's dwelling place, which turns out to be a pile of gold buried at the roots of a tree. Two of the revellers stay to guard the gold while their friend goes into town, and they agree to murder him so that there will be one less to share the treasure. The third reveller has had the same idea and returns bringing poisoned wine. The two others kill him and then drink the wine, and the directions given by the old man as to the dwelling place of Death are proven to be correct.

Around this spare but effective framework Chaucer succeeded in building a short story that Poe could not have bettered for horror or de Maupassant for pace. There is not a line of action or a word of dialogue that does not contribute directly to the climax.

The story opens with the clink of a bell as a corpse is carried by the tavern door, and a mounting sense of the macabre is kept to the end. There is an added note of the supernatural in the figure of the old man who points out the path to the gold, for he wants to die and cannot. He keeps his own coffin waiting in his bedroom, and longs for burial.

> "Upon the ground, which is my mother's gate,
> I knocke with my staff, both erly and late,
> And seye, 'Leve mother, let me in.'"

293

Chaucer achieves, also, a skillful use of commonplace details to heighten the sense of the macabre by contrast. When the third reveller goes to an apothecary to buy the poison he is careful to explain that he has been troubled by rats and that there is a pole-cat in his chicken yard.

This perfectly maintained atmosphere of the macabre combines with a faultless narrative technique to give the reader the equivalent of a Dance of Death performed by a well-articulated skeleton. That this effect could be achieved by a poet like Geoffrey Chaucer, whose narrative talents lay in the direction of clear, realistic coloring and leisurely development of character, shows that very little is impossible to an intelligent and self-disciplined writer who is also a genius.

The Pardoner closes his *exemplum* with a flourish by inviting the men and women of his congregation to come up to his pulpit and do penance for their sin of loving money by giving him their coins and spoons and rings. Then, still with his bitter grin at all fools, the Pardoner leaves his imaginary church and offers his services to his fellow pilgrims. He has the "heigh power" to assoil them of sin, which will come in useful if one or two of them should happen to fall from their horses and break their necks.

The Host is to be offered the first pardon, on the basis that he is the one most thoroughly enveloped in sin, and the Host is very angry. He knows that he is no match for the brilliant, scathing intellect that is lodged under the Pardoner's limp yellow hair, and he therefore defends himself in the only way he knows. He makes so brutal a reference to the Pardoner's physical deficiencies that the Pardoner is for once rendered speechless. The Knight is obliged to take over temporarily the function of master of ceremonies and make peace between the two men before the little company can once more ride cheerfully on its way.

The next fragment in *The Canterbury Tales* begins with a story told by the Shipman. It is a mildly clever little tale of how a monk played a trick on a merchant, and is chiefly interesting because Chaucer wrote it first for the Wife of Bath.

The characterization of the narrator is extremely commonplace,

and the author is so anxious to have it understood that women are
extravagant that he labors the point unnecessarily:

> "The sely [hapless] husband, algate he moot paye,
> He moot us clothe, and he moot us arraye,
> Al for his owne worshipe richely,
> In which array we daunce jolily."

This is a long way from Chaucer's final version of the Wife of
Bath, ramping about delightedly in her "gaye scarlet" and firmly
convinced that it is a man's natural function to give his wife all his
money to spend on her clothes. It was a great day for *The Canterbury Tales* when Chaucer decided on a different and much more
subtle approach to the Wife of Bath and gave her original story to
the Shipman; but it is always interesting to get a view of Chaucer's
workshop and discover how little of his success was due to accidental inspirations and how much of it was due to hard work and a
constant willingness to experiment.

The Shipman's profession naturally put him at odds with the
whole tribe of merchants, and the tale of how a merchant was out-
witted serves suitably enough for him except for Chaucer's over-
sight in the use of "we." The Shipman's Tale, however, is not the
masterpiece the Host believes it to be. The Host is so susceptible
to even a moderately good story that he must have made an ideal
master of ceremonies.

The Host was a good man for the post in other ways also. After
an oath and a bellow of delight to express his approval of the Shipman's Tale, he turns with an abrupt change of manner to the
Prioress and speaks "as curteisly as it had been a maid." He would
very much like the Lady Prioress to tell the next tale, if such a
request would not inconvenience her in any way. "Now wil ye
vouche sauf, my lady deere?" The lady will vouchsafe gladly, and
the next story in *The Canterbury Tales* is hers.

Chaucer is even more a master of sudden changes in mood than
the Host. The story that follows the Shipman's rather coarse contribution is a small, flawless jewel offered by an innocent heart to
the glory of Our Lady. It is purely medieval in tone, but medieval
in the holy, trusting sense that the Prioress herself was medieval.

295

It is childlike in its unconscious cruelty and its simple division of the world into black and white, and yet it is as lyrically exalted as the spire of a Gothic cathedral.

There is an exquisite preliminary invocation to the Virgin, perhaps the most perfect single piece of pure poetry in Chaucer. Then the Prioress tells the story of a widow's son, only seven years old, who is attending day school. She lingers over her description of the "litel child, his litel book learnynge," and how he memorizes a song in praise of the Virgin for the Christmas season. He sings it going to and from school, and the Jews murder him because they cannot bear the song. But the Blessed Virgin, by a special miracle, permits him to go on singing the song he learned in her praise until his mother finds his dead body where the "cursed Jews" have hidden it.[2]

The Prioress' Tale is the one occasion in Chaucer's career when he managed to produce a perfect piece of art upon a religious subject. This does not mean, however, that Chaucer had at last achieved the fusion between his identity as an artist and his identity as a medieval Christian that had eluded him when he wrote *Troilus and Criseyde*. It is not Chaucer as a Christian who appears in the tale of the Prioress, any more than it is Chaucer as a pagan who appears in the portrait of the Wife of Bath. The motivating force in either case is Chaucer the realist. The Prioress' Tale is exactly as realistic as the Wife of Bath's because everything in it is exactly as she would have said it. The warmhearted maternal sympathy is hers, the innocence and the delicacy. There is even her courteous little reproof to the tale that preceded hers. The abbot in her story is not in the least like the ecclesiastic in the Shipman's Tale; he is a holy man, "as monkes been, or elles ought to be."

This is not to say that Chaucer did not sympathize fully with the

[2] The Prioress would speak of cursed Jews as naturally as cursed Turks. Anyone not a Christian was automatically damned, and the Jews were particularly damned because they had murdered the Lord Himself.

Even Chaucer would think of Jews as a diabolical abstraction, for it is doubtful if he ever saw a real one in his life. The Jews had been banished from England a century earlier, and Chaucer had no more reason for questioning the justice of their exile than he had for regretting that his home in Aldgate had been rebuilt in part with material from the ruined homes of the martyred "Hebrayk people."

tale the Prioress told, for of course he did. He was a man of his time in his religion, and he believed saints' legends with the best of them. But his approach to the story is not through the legend itself but through the character and personality of the Prioress. He approached it not as a Christian but as an artist, and it is as an artist that he made the tale immortal.

The Prioress' Tale moves the whole company deeply, and to cheer them up the Host looks around for something to make them smile. His eye alights upon "Geoffrey," whom even a less experienced man than the Host would recognize at once as born to be teased. The host offers some free comments on Geoffrey's manners and his waist measure, and then orders him to begin his tale in the peremptory manner that adults use towards the young. Geoffrey remains humble and eager to oblige. He only knows one story, a rhyme he learned long ago, but he proffers this hopefully to the company.

Geoffrey is as much Chaucer's literary creation as the Pardoner or the Prioress, and Chaucer gives him the kind of story that is perfectly suited to his limited supply of brains. He is about on the same mental level as the group of Athenian workmen who tried to produce a version of Pyramus and Thisbe with equally good intentions, and the result is that, next to Shakespeare's interlude in *A Midsummer Night's Dream*, Chaucer's tale of Sir Thopas is the funniest parody in the realm of serious English literature.

To realize fully the murderous delicacy of Chaucer's performance it would be necessary to read half a dozen of the Middle English metrical romances that he is parodying here; but even a casual reading of Geoffrey's contribution shows the inimitable combination of the sober and the absurd that makes Sir Thopas a thing of such delight.

It was of course easy enough for an accomplished craftsman to gently overemphasize the silly jogtrot of the originals.

> Listen, lordes, in good entent,
> And I wil telle verrayment
> Of mirthe and of solas;
> Al of a knyght was fair and gent
> In battle and in tourneyment,
> His name was sire Thopas.

Sir Thopas was born in the far-off, romantic land of Flanders (about the equivalent to an American reader of the far-off, romantic town of Detroit). He is indeed a lovely man; his golden beard comes to his girdle, his face is as white as the finest bread and he has a seemly nose. All the maidens sigh for his love when they should be asleep; but they sigh in vain for he is a very pure individual. He spends his spare time pricking through the forest in defiance of wild beasts like hares and deer. It is truly a forest of romance, for it is full of herbs like licorice and nutmeg and the birds sing so sweetly that even the sparrow hawk joins the song.

Sir Thopas experiences an adventure with a giant and a fairy queen, with a suddenness that gently underlines the somewhat jerky narrative style of Chaucer's originals. Then the tale takes exactly the same number of stanzas to describe, inch by inch, all the details of Sir Thopas' armor, for this is the sort of thing that no self-respecting English metrical romance would dream of omitting.

We then begin cheerily on Fit the Second, which begins at a point that is quite indistinguishable from Fit the First. Sir Thopas goes pricking off again, and is checked in the middle of a sentence by a yell of remonstrance from the Host. He offers the frank statement that Geoffrey is making his ears ache.

Geoffrey is completely baffled by the Host's attitude.

> "Why so?" quod I, "why wiltow lette [hinder] me
> Moore of my tale than another man
> Syn that it is the beste rhyme I kan?"

The Host refuses to argue the case; he informs Geoffrey firmly that there will be no more rhyming but that Geoffrey may, if he wishes, tell the company a tale in prose.

Luckily Geoffrey happens to know a "litel treatise" in prose that is full of instructive material. It is also full of proverbs—more than the assembled company probably ever "herd bifoore"—but it is nevertheless a merry tale.

A modern reader would not be likely to attach such a label to the story of Melibeus and his noble wife Prudence. Nevertheless, it must have been very popular in its own day for even the most

298

fragmentary versions of *The Canterbury Tales* in the fifteenth century usually include the "tale of Melibee."

The story is of a man who is dissuaded from taking vengeance upon his enemies by the overwhelming array of proverbs and wise counsels marshaled by his wife. It had been composed in the preceding century by an Italian judge, who was in the habit of giving each of his sons a guide to virtuous living as they came of age. This story went to his third son, who was training to be a surgeon. It was enormously popular in that age of self-conscious morality, and it had already been translated into French, Italian, Dutch and German before Chaucer translated it into English. Chaucer was never wholly at his ease in prose; but it can be said of his tale that at least its morality is impeccable and that it contains about a hundred and fifty proverbs.

The tale of the virtuous wife Prudence causes the Host to think with sorrow of his own wife. Her name is Godelief and she is not the kind of a woman to counsel patience. When someone has failed to bow to her in church, she rushes home and demands that her husband avenge her at once. She calls him a coward ape and offers him her distaff so that he can sit down to spin, because he does not at once rush out, knife in hand, upon the offending neighbor.

The Host finally drags himself from a consideration of his own marital problems and asks the Monk for a story. The Monk would have followed the Knight if the Miller had not interfered, but now it is a day's journey from London and the Monk has not yet had his turn.

Even now the Monk is not treated with the dignity due his rank. The Host trots out his favorite joke, comparing the virility of the churchman with the fact that ordinary men like himself are "shrympes." The Host means this disgraceful jest as a compliment, but the Monk becomes increasingly dignified under such treatment and evidently resolves to raise the tone of the pilgrimage singlehanded.

The Monk tells the assembled company a series of tragedies, a tragedy being, as he explains in his stately manner, the story of someone who began his life in prosperity and ended it in disaster. These victims of fate range from Lucifer to Julius Caesar, from

Adam to Hercules, and from Nebuchadnezzar to Bernabo Visconti.

Each anecdote is handled so briefly that Chaucer gives himself no room for any kind of character development, with the possible exception of his adaptation of Dante's story of Ugolino. Ugolino starved to death in prison along with his three little boys, and Chaucer had a sympathetic and affectionate spirit whenever he came to children.

Chaucer probably began his series of tragedies with a sober enough intent; but the effort of writing a number of stories on the same theme eventually wore him down, as did a similar experience in *The Legend of Good Women*. In the *Legend*, since he was writing in his own person, he could do nothing but stop writing, but in *The Canterbury Tales* he had the pleasure of letting his garrulous Monk be checked by another character.

It is the Knight who finally grows desperate and tells him to stop. The Knight likes cheerful stories and he has endured seventeen tragedies from the Monk with no guarantee that the worthy man will cease until he has run through the hundred tales he says he keeps in his cell. The Host chimes in with the remark that it is only the bells on the Monk's bridle that have been keeping him awake and offers him a much better idea for a story.

"Sir, saye somwhat of huntyng, I yow praye."

The Monk, lofty to the end, refuses, and the Host's eye lights upon another son of the Church. This is one of the three priests who are riding as escort to the Prioress and her sister-nun. His existence is noted in the Prologue and nothing more, for the idea of the personality of the Nun's Priest evidently came to Chaucer late. That it came to him at all is cause for gratitude, for his mock-heroic tale of the cock and the hen is perhaps the most delightful piece of comedy Chaucer ever produced.

The Nun's Priest, happy man, was very like Chaucer himself in the uncritical delight he took in the activities of mankind. So alike, in fact, are the creator and his creation, especially in the numerous sidelong comments scattered through the tale, that it is difficult to know where one man leaves off and the other begins. At any rate, the story is charming and so is the man who tells it.

300

The Nun's Priest's Tale is especially characteristic of Chaucer in its ability to tell an elaborate joke with a straight face. The language is elegant, the emotions are lofty and the sentiments learned. Pope used the same device when he employed the full battery of classical epic technique to hymn the world-shaking events that ensued when a London lady lost a lock of her hair; and *The Rape of the Lock* is the one example of the mock-heroic in English that can safely be introduced into the same company as the Nun's Priest's Tale.

The story opens with the same kind of brilliant, exact painting of scene and characters that enlivened the Miller's Tale. The owner of the hero and the heroine comes to life before the reader's eyes—an old dairy-woman with three pigs and a sheep named Moll. The reader even knows what she has for breakfast.

Within her chicken yard is a cock named Chauntecleer; and Chaucer's description of him is not only a masterpiece of exact observation of a real rooster but somehow contrives to make Chauntecleer as gallant as one of Froissart's knights.

> His comb was redder than the fine coral,
> And batailled as it were a castle wal;
> His bill was blak, and as the jet it shoon;
> Like azur were his legges and his toon; [toes]
> His nayles whiter than the lily flour,
> And like the burned gold was his colour.

Chauntecleer's favorite wife was named Pertelote. "Curteys she was, discreet and debonaire" and had been thus ever since she came of age when she was seven days old.

Madame Pertelote awakes one morning to find her husband, who sleeps on the perch beside her, behaving in a way that no gentleman should permit himself. He has been frightened by a bad dream, and, as a true son of the Middle Ages, Chauntecleer takes dreams very seriously. A large yellow beast with glowing eyes and black hairs on its tail appeared in his slumbers, and Chauntecleer fears that this is an omen.

Madame Pertelote does not agree with him. It is her opinion that her husband has been overeating. She is instructive enough on the subject of humours (the basis of all medieval medical practice) to overwhelm any lesser fowl, and ends by recommending a digestive of worms to be followed by a laxative of laurel and herbs and dogwood berries.

In an unwise moment, however, Madame Pertelote makes an appeal to literary authority by quoting Cato on the subject of the worthlessness of dreams. Her husband seizes on the opening, for where Madame Pertelote can quote only a schoolroom authority like Cato, Chauntecleer can quote a dozen "olde bookes" she never heard of. For nearly two hundred lines he defends the dignity and worth of his dream, as a warning vision vouchsafed him from on high, reinforcing his position with quotations from the ancients and relevant anecdotes. He ends with the clinching argument that in any case he does not like laxatives. "I hem defy," proclaims Chauntecleer, somewhat carried away by his own oratory.

Nevertheless he is too good a husband and too courtly a lover to end a discussion with his lady on so jarring a note. He agrees to forget his dream in thinking of the entrancing scarlet color around her eye, and he quotes that beautiful old Latin saying, *"Mulier est hominis confusio,"* (Woman is the confusion of man), which he then gracefully translates for his dear wife.

> "Madame, the sentence of this Latyn is,
>   'Womman is mannes joye and al his bliss.' "

After this Chauntecleer feels so gay that nothing can stop him, and "with a chuk" he roams gallantly up and down and unearths bits of corn for his seven wives.

There is, says the Nun's Priest, a tendency for worldly joy to vanish; and this is so striking a thought, he adds, that someone really ought to write it down. In this otherwise merry month of May, "Chauntecleer the faire" is faced with a dreadful doom. An animal with yellow hide and black-tipped ears, exactly like the one he saw in his vision, has broken through the old lady's fence of sticks and lies waiting for him among the herbs.

In describing the fox, the Nun's Priest delivers an apostrophe to similar traitors of antiquity, from Iscariot to Genelon. He then adds an equally solemn discussion of predestination, which is a subject discussed with "grete altercation" in the theological colleges and is especially suitable to this tragic moment.

Unaware of the doom that is so soon to strike, Pertelote and her sister wives are bathing in the sand and Chauntecleer is singing as merrily as any mermaid in the sea. Casting his eye upon a butterfly among the herbs, he suddenly sees the fox. The fox is very cordial. He well remembers Chauntecleer's dear mother and father and how much he enjoyed entertaining them both in his little home. He speaks of the elder cock's musical renditions, delivered on "tip-toon" with his neck stretched out and his eyes closed. Chauntecleer tries out the same technique, and as soon as his eyes are closed the fox seizes him and carries him off.

The Nun's Priest mourns his capture in some noble stanzas, evoking first destiny and then Venus and then Geoffrey de Vinsauf. If only he had that great master's rhetorical experience a wonderful bit of writing might result at this point; for this tragedy took place upon a Friday.

> "O Gaufred, deere maister soverayn . . .
> Why ne hadde I now thy sentence and thy lore
> The Friday for to chide, as diden ye?" [3]

Chauntecleer's seven wives take up the burden, with an outcry the like of which had not been heard since the fall of Troy. Pertelote wails like the queen of ruined Carthage and the other hens mourn as did the wives of the senators when Nero burned Rome.

The noise rouses the old lady and her daughters, and everyone rushes out to chase the fox.

> "Ran Colle oure dogge, and Talbot, and Gerland,
> And Malkyn with a dystaf in hir hand;
> The cow and calf, and eek the verray hogges."

[3] This mild dig at the rhetoricians is reminiscent of Thackeray's treatment of a fellow novelist in *The Rose and the Ring*, when he is engaged in describing the passion of a monarch among the egg-cups. "Had I the pen of G. P. R. James, I would describe Valoroso's torments in the choicest language."

The hogs, frightened by the shouting, squeal like fiends in hell. The ducks begin to quack, the geese fly up over the trees, and the swarm of bees escape from their hive. Someone found a trumpet and "powped" upon it, and the noise was worse than at any time since the Peasants' Revolt.

Chauntecleer, always the gentleman, retains his self-possession even in an exceedingly difficult position. He suggests to his captor that so motley a crew should be defied with proud words, and when the fox opens his mouth to begin the defiance Chauntecleer neatly flies away. The net result is that the cock resolves not to be so eager to believe flattery and the fox resolves not to open his mouth next time when he has nothing to say.

All this is Chaucer at his most characteristic, even to the courteous and unlabored little moral at the end. It is the mood in which he enjoys everything and respects nothing. He can include in the same comedy Macrobius on dreams, Bishop Bradwardine on free will, a medical treatise on the humours, and a dozen other aspects of his reading that went into his head as sober learning and came out as something quite different.

As for the grace of the thing, the perfect balance of the whole in spite of the cheerful diversity of its parts, it shows what a perfect craftsman the author of *The Parliament of Birds* had become without losing his originality, his wit, or his incomparable touch with anything in feathers.

The Second Nun, who was in the company of the Nun's Priest and the Prioress, probably did not sympathize with this light treatment of Bishop Bradwardine and Judas Iscariot. Chaucer did not expend much thought upon the Second Nun and he gave her a story he already had on hand, a routine saint's legend of the kind any nun might suitably tell.

Saint Cecilia was one of the noblest of saints, but, like the equally virtuous Constance she could hardly be called a real woman. Her blessed life and supernatural rescue from martyrdom gave Chaucer no opportunity to exercise his talent for portraying real human beings. The chief distinction of the Second Nun's Tale is that it translates the commonplace Latin prose of the original into some very fine verse, and there are stanzas in it that for musical beauty almost match those of the Prioress' Tale. But the Prioress' Tale is lit at every turn by the mind of a real woman, while the Second Nun's Tale, like the *A.B.C.* of Chaucer's youth, is hardly more than a devotional exercise.

In this it is in striking contrast to the tale that follows, which is so colored by the mind and personality of its narrator that the story itself is the least of it. It is not the Canon's Yeoman's Tale that the reader remembers but that wonderful fool, the Canon's Yeoman himself.

The Canon and his Yeoman, or servant, were not members of the original party of pilgrims but caught up with them at Boughton under Blee. Although the Canon is dressed "light for sumer" and has a burdock leaf under his hood to keep his head cool, he and his servant are running with sweat and their horses are flecked with foam.

Hot as he is, the Yeoman promptly embarks on a sales talk, for his master is an alchemist and could, if he liked, pave the whole road from here to Canterbury with gold and silver. The Host feels this would be a remarkable achievement, since the Canon's torn and shabby clothes indicate that his magical abilities have not been of much financial use personally. The Yeoman is delighted to find himself among skeptics and expands under a magnificent opportunity to give his exact opinion of the trade of alchemy, while the Canon steals rapidly away because there is nothing else for him to do under the circumstances.

The Yeoman's opening remarks are like the Pardoner's in the sense that he sets out to expose his profession, but the Yeoman is more like the Wife of Bath in the sense that he is unaware that he is also exposing himself. He is no intellectual; he merely wants to explain his grievances and has at last found a sympathetic audience.

The Yeoman thinks very well of himself, and could almost weep when he thinks how he has been mistreated. Seven years he has worked in the Canon's laboratory and all he has acquired for his pains is a ruined complexion, an old stocking for a cap, a smattering of alchemical terminology, and a terror of the "cursed craft" which nevertheless fascinates him in spite of himself.

The Yeoman has been the Canon's chief assistant in his experiments. He was the one who laid the fire and then swept up the pieces when they blew up, as they invariably did. He gives a touching picture of one of these explosions and the way the metals burst from the retort and "lepe into the roof." Everyone then stands around and argues as to what caused the experiment to blow up this time. Some think the wood on the fire was wrong. Some think the fire was blown up incorrectly. ("Then was I feared, for that was myn office.") And the Canon's own opinion is that the pot was clearly inferior. Then they sweep the mess up, sift it, and hopefully begin all over again.

The Yeoman's rag bag of a mind is a confused jumble of self-pity, hatred for his master, an awed respect for the mysterious occupation of alchemy and a cocky display of erudition. Throughout the whole of his lecture he keeps bringing in stray bits of information that he has forgotten to mention before.

> "Yet forgat I to maken rehersaille
> Of waters corosif, and of lymaille,
> And of bodies mollificacioun,
> And also of hir induracioun;
> Oiles, ablucions, and metal fusible. . . ."

Never did a man have a better collection of technical jargon in his head or less idea of what he was talking about.

The Canon's Yeoman's Tale is not so much a tale as a continuation of the characterization of the Canon's Yeoman himself. It is an account of how a good priest was tricked by a wicked canon into paying forty pounds for a worthless alchemical formula, and the Yeoman, intent on his tale, is not aware that he is displaying at every turn his own stupid and vindictive little mind.

The Yeoman's chief idea is to display the wickedness of the whole race of canons who go in for alchemy, and every few lines he stops off to explain anxiously that the canon is the villain of the piece. Of course he actually is not. He is merely a good sleight-of-hand artist, and it is the priest's greed, his unethical desire to get something for nothing, that forms the basis of the story. But in the Yeoman's estimation the priest is a very good man, one of "Christes peple" and the innocent victim of a black-hearted knave. The canon, however, is a "fiend." He is also the "roote of all treacherie," a "wrecche," "this false chanoun—the foule fiend hym fetch," "this cursed man," the "roote of all cursednesse," and so on. In case anyone still misses the point, the Yeoman also adds parenthetical comments pointing out the canon's villainy. "Now tak heede of this chanoun's cursednesse!" "Taketh heede now, sires, for Goddes love!"

All this anxious pointing out of the wickedness of the canon is not so much the Yeoman's characterization of the canon as Chaucer's characterization of the Yeoman. It is a curious misunderstanding of Chaucer's adult and objective art that anyone should think he wrote the story because he himself had been tricked by an alchemist and was angry about it. It is not Chaucer who is angry. It is the sweating fool on horseback whom the pilgrims met near Boughton under Blee.

To the end, the Yeoman remains true to his own muddled little mind. He becomes involved in the metaphysical aspects of what he calls the "slidynge science" and manages to become quite as confused as when he listed all the technical terms he knew. He wrestles briefly with Arnold de Villa Nova, Hermes Trismegistus and Plato, and comes to no result at all. But, as he himself candidly admits, the "wit that men have now-a-dayes" is not considerable, and this remark may well serve as a suitable epitaph for the Canon's Yeoman.

The final fragment of *The Canterbury Tales* was designed to coincide with the pilgrims' arrival in Canterbury and it begins with the enchanting little geographical comment that is so characteristic of Chaucer's easy friendliness with his readers.

> Wot ye not where ther stant a litel toun
> Which that y-cleped is Bobbe-up-and-doun,
> Under the Blee, in Caunterbury way?

Now that the houses of Canterbury are in sight, the Host concludes it is time the Cook should tell a tale.[4]

---

[4] The Cook had already begun one tale earlier in the pilgrimage. Perhaps Chaucer intended to give the tale of Perkin Reveller to another character, or, since it was unfinished, to omit it. Or perhaps the Cook is being asked here for his second tale, since each pilgrim was supposed to tell two stories on the way to Canterbury.

The Cook is in a bad way. He is so sleepy he can hardly sit his horse, as the Manciple points out. There was no need, however, for the Manciple to conclude that the Cook was drunk, much less to call him a "stynking swine." The Cook is so furious he promptly falls off his horse and it takes the combined efforts of the pilgrims and "grete shoving both to and fro" before he can be hoisted into the saddle again.

Since the Cook is incapable of a tale the Manciple tells one instead. The Manciple's is a moral tale of a crow who talked out of turn and was punished by having all his snowy feathers turn black. In case anyone might miss the point of his discourse, the Manciple then continues with all the advice his old mother used to give him on the wisdom of keeping one's mouth shut—nearly fifty lines of a smug unctuousness that comes well from a gabby little meddler like the Manciple. Like most of Chaucer's characters the Manciple has a happy inability to see himself as others see him, and if anyone had mentioned the matter to him he would doubtless have replied indignantly that he spent his life obeying his old mother's commands to the letter.

The next, and last, tale is the Parson's. Chaucer had the general framework of *The Canterbury Tales* clear in his mind and when he wrote this final link in the tales he was assuming that all the missing tales would shortly after be fitted in. Therefore the Host remarks that every member of the company has been heard from except the Parson. "Every man, save thou, hath toold his tale."

The Parson is in an unbending mood. In answer to the Host's innocent hope that he will give them a cheerful tale the Parson replies austerely that he has no wish to "tellen fables and swich wrecchednesse." Also, he will tell his tale in prose, for he has a very low opinion of verse. On the other hand, he promises that it will be a "merrie tale" and one that will bring the pilgrimage to a fitting conclusion. The Host is full of anticipation but requests him to tell his story briefly, for the sun is going down.

The sun is indeed going down, and it never rises again upon *The Canterbury Tales*.

Chaucer had an excellent idea in mind when he planned the Parson's Tale to close the series. He was going to remind his readers of a greater pilgrimage than the one to Canterbury,

> To shewe you the way, in this viage,
> Of thilke parfit glorious pilgrimage
> That highte Jerusalem celestial.

The Parson, whose gentle holiness had already been indicated in the Prologue, was unquestionably the right man to round out *The Canterbury Tales* and give them his benediction.

The difficulty was that no parson could give them his benediction. Chaucer knew very well, and did not need a churchman to tell him, that even symbolically there was little connection between the soul's pilgrimage to heaven and his rowdy troop of earthlings riding to Canterbury.

Dearly as he loved his characters, he knew that his love was a sin. In the "foul prison of this life," as the Knight puts it, a good Christian should be intent only on the welfare of his own soul and have no eyes for the fascinating oddities of his fellow prisoners. Above all he should never believe them to be important as Chaucer believed them to be important. For Chaucer was a poet of the earth, and his religion taught him that the earth was sin.

Therefore Chaucer wrote the interminable piece of prose that calls itself the Parson's Tale. It is a sermon on penitence, divided and subdivided in the usual medieval manner, with a long additional treatise on the seven deadly sins. It is written in the laborious style that was Chaucer's usual one in prose, heavy, full of effort and painfully in earnest. It is a man flogging his pen to do something he knows should be done, and the words that obey him with such enchanting grace when he writes of the things he loves now plod like hooded penitents while he writes of sin.

Still worse is to come. It was obviously not the subject of sin in general that haunted Chaucer's mind when he started his essay on penitence. It was his own particular sin, the sin of having spent a lifetime as a poet loving the wrong things.

The final words of the Parson's Tale are "mortificacion of synne," and Chaucer proceeds to mortify it. He takes his leave of the readers of *The Canterbury Tales* in words that are tragic under the circumstances. For it is a painful thing, and required in no court of law, that a man should testify against himself.

This is Chaucer's testimony:

I beseech yow mekely, for the mercy of God, that ye
pray for me that Christ have mercy on me and forgive
me my giltes; and namely of my translacions and
enditynges of worldly vanitees, the which I revoke
in my retracciouns.

Then Chaucer goes on to summon to the bar, by name, all his sins.
They are as follows: *The Book of the Duchess, The House of
Fame, The Parliament of Birds,* all the shorter lyrics that treat of
love, *Troilus and Criseyde, The Legend of Good Women,* and
every section of *The Canterbury Tales* that does not deal with
saints' legends or lessons in morality.

These are the sins for which Chaucer prayed Jesus Christ to
forgive him. They include the whole body of his poetry except
for the "bookes of legendes of seintes, and homilies, and moralitee,
and devocion." They include the whole of his art. They include,
almost, the whole of his life.

Chaucer wrote this retraction "so that I may be oon of hem at
the day of doom that shall be saved." No reader is going to be-
grudge Chaucer his peace of mind, and every grateful admirer of
Pandarus and the Eagle and the Wife of Bath may well pray that
their creator found the soul's peace he was searching for. He gave
happiness to so many people that he was certainly entitled to some
measure of it for himself.

Any man who outstrips his century is likely to find himself at
war with his century, and Chaucer was no exception either to the
privilege or to the penalty. He made one choice with his mind,
and it is to be hoped that through it he found quietness of spirit.
But he made another choice with his heart, and it is the choice of
his heart that endures. No formal retraction on a bit of paper
could blot out Pertelote and the Carpenter's Wife and the Miller
and the Franklin and the Wife of Bath, any more than an earlier
retraction could blot out Pandarus and Criseyde. Chaucer never
burned the papers on which they lived and moved and breathed,
and no written act of recantation could destroy what his love had
already made immortal.

CHAPTER XX

HAUCER did not finish *The Canterbury Tales*, but he allowed some of its sections to circulate among his friends. The Wife of Bath naturally bounced her way into everyone's affections, and Chaucer himself invokes her as an authority in a short poem he wrote to a friend of his.

The poem is a ballade on the subject of marriage and was sent to a man named Bukton, presumably after his intent to marry had just been announced. The recipient of the ballade was probably Sir Peter Bukton of Yorkshire or Sir Robert Bukton of Suffolk; but whoever he was, Chaucer was on sufficiently intimate terms with him to trust him to understand a joke.

Chaucer's last warning to a once happy bachelor depends for its comedy on the same kind of solemn overemphasis that he used in the tale of Chauntecleer. He writes with deep gravity, as one man to another, of the deadly peril common to all men, and finally offers his friend the Wife of Bath's views on the subject as a last resort to save him from rushing madly into the dire captivity of matrimony. The tone is about the same as the one achieved at a farewell dinner given by the groom's bachelor friends, except that Chaucer is a major poet; and if "maister Bukton" was the man he should have been, he must have derived more enjoyment out of Chaucer's little offering than out of any other wedding present he received.

Chaucer's friends were a fortunate group of people. The kind of banter that is usually lost over a dinner table Chaucer tucked into the intricate shape of a ballade and gave his friends to keep. He gave one of the Scogans, for instance, a portly grey-haired gentleman like himself, a ballade of reproof on the conduct of his love affairs.[1]

[1] This was probably Sir Henry Scogan. After Sir Henry became tutor to the sons of Henry IV he wrote them a ballade of good advice that quotes one of Chaucer's poems entire and refers to him several times as "maister."

Again there is the solemn overemphasis and the portentous gravity. The eternal statutes of heaven have been shattered, for never was rain intended to come from the fifth sphere where Venus resides. But Scogan has broken Venus' heart and the bright goddess is drowning the earth in her tears; for Scogan has rebelled against the laws of love and has told his lady he will stop being her servitor at Michaelmas unless she takes pity on him. It is not so much Scogan about whom Chaucer is concerned as certain friends of his who also are "hoar and rounde of shape." The goddess' son Cupid may end by being annoyed with all portly and grey-haired men, who otherwise "ben so likely folk in love to speed," and it is Chaucer's contention that men of "oure figure" ought to be more careful.

After having given this remarkable explanation of a recent spell of heavy rain, Chaucer becomes even more grave in his tone. He warns Scogan against dreaming for a moment that he can dismiss the whole thing as a joke and that his old friend is trying to "rhyme and play" in his dotage. As a matter of fact he does not make rhymes any more, says Chaucer in faultless rhyme. His time for such things ended with his youth. He now inhabits a solitary wilderness, forgot by all, and may his friend sometimes think of him there. Farewell.

This sort of private joke demands a common background in Chaucer's readers. It was written to be read by men who had been brought up on the amatory vaporings of the French school of love poetry and who would know a good parody if they saw one, just as Sir Thopas was written to be read by men who were familiar with Middle English metrical romances. The same is true of Chaucer's ballade to Bukton, and no medieval reader would be likely to make the mistake some modern readers have made and take either of them seriously. A joke is a risky thing to transmit to another century, especially the Chaucerian brand of humor which is invariably delivered with a straight face, and to read Chaucer successfully it is necessary to return to his own century with him as far as the general background of his work is concerned.

It is not only Chaucer's comic poems that make this sort of demand upon his readers. He wrote a beautiful ballade called *Truth* which at one time used to be criticized because the envoi was addressed to "thou vache," which is French for cow. It was not Chaucer's taste that was at fault but the information of his critics. Any of Chaucer's contemporaries would have known at once that Chaucer was not addressing his poem to a cow; he was addressing it to Sir Philip de la Vache, the son-in-law of Sir Lewis Clifford.

The ballade is a serious and affectionate one, and it contains the most explicit statement any reader is likely to find of Chaucer's own creed. Chaucer valued the word "truth." Its contemporary spelling is "trouthe," which carries with it the additional connotation of fidelity, or good faith, and was the quality that both Criseyde and the heroine of the Franklin's Tale valued so highly.

To Chaucer this word was the basis of all self-respect, and especially of the self-sufficiency he had learned from Boethius.

> Flee from the press, and dwelle with soothfastnesse,
> Suffice unto thy good, though it be small.

"Rule wel thyself." Do not try to compete with other men, but keep to your own standards of conduct. Do not try to reform them; reform yourself, and keep to the best that is in you.

This is not the kind of advice that would have suited a reformer like Wyclif, but Chaucer was no reformer. He believed that it was useless for a man to "tempest" himself to change the world, since lasting change could only come through the self-reform of the individual. He believed also, and it is a heroic conception, that truth is a strong enough force to act as a man's whole deliverance if only it is trusted.

> Hold the high wey, and let thy ghost [spirit] thee lead,
> And truth shall thee deliver.

It is curious that this advice should have been delivered to Clifford's son-in-law, for Sir Lewis was laboring hard in the nineties to "redresse" the crookedness of the world. In 1395 his activities, and those of the Lollard Knights in general, came to a climax. Sir Lewis Clifford, Sir Richard Stury and some other friends of Chaucer tacked up publicly on the door of St. Paul's Cathedral the famous Lollard Conclusions. The Conclusions called for a radical program of religious and social reform, condemning among other things war, capital punishment, religious images, church endowments, pilgrimages and the celibacy of the clergy.[2]

The Lollard Conclusions so shocked the bishops that they hurried to Ireland to complain directly to King Richard, and Richard returned to exact an oath from Stury that he would never do such a thing again on pain of death.

The weight of medieval church authority was very heavy, and when it descended on Sir Lewis Clifford it was too much for him. He recanted, and his subsequent state of mental agony is testified to by his tragic will of 1404.

> I, Lowys Clifford, fals and traytor to my Lord God
> and to all the blessed company of Hevene, and unworthi
> to be cleped a Christen man, make and ordeyne my
> Testament . . . I most unworthi and Goddis traytor,
> recommaunde . . . my wrechid carcass to be buried in
> the ferthest corner of the chircheyard . . . that on
> my stinking carcass be but a black cloth . . . ne stone . . .
> whereby any man may wit where my stinking carcass
> lieth.

That such a mood could come upon a good and honorable man like Sir Lewis Clifford shows how inevitable it was that Geoffrey Chaucer should end *The Canterbury Tales* by retracting the whole of it.

That innocent and gracious lady, Queen Anne, died under a lesser shadow of the same terror, for she was obliged to repent on her deathbed of the sin of having been too fond of parties. She died rather suddenly at the royal manor of Sheen in the Whitsuntide season of 1394, and she left her young husband almost frantic

---

[2] This last was a graver social problem than might appear at first glance. Nearly all government clerks, for instance, were in minor orders. This meant that the average Westminster accountant could not marry and settle down to a wife and family but lived with the other clerks in a series of male dormitories or "households." The results achieved by this kind of artificial segregation among normal young men are sufficient to explain the Lollard objection to the celibacy of the clergy.

with grief. He tore down Sheen because she had died there and it was almost a year before he was willing to revisit any of the places where they had been happy together.

Richard gave his wife a magnificent funeral, with the greatest display of wax lights that had ever been seen in England. He also gave her an unquiet one. The Earl of Arundel, Gloucester's great ally, arrived late, and Richard was so furious at the insult to his adored Anne that he snatched a wand from a verger and knocked the Earl to the ground. From the ecclesiastical point of view Arundel's blood polluted the Abbey, and the whole ceremony had to be suspended until the Abbey could be reconsecrated. Every excuse can be made for Richard, for he was only twenty-seven years old and incapable of hiding at the moment either his hatred of Arundel or his love for Anne.

This same year of 1394 saw the burial of Richard's aunt by marriage. Constance of Castile, the wife of John of Gaunt, died on the fifth of June, and the Duke of Lancaster set out as soon as he decently could to get a dispensation from the Pope so that he could marry Katherine Swynford. He married her in Lincoln, and Chaucer's sister-in-law took precedence over every woman in England except the Queen. The Duke of York was pleased with his brother's marriage in his easygoing and kindly way, but the Duke of Gloucester was furious. As for the Duchess of Gloucester, she and the Countess of Arundel both swore they would never honor the upstart by calling her sister.

King Richard himself married again almost at once, but the marriage was nothing but a political arrangement. His bride was a self-contained little girl of eight years named Isabella, the daughter of the King of France. Sir Lewis Clifford and Sir John Clanvowe were two of the three ambassadors who helped arrange the union, and Richard went to Calais to be married as the climax of a glittering series of festivities that were planned for him by the French.[3]

[3] Deschamps was not invited to the ceremonies, and it was the shock of his life. He, the self-appointed historiographer royal, who had devoted such a large part of his poetic career to recording the births, deaths and marriages of the great! He was so furious about it that he broke his pen.

The new Queen of England was installed with suitable ceremonies, but there was nothing an eight-year-old child could do for
King Richard. His unstable emotionalism had been very largely
held in check by his love for Anne; now it could find no permanent
object to attach itself to, and the unhappy Richard plunged deeper
and deeper into a riot of extravagance whose origin was certainly
despair.

The court took its tone from the King. There was already a
weariness in court life in the nineties, a bored *fin de siècle* point of
view in which pessimism was fashionable and enthusiasm was child-
ish and old-fashioned. The tone came from France, where Deschamps was writing ballades whose shallow gloom made them increasingly popular, and the pleasure-seeking court of Richard was
in the same state of unsatisfied weariness.

Meanwhile the fashions grew increasingly fantastic. New styles
in hats and hairdressing followed each other with bewildering
rapidity, and clothing became very strange. Gowns were either
voluminous or so tight that it was impossible to bend over without
forethought, and a ruff-like collar was introduced which buttoned
up so high on the neck that it must have been a plague to the ears
of men. Taxes soared, and there was a general sense of social irresponsibility that the more sober elements in the country eyed with
deep misgiving.

It was probably at about this time that Chaucer wrote the ballade called *Lack of Steadfastness*. Chaucer was not Gower, and he
was seldom moved to comment unfavorably upon the state of the
world. But so open was the scramble for money and position
around Westminster and so universal the contempt for the old-
fashioned virtue of honesty that even Geoffrey Chaucer was obliged
to protest as a troubled century drew to its unlamented end.

Lack of Steadfastness is a kind of companion piece to Chaucer's
ballade on *Truth*, for it illustrates what happens when the com-
modity that Chaucer recommended to Sir Philip de la Vache is no
longer valued. There was once a time in England, says Chaucer,
when a man's word could be trusted.

> Somtyme this world was so stedfast and stable
> That mannes word was obligacioun.

But now the world is turned upside down, no man can trust his neighbor, and "all is lost for lak of stedfastnesse."

In this particular matter royalty itself has not set a very good example, and Chaucer addresses his envoi to King Richard.

> O prince, desire to be honorable,
> Cherish thy folk and hate extorcioun . . .
> Dread God, do law, love truth and worthinesse,
> And wed thy folk again to stedfastnesse.

This to Richard Plantagenet, who in the latter years of the decade was distinguishing himself by a lack of steadfastness that even the Stuart kings at their most irresponsible could hardly have matched.

All that was steadfast in Richard by now was his hatred for the Earl of Arundel and the Duke of Gloucester. He never forgot they had murdered Simon Burley and sent Robert de Vere into exile. When de Vere died abroad Richard sent for his body so that it might be buried in his native Essex, and had the coffin opened so that he might stroke the dead man's face.

In 1397 Richard decided that eight years of constitutional rule had at last made him strong enough to avenge his friends. He attacked suddenly, and successfully, for his military position was secure. Gloucester and Arundel were indicted for treason, and paid for the acts of the Merciless Parliament with their lives.

No one else died in Richard's hour of revenge, so that in one sense he was more moderate than Gloucester had been; and the murder of one's relatives was not so uncommon in medieval times that his subjects would have failed to forgive him. Unfortunately Richard grew giddy with success. He made the fatal mistake of deciding that he was an all-powerful monarch whom no one could withstand. Like the unlucky Stuarts he subscribed wholeheartedly to the doctrine of the divine right of kings; and, like the Stuarts, he was to find that the people of England did not agree with him.

Blindly unaware of the temper of the nation, Richard raced down the short road to ruin. He had never practiced self-discipline in his life, and now there was no one to oppose him. Rid of Gloucester and with two thousand archers in his personal pay, he was free to do what he liked. He was free to create five dukes in

317

one day, to condemn John of Gaunt's son to banishment, to spend thirty thousand marks on the jewels for a single coat. If he lacked money to pay for the coat he was free to raise more, since an intimidated Parliament had handed over to him its hard-won control of taxation. Richard had other methods of raising money, such as compelling individuals and corporations to make out blank checks that were filled in by the Crown; and it was in a large measure this financial irresponsibility that brought about his downfall. The purse of the average Englishman is a very susceptible part of his nature.

Richard's crowning act of imbecility occurred in March of 1399. John of Gaunt had just died in the Bishop's palace at Holborn, leaving to his nephew the King "the cup of gold which my dear wife Katherine gave me on New Year's Day" and leaving to his son, the exiled Henry of Derby, the title to the vast Lancastrian estates. With the insanity of a man almost literally drunk with power, Richard confiscated the whole of Henry's property.

Richard ought to have remembered, as Froissart remarks, that Henry of Lancaster was the most popular man in England; he became at once not only a martyr but a rallying point for the gathering anger of the whole realm, and there was almost no one willing to oppose him when he returned to England to claim his inheritance. Richard made a few futile gestures of defiance and then surrendered himself to his cousin.

The King was dethroned in the dignified and constitutional manner with which Englishmen are able to manage the most unorthodox performances. A committee of learned men were gathered together to discuss Henry's claims to the throne, and to no one's surprise Henry's claims were found to be legitimate. He came to the throne as a constitutional monarch—by "free election," as Chaucer puts it—and he proved to be a workmanlike, practical, sensible sort of king who had no illusions about the temper of his people.[4]

Richard, who invariably behaved unexpectedly, accepted his de-

[4] Even the author of *Piers Plowman*, who was an old-fashioned conservative in many things, said of the king that it was the "myght of the communes made hym to regne."

thronement with noble calm. Although he indulged in some private dramatics in the Tower he handed over his crown with placid dignity, and his almost feminine pallor and grace must have made a striking contrast to his thickset cousin of Lancaster.

Richard was deposed in the Great Hall at Westminster, which he had begun rebuilding with an artist's fervor two years earlier. It was his last sight of it. He died in prison and was temporarily buried at Langley among the Dominican friars. It is to be regretted he could not have been placed in the Abbey of Westminster, with Anne at his side, in the marble tomb that Henry Yevele had designed for him; but there is little in Richard's life that is not to be regretted, with so much promising material gone tragically to waste. At any rate, he lies in the Abbey now, his effigy clasping hands with Anne's and the Duke of Gloucester beside them.

Richard's little French queen was sent back to her father with her dowry intact, and among the Englishmen who escorted her to Calais were Sir Philip de la Vache and Sir Thomas Clanvowe.[5] Before her departure Isabella was in custody at Wallingford, where Thomas Chaucer had been newly created Constable of the Castle. Thomas Chaucer had been intimately associated with the house of Lancaster ever since he had entered Gaunt's service as a young man in 1389, and when Gaunt's son became king Thomas Chaucer entered upon a long and prosperous career as a public official.

Geoffrey Chaucer's relations with the house of Lancaster were naturally not as close as those of his son, but Chaucer had always been on excellent terms with Henry of Derby. One of his gifts from him had been a scarlet robe, trimmed with fur, valued at about six hundred dollars in modern money; and he had evidently done him various small services throughout the decade.[6] Less than three weeks after Henry IV was crowned he confirmed the annuity that Chaucer had been receiving from Richard, "of our especial

[5] Sir Thomas was the son of Chaucer's friend, Sir John Clanvowe, and it is just possible that it was the son rather than the father who wrote *The Cuckoo and the Nightingale*.

[6] For instance, Chaucer collected ten pounds for Henry in the middle of the decade, receiving it from the clerk of Henry's wardrobe to deliver it into Henry's hands.

favor and in return for the service which our beloved esquire, Geoffrey Chaucer, hath bestowed and will bestow on us in time to come." He gave his beloved esquire also an extra annuity of forty marks.

It was to Henry IV that Chaucer addressed his delightful ballade, the *Complaint to his Purse*. It is not likely that Chaucer was begging the King for money, any more than in his ballade to Bukton he was seriously requesting his friend to stay a bachelor. But the poem does show that Chaucer was on sufficiently intimate terms with the new king to expect him to share a joke.

Like the ballade to Scogan, the *Complaint to his Purse* is a parody on courtly love. It is an authentic love complaint, of the kind that Chaucer was taking seriously when he wrote *The Complaint of Venus, The Complaint of Mars,* the complaint of Anelida and so forth. But here he parodies the whole race of complaints by taking his purse for his "lady deere" and pouring out to it protestations of undying passion. Chaucer's purse is the light of his life, his treasure, and his heart's star. Its color is as bright as the sun (a stock comparison for the gold of a woman's hair) and Chaucer will go down to his grave a tragic victim of unrequited love unless his dear one has pity on him.

No poet had ever treated the sacred subject of finances like this before. The usual attitude was the one exemplified by Deschamps, who wrote one ballade to point out that his payment of five sous a day was not enough, another to indicate that he needed some winter wood, and another to remind a prince that a new horse which had been promised was not forthcoming. This habit of proffering rhymed bills and expense accounts in sober earnest was shared by Lydgate and Hoccleve, and it was apparently only Chaucer who saw something mildly funny in the practice.

Henry IV was crowned in September of 1399, and three months later Chaucer settled down permanently at Westminster. He rented a little house in the garden of St. Mary's chapel, on the Abbey side of the wall but not far from the palace gate. The rent was fifty-three shillings and fourpence a year, and with the same optimism that made him plan a hundred and twenty stories for

The Canterbury Tales he took the little house on a fifty-three year lease.

The optimism was ill-founded. Chaucer collected his last pension from the Exchequer on the fifth of June, 1400, and according to the inscription on his tomb he died on the twenty-fifth of October.

Perhaps Chaucer died of the plague, for 1400 was a plague year. It is to be hoped that he died quickly for he did not die in peace. Deschamps once spoke of the way the unending ringing of bells can trouble a sick man, but it was more than the heavy bells of Westminster Abbey that Chaucer heard ringing in his ears.

Chaucer was still trying to make his peace with heaven, and as the hour of the final rites approached he was overwhelmed by his sense of sin. According to the testimony of Gascoigne, he was no longer content with having retracted all his poetry. He wanted to call it back and destroy it, because most of it was based upon the evil subject of the love of men and women. And of this, Gascoigne, a distinguished Oxford churchman of the period, grimly approved, for he compares Chaucer's deathbed repentance with the final hours of still another traitor to Christianity—Judas Iscariot.

Chaucer was buried in the cloister of Westminster Abbey in the place now called the Poets' Corner, not because he was one of the greatest poets England would ever know but because he had been a tenant of the Abbey grounds. His friends sent up a heartfelt prayer for the safety of his soul, and Hoccleve even pointed out to the Virgin that Chaucer had frequently written lines in her praise and therefore she ought to intercede for him.

So died Geoffrey Chaucer, trying to the last to make his peace with his century and the God of his century. He left behind him the men and women he had created and they went on without him, subject neither to medieval laws nor to medieval penalties. The condemnation is forgotten, but Criseyde and the Wife of Bath are not. They are more real now than any of Chaucer's contemporaries, and they will continue to be real five hundred years hence.

An admirer of Chaucer's poetry put up a small memorial to him in stone. It has since been lost. Stone is not a very permanent substance, as any Clerk of the Works knows. Chaucer built his own best memorial, for he was a careful workman building in a stronger medium than stone; and although the three kings whom he served lie under tombs of marble and alabaster Chaucer has a better monument than theirs.

This would have surprised Chaucer. He had no reason to expect immortality for his poetry, for according to the standards of his century he had chosen both the wrong subject and the wrong medium. The subject was a sinful one, and the medium despised and unstable.

Setting himself against the weight of medieval authority, Chaucer wrote of English men and women and wrote in the English tongue. He did not do it for approval or for money or for fame. He did it for love, and there is the evidence of six centuries to show that a love like that is not betrayed.

SELECTED BIBLIOGRAPHY

GENERAL BACKGROUND

SYDNEY ARMITAGE-SMITH, *John Of Gaunt*, London: Constable and Company, 1904.

SYDNEY ARMITAGE-SMITH, *John Of Gaunt's Register*, 2 volumes, London: Royal Historical Society, 1911.

ELIAS ASHMOLE, *The History Of The Most Noble Order Of The Garter*, London: A. Bell, 1715.

MARY BATESON, *Medieval England*, New York: G. P. Putnam's Sons, 1904.

WALTER GEORGE BELL, *Fleet Street In Seven Centuries*, London: Pitman and Sons, 1912.

GEORGE FREDERICK BELTZ, *Memorials Of The Order Of The Garter*, London, 1841.

WALTER BESANT, *Medieval London*, 2 volumes, London: A. C. Black, 1906.

WALTER BESANT, *Westminster*, New York: Frederick A. Stokes and Company, 1895.

P. M. BOISSONNADE, *Life And Work In Medieval Europe*, translated by Eileen Power, London: K. Paul, Trench, Trübner and Company, 1927.

THOMAS BRYDSON, *A Summary View Of Heraldry In Reference To The Usages Of Chivalry*, Edinburgh: Mundell and Son, 1795.

Cambridge Medieval History, Volume VII, Cambridge: Cambridge University Press, 1932.

WILLIAM WOLFE CAPES, *The English Church In The Fourteenth and Fifteenth Centuries*, London: Macmillan and Company, 1909.

CHRONICLES: Adam of Usk, *Chronicon*, edited by Edward Maunde Thompson, London: Henry Frowde, 1904.

    The Anonimalle Chronicle, edited by V. H. Galbraith, Manchester: Manchester University Press, 1927.

    The Brut, Or The Chronicles Of England, edited by F. W. D. Brie, 2 volumes, London: K. Paul, Trench, Trübner and Company, 1908.

    John Capgrave, *The Chronicle Of England*, edited by F. C. Hengeston, London, 1858 (*Great Britain Public Record Office, Chronicles and Memorials, No. 1*).

    Chronique De La Traison Et Mort De Richard Deux, edited by Benjamin Williams, London, 1846.

    Robert Fabyan, *The New Chronicle Of England And France*, edited by Henry Ellis, London, 1811.

    John Froissart, *Chronicles*, translated by Thomas Johnes, 12 volumes, London, 1805–06.

Ralph Higden, *Polychronicon, Together With The English Translation Of John Trevisa*, edited by Churchill Babington, London, 1865–86 (*Great Britain Public Record Office, Chronicles and Memorials, No. 41.*)

"An Historicall Relation Of Certain Passages About The End Of King Edward The Third And Of His Death" presented by Thomas Amyot, *Archaeologia*, 1829.

John of Reading, *Chronica*, edited by James Tait, Manchester: Manchester University Press, 1914.

John Stow, *Annales Or A Generall Chronicle Of England*, London: R. Meighen, 1631.

Thomas Walsingham, *Chronica Monasterii S. Albani*, edited by Henry Thomas Riley, Volumes I and II, London: Longmans, Green and Company, 1863–64 (*Great Britain Public Record Office, Chronicles and Memorials, No. 28*).

M. V. CLARKE, *Fourteenth Century Studies*, Oxford: Clarendon Press, 1937.

M. V. CLARKE, *Medieval Representation And Consent*, London: Longmans, Green and Company, 1936.

W. COBBETT, *Parliamentary History Of England*, Volume I, London: R. Bagshaw, 1806.

JOHN COLLINSON, *The History And Antiquities Of The County Of Somerset*, Volume II, Bath: R. Cruttwell, 1791.

IVY M. COOPER, "The Meeting-Places Of Parliament In The Ancient Palace Of Westminster," *British Archaeological Association Journal*, 1938.

G. G. COULTON, *Chaucer And His England*, London: Methuen and Company, 1937.

CHARLES CREIGHTON, *A History Of Epidemics In Britain*, Volume I, Cambridge: Cambridge University Press, 1891.

EDMUND CURTIS, "The Viceroyalty Of Lionel, Duke Of Clarence, In Ireland," *Journal of the Royal Society of Antiquarians of Ireland*, 1918.

EDWARD L. CUTTS, *Parish Priests And Their People In The Middle Ages In England*, London: Society For Promoting Christian Knowledge, 1898.

H. C. DARBY, *An Historical Geography Of England Before 1800*, Cambridge: Cambridge University Press, 1936.

Dictionary Of National Biography, London: Oxford University Press, 1921–22.

WILLIAM DUGDALE, *The History Of St. Paul's Cathedral*, London: Edward Maynard, 1716.

FRANCIS A. GASQUET, *The Black Death Of 1348 And 1349*, London: George Bell and Sons, 1908.

RICHARD GOUGH, *British Topography*, Volume I, London: T. Payne and Son, 1780.

324

N. S. B. GRAS, *The Early English Customs System*, Cambridge: Harvard University Press, 1918.

N. S. B. GRAS, "Economic Rationalism In The Late Middle Ages," *Speculum*, 1933.

HUBERT HALL, *A History Of The Custom-Revenue In England*, Volume I, London: Elliot Stock, 1885.

HENRY HALLAM, *View Of The State Of Europe During The Middle Ages*, 3 volumes, London: John Murray, 1860.

THOMAS DUFFUS HARDY, editor, *Modus Tenendi Parliamentum*, London: G. E. Eyre and W. Spottiswoode, 1846.

THOMAS DUFFUS HARDY, *Syllabus Of Rymer's Foedera*, Volumes I and II, London: Longmans, Green and Company, 1869 and 1873.

JOHN H. HARVEY, "The Medieval Office Of Works," *Journal of the British Archaeological Association*, 1941.

EDWARD HASTED, *History Of Kent*, edited by Henry Drake, London: Mitchell and Hughes, 1886.

GORDON HOME, *Old London Bridge*, London: John Lane, 1931.

JOHAN HUIZINGA, *The Waning Of The Middle Ages*, London: Edward Arnold and Company, 1937.

J. E. A. JOLLIFFE, *Constitutional History Of Medieval England*, London: A. and C. Black, 1937.

FRANCIS M. KELLY AND RANDOLPH SCHWABE, *A Short History Of Costume And Armour, Chiefly In England, 1066–1800*, London: B. T. Batsford, 1931.

RAYMOND LINCOLN KILGOUR, *The Decline Of Chivalry As Shown In The French Literature Of The Late Middle Ages*, Cambridge: Harvard University Press, 1937.

DOUGLAS KNOOP AND G. P. JONES, *The Medieval Mason*, Manchester: Manchester University Press, 1933.

HENRY CHARLES LEA, *A History Of The Inquisition Of The Middle Ages*, 3 volumes, New York: The Macmillan Company, 1922.

G. LECHLER, *John Wycliffe And His English Precursors*, translated by P. Lorimer, London, 1884.

LEOPOLD WICKHAM LEGG, *English Coronation Records*, London: Archibald Constable and Company, 1901.

WILLIAM JOHN LOFTIE, *Memorials Of The Savoy*, London: Macmillan and Company, 1878.

JEAN LULVES, *Calais Sous La Domination Anglaise, 1347–1558*, Berne: F. Wyss, 1917.

DOROTHY MUIR, *A History Of Milan Under The Visconti*, London: Methuen and Company, 1924.

NICHOLAS HARRIS NICOLAS, editor, *De Controversia In Curia Militari Inter Ricardum Le Scrope Et Robertum Grosvenor, Milites,* 2 volumes, London, 1832.

NICHOLAS HARRIS NICOLAS, *A History Of The Royal Navy,* London, 1847.

CHARLES OMAN, *A History Of The Art Of War In The Middle Ages,* Volume II, New York: E. P. Dutton and Company, 1937.

CHARLES OMAN, *The History Of England, 1377–1485,* London: Longmans, Green and Company, 1910 (*The Political History Of England,* Volume IV).

G. R. OWST, *Literature And Pulpit In Medieval England,* Cambridge: Cambridge University Press, 1933.

SIDNEY PAINTER, *French Chivalry,* Baltimore: Johns Hopkins Press, 1940.

CHARLES PENDRILL, *London Life In The Fourteenth Century,* London: G. Allen and Unwin, 1925.

HENRI PIRENNE, *Economic And Social History Of Medieval Europe,* New York: Harcourt, Brace and Company, 1937.

EILEEN POWER, *The Wool Trade In English Medieval History,* London: Oxford University Press, 1941.

BERTHA HAVEN PUTNAM, *Proceedings Before The Justices Of The Peace In The Fourteenth And Fifteenth Centuries,* London: Spottiswoode, Ballantyne and Company, 1938.

JAMES H. RAMSAY, *Genesis Of Lancaster,* 2 volumes, Oxford: Clarendon Press, 1913.

EDITH RICKERT, "Extracts From A 14th Century Account Book," *Modern Philology,* 1926.

H. T. RILEY, editor, *Memorials Of London And London Life,* London: Longmans, Green and Company, 1868.

JAMES E. THOROLD ROGERS, *Six Centuries Of Work and Wages,* Volume I, London: 1884.

ERNEST L. SABINE, "City Cleaning In Medieval London," *Speculum,* 1937.

GAETANO SALVEMINI, "Florence In The Time Of Dante," *Speculum,* 1936.

LOUIS F. SALZMAN, *English Life In The Middle Ages,* London: H. Milford, 1926.

LOUIS F. SALZMAN, *English Trade In The Middle Ages,* Oxford: Clarendon Press, 1931.

GEORGE SARTON, *Introduction To The History Of Science,* Volume II, Baltimore: Williams and Wilkins Company, for the Carnegie Institution of Washington.

REGINALD R. SHARPE, *Calendar Of Coroners' Rolls Of The City Of London, 1300–1378,* London: R. Clay and Sons, 1913.

REGINALD R. SHARPE, *Calender Of Letter-Books Of The City of London, Letter Book F, Letter Book H,* London, 1904 and 1907.

326

REGINALD R. SHARPE, *London And The Kingdom*, London: Longmans, Green and Company, 1894.

ANDRÉ SIMON, *History Of The Wine Trade In England*, Volume I, London: Wyman and Sons, 1906.

W. SPARROW SIMPSON, "Some Early Drawings Of Old St. Paul's," *Journal of the British Archaeological Association*, 1881.

F. M. STENTON, "The Road System Of Medieval England," *Economic History Review*, 1936.

JOHN STOW, *Survey Of London*, edited by William J. Thoms, London: Whittaker and Company, 1842.

GRACE STRETTON, "Some Aspects Of Medieval Travel," *Transactions of the Royal Historical Society*, 1924.

A. H. THOMAS, "Illustrations Of The Medieval Municipal History Of London From The Guildhall Records," *Transactions of the Royal Historical Society*, 1921.

A. H. THOMAS, "Life In Medieval London," *Journal of the British Archaeological Association*, 1929.

ROBERT RICHARD TIGHE AND JAMES EDWARD DAVIS, *Annals Of Windsor*, Volume I, London, 1858.

T. F. TOUT, *Chapters In The Administrative History Of Medieval England*, 6 volumes, Manchester: Manchester University Press, 1920.

T. F. TOUT, *The Collected Papers Of Thomas Frederick Tout*, 3 volumes, Manchester: Manchester University Press, 1934.

T. F. TOUT, "Literature And Learning In The English Civil Service In The Fourteenth Century," *Speculum*, 1929.

T. F. TOUT, *The History Of England, 1216–1377*, London: Longmans, Green and Company, 1905 (*The Political History Of England*, Volume III).

G. M. TREVELYAN, *England In The Age Of Wyclif*, London: Longmans, Green and Company, 1899.

G. J. TURNER, editor, *Select Pleas Of The Forest*, London: Selden Society, 1901.

GEORGE UNWIN, *Finance And Trade Under Edward III*, Manchester: Manchester University Press, 1918.

GEORGE UNWIN, *The Gilds And Companies Of London*, London: Methuen and Company, 1909.

KENNETH H. VICKERS, *England In The Later Middle Ages*, London: Methuen and Company, 1937.

H. WALLON, *Richard II*, 2 volumes, Paris: L. Hachette et Cie., 1864.

FRANCIS WATT, *Canterbury Pilgrims And Their Ways*, London: Methuen and Company, 1917.

W. T. WAUGH, "The Lollard Knights," *Scottish Historical Review*, 1914.

327

THEODORE OTTO WEDEL, *The Medieval Attitude Towards Astrology*, New Haven: Yale University Press, 1920.

JAMES FIELD WILLARD, "Inland Transportation In England During The Fourteenth Century," *Speculum*, 1926.

E. WILLIAMS, *Early Holborn And The Legal Quarter Of London*, 2 volumes, London: Sweet and Maxwell, 1927.

HERBERT B. WORKMAN, *John Wyclif*, 2 volumes, Oxford: Clarendon Press, 1926.

LITERARY BACKGROUND

CHARLES SEARS BALDWIN, *Medieval Rhetoric And Poetic*, New York: The Macmillan Company, 1928.

CHARLES SEARS BALDWIN, *Three Medieval Centuries Of Literature In England*, Boston: Little, Brown and Company, 1932.

SARAH F. BARROW, *The Medieval Society Romances*, New York: Columbia University Press, 1924.

ALBERT CROLL BAUGH, *A History Of The English Language*, New York: D. Appleton-Century Company, 1935.

H. S. BENNETT, "The Author And His Public In The Fourteenth And Fifteenth Centuries," *Essays and Studies by Members of the English Association*, Oxford: Clarendon Press, 1938.

HALDEEN BRADDY, "Sir Oton De Graunson, 'Flour Of Hem That Make In Fraunce,' " *Studies in Philology*, 1938.

HALDEEN BRADDY, *Three Chaucer Studies*, London: Oxford University Press, 1932.

BERTRAND H. BRONSON, "Chaucer's Art In Relation To His Audience," *Five Studies in Literature*, Berkeley: University of California Press, 1940.

W. F. BRYAN AND GERMAINE DEMPSTER, *Sources And Analogues Of Chaucer's Canterbury Tales*, Chicago: University of Chicago Press, 1941.

THOMAS CAMPBELL, *Life Of Petrarch*, 2 volumes, London: H. Colburn, 1841.

GEOFFREY CHAUCER, *Complete Works*, edited by F. N. Robinson, Boston: Houghton Mifflin Company, 1933.

CHRÉTIEN DE TROYES, *Cligés*, translated by L. A. Gardiner, London: Chatto and Windus, 1912.

WALTER CLYDE CURRY, *Chaucer And The Medieval Sciences*, New York: Oxford University Press, 1926.

EUSTACHE DESCHAMPS, *Oeuvres Completes*, ed. par Saint-Hilaire, 11 volumes, Paris: Firmin Didot et Cie., 1878–1903.

OLIVER FARRAR EMERSON, *Chaucer Essays And Studies*, Cleveland: Western Reserve University Press, 1929.

OLIVER FARRAR EMERSON, "Chaucer's First Military Service," *Romanic Review*, 1912.

328

DEAN SPRUILL FANSLER, *Chaucer And The Roman De La Rose*, New York: Columbia University Press, 1914.

EDMOND FARAL, *Les Arts Poétiques Du XIIe Et Du XIIIe Siècle*, Paris: E. Champion, 1924.

WILLARD FARNHAM, "England's Discovery Of The Decameron," *Publications of the Modern Language Association*, 1924.

ROBERT DUDLEY FRENCH, *A Chaucer Handbook*, New York: F. S. Crofts and Company, 1927.

JEAN FROISSART, *Oeuvres: Poésies*, 3 volumes; Bruxelles: V. Devaux et Cie., 1870–72.

MARGARET GALWAY, "Geoffrey Chaucer, J. P. and M. P.," *Modern Language Review*, 1941.

R. C. GOFFIN, "Chaucer And Elocution," *Medium Aevum*, 1935.

R. K. GORDON, editor, *The Story Of Troilus As Told By Benoit De Sainte-Maure, Giovanni Boccaccio, Geoffrey Chaucer And Robert Henryson*, London: J. M. Dent and Sons, 1934.

JOHN GOWER, *Complete Works*, edited by G. C. Macaulay, 4 volumes, Oxford: Clarendon Press, 1899.

CHARLES HALL GRANDGENT, *Dante*, New York: Duffield and Company, 1916.

ELEANOR PRESCOTT HAMMOND, *Chaucer; A Bibliographical Manual*, New York: The Macmillan Company, 1908.

CHARLES HOMER HASKINS, *The Renaissance Of The Twelfth Century*, Cambridge: Harvard University Press, 1927.

R. B. HEPPLE, *Medieval Education In England*, London: G. Bell and Sons, 1932.

THOMAS HOCCLEVE, *Works*, edited by F. J. Furnivall, 3 volumes, London: K. Paul, Trench, Trübner and Company, 1892–1925.

H. C. HOLLWAY-CALTHORP, *Petrarch, His Life And Times*, London: Methuen and Company, 1907.

KARL JULIUS HOLZKNECHT, *Literary Patronage In The Middle Ages*, University of Pennsylvania thesis, Philadelphia, 1923.

JAMES ROOT HULBERT, *Chaucer's Official Life*, University of Chicago thesis, Menasha, Wisconsin: The Collegiate Press, 1912.

EDWARD HUTTON, *Giovanni Boccaccio*, London: John Lane, 1910.

BERNARD L. JEFFERSON, *Chaucer And The Consolation Of Philosophy Of Boethius*, Princeton: Princeton University Press, 1917.

J. J. JUSSERAND, *A Literary History Of The English People*, New York: G. P. Putnam's Sons, 1906.

W. P. KER, *Epic And Romance*, London: Macmillan and Company, 1931.

W. P. KER, *Essays On Medieval Literature*, London: Macmillan and Company, 1905.

W. P. KER, *Form And Style In Poetry*, London: Macmillan and Company, 1928.

ALFRED ALLAN KERN, *The Ancestry Of Chaucer*, Baltimore: Lord Baltimore Press, 1906.

GEORGE LYMAN KITTREDGE, "Chaucer And Some Of His Friends," *Modern Philology*, 1903.

GEORGE LYMAN KITTREDGE, "Chaucer's Lollius," *Harvard Studies In Classical Philology*, Cambridge: Harvard University Press, 1917.

RUSSELL KRAUSS, *Chaucerian Problems*, Lancaster: The Lancaster Press, 1932.

ERNEST P. KUHL, "Chaucer And Aldgate," *Publications of the Modern Language Association*, 1924.

A. F. LEACH, *The Schools Of Medieval England*, New York: The Macmillan Company, 1915.

C. S. LEWIS, *The Allegory Of Love; A Study In Medieval Tradition*, Oxford: Clarendon Press, 1936.

Life Records Of Chaucer, second series: 12, 14, 21, 32. Chaucer Society Publications.

CAMILLE LOOTEN, *Chaucer, Ses Modèles, Ses Sources, Sa Religion*, Lille: Facultés Catholiques, 1931.

THOMAS R. LOUNSBURY, *Studies In Chaucer*, 3 volumes, New York: Harper and Brothers, 1892.

JOHN LIVINGSTON LOWES, *Convention And Revolt In Poetry*, London: Constable and Company, 1930.

JOHN LIVINGSTON LOWES, *Geoffrey Chaucer And The Development Of His Genius*, Boston: Houghton Mifflin Company, 1934.

GUILLAUME DE MACHAULT, *Oeuvres*, Reims: P. Regnier, 1849.

JOHN MATTHEWS MANLY, "Chaucer And The Rhetoricians," *Proceedings of the British Academy*, London: Oxford University Press, 1926.

JOHN MATTHEWS MANLY, *Some New Light On Chaucer*, New York: Henry Holt and Company, 1926.

FRANK JEWETT MATHER, "On The Asserted Meeting Of Chaucer And Petrarch," *Modern Language Notes*, 1897.

THEODORE MAYNARD, *The Connection Between The Ballade, Chaucer's Modification Of It, Rime Royal And The Spenserian Stanza*, Washington, D. C.: Catholic University of America, 1934.

WILLIAM A. NITZE AND E. PRESTON DARGAN, *A History Of French Literature*, New York: Henry Holt and Company, 1927.

HOWARD ROLLIN PATCH, *The Tradition Of Boethius*, New York: Oxford University Press, 1935.

L. PETIT DE JULLEVILLE, *Histoire De La Langue Et De La Littérature Française*, Volume II, Paris: A. Colin et Cie., 1896.

GEORGE A. PLIMPTON, *The Education Of Chaucer*, London: Oxford University Press, 1935.

ROBERT A. PRATT, "Chaucer And The Visconti Libraries," *ELH, Journal of English Literary History*, 1939.

330

GEORGE HAVEN PUTNAM, *Books And Their Makers During The Middle Ages*, Volume I, New York: G. P. Putnam's Sons, 1896.

EDWARD KENNARD RAND, *Ovid And His Influence*, Boston: Marshall Jones Company, 1925.

VINCENT B. AND LILLIAN J. REDSTONE, "The Heyrons Of London," *Speculum*, 1937.

EDITH RICKERT, "Was Chaucer A Student At The Inner Temple?" *Manly Anniversary Studies In Language And Literature*, Chicago: University of Chicago Press, 1923.

JAMES HARVEY ROBINSON, *Petrarch, A Selection From His Correspondence With Boccaccio And Other Friends*, New York: G. P. Putnam's Sons, 1898.

The Romance Of The Rose by W. Lorris and J. Clopinel, Englished by F. S. Ellis, 3 volumes, London: J. M. Dent and Sons, 1900.

R. K. ROOT, *The Book Of Troilus And Criseyde*, Princeton: Princeton University Press, 1926.

R. K. ROOT, "Publication Before Printing," *Publications of the Modern Language Association*, 1913.

MARTIN B. RUUD, *Thomas Chaucer*, Minneapolis: University of Minnesota Press, 1926.

W. H. SCHOFIELD, *English Literature From The Norman Conquest To Chaucer*, New York: The Macmillan Company, 1906.

WILBUR LANG SCHRAMM, "The Cost Of Books In Chaucer's Time," *Modern Language Notes*, 1933.

J. BURKE SEVERS, *The Literary Relationships Of Chaucer's Clerk's Tale*, New Haven: Yale University Press, 1942.

EDGAR FINLEY SHANNON, *Chaucer And The Roman Poets*, Cambridge: Harvard University Press, 1929.

KENNETH SISAM, *Fourteenth Century Verse And Prose*, Oxford: Clarendon Press, 1921.

WALTER W. SKEAT, *Chaucerian And Other Pieces, Being A Supplement To "The Complete Works Of Geoffrey Chaucer,"* Oxford: Clarendon Press, 1897.

ROBINSON SMITH, *Earliest Lives Of Dante, Translated From The Italian Of Giovanni Boccaccio And Leonardo Bruni Aretino*, New York: Henry Holt and Company, 1901.

CAROLINE SPURGEON, *Five Hundred Years Of Chaucer Criticism And Allusion*, 7 volumes, London: Oxford University Press, 1914–25.

J. S. P. TATLOCK, "Chaucer's Merchant's Tale," *Modern Philology*, 1936.

J. S. P. TATLOCK, "The Epilog Of Chaucer's Troilus," *Modern Philology*, 1921.

J. S. P. TATLOCK, "The Middle Ages—Romantic Or Rationalistic?" *Speculum*, 1933.

J. S. P. TATLOCK, *The Scene Of The Franklin's Tale Visited*, London: Oxford University Press, 1914.

JAMES WESTFALL THOMPSON, *The Medieval Library*, Chicago: University of Chicago Press, 1939.

LYNN THORNDIKE, "Elementary And Secondary Education In The Middle Ages," *Speculum*, 1940.

J. R. R. TOLKIEN, "Chaucer As A Philologist: The Reeve's Tale," *Transactions of the Philological Society*, 1934.

PAGET TOYNBEE, *Dante Studies*, Oxford: Clarendon Press, 1921.

INDEX

INDEX

338

Holborn, 57-58, 118n., 255, 318
Holderness, 241
Homer, 114, 166n.
Horace, 166n.
Host, the (Harry Bailly), 203n., 243n., 248, 259, 262, 264, 267, 279, 280, 282, 291, 294, 295, 297, 298, 299, 300, 305, 307, 308
House of Fame, The, see Chaucer, works of
Hundred Years War, 21, 44-49, 95-97, 124, 143, 196, 212-213
Huntingfeld, William, 228, 229
Huss, John, 202
Hustings, Court of, 16

Il Filostrato, see Boccaccio, Giovanni
Inner Temple, 58
Inns of Chancery, 57, 58
Inns of Court, 57, 58, 255
Inquisition, the, 205, 205n.
Insulus, Alanus de, 132, 132n.
invasion scare, 143, 212-213
Ipswich, 11, 12, 16
Ireland, 40, 43, 54, 95, 314
Isabella of Castile, Duchess of York, 97, 203
Isabella of France, 315, 316, 319
Isabella, Queen Mother, 15, 16
Isabelle, Princess of England, 23, 40
Iscariot, Judas, 302, 304, 321
Isle of Wight, 143
Italian influence on Chaucer, see Chaucer, as a writer
Italian vernacular, 83-84, 103, 103n., 104, 126-127

Jacquerie, the, 205
Jane Eyre, 244n.
Jankin, 274-275
January, 283-284
Jean de Meun, see Meun, Jean de
Jerusalem, 254
Jews, 114, 214, 296, 296n.
Joan of Kent, Princess of Wales, 53-54, 95, 118, 122, 190, 198, 202, 211n.
John, King of France, 26, 44, 48, 51, 150
John of Blois, 135
John of Gatesden, 253

John of Gaunt:
    life, 22, 42-43, 53, 96-99, 119, 196, 197, 219n., 228, 231n., 233, 315, 318; political activities, 49, 119n., 123, 143, 200, 202n., 210, 211, 213, 221; relation to Katherine Swynford, 59-60, 98-99, 146, 219, 315; relation to Chaucer's family, 60, 99, 146, 147n., 148, 319; relation to Chaucer, see Chaucer, personal life of
John of Northampton, 142, 220
John of Salisbury, 166n.
Josephus, 114
justices of the peace, 206-210, 221, 252; see also Chaucer, public life of

Katherine of Lancaster, 221, 231n.
Keats, John, 246
Kent, county of, 197, 199, 212, 216, 219; Chaucer's connection with, 26, 148, 206-210, 211, 213, 217n., 218, 221, 228, 230, 252, 254
Kent, John, 140, 148, 150
Kilkenny, Statute of, 54
King's Butler, 23-24, 147, 230
King's Esquire, see Chaucer, public life of
King's Wardrobe, 22, 47, 56, 105n.
Knight, the, 246, *249,* 259, 294, 299, 300, 309

labor unrest, 102, 205; see also Peasants' Revolt
Lack of Steadfastness, see Chaucer, works of
l'Allemand, Evrard, 67
Lambeth Council, 202
Lancaster, House of, 16, 98, 211, 319
Lancaster, Blanche of, see Blanche of Lancaster
Lancaster, Constance of, see Constance of Castile
Lancaster, first Duke of, see Henry, Duke of Lancaster
Lancaster, second Duke of, see John of Gaunt
Lancaster, Earl of, see Henry, Earl of Lancaster
Lancaster, Elizabeth, see Elizabeth of Lancaster

341

Mile End, 197
Milleford, 231
Miller, the (Robin), 200, 239, 243, 244,
    249, *255*, 258, 264, 268, 275, 283,
    284, 299
Milton, John, 80, 89, 240
miracle plays, 191, 262
Miroir de l'Omme, see Gower, John
Miroir de Mariage, 277n.
Mohun, Lady Joan, 231n.
money, buying power of, 7-8, 14n.; account-
    ing, 37, 140-141, 225
Monk, the, 239, 243, *251*, 256, 263, 299,
    300
Monmouth, Geoffrey of, *see* Geoffrey of
    Monmouth
Montreuil, 120-121
Moorfields, 31
Mortimer, 15-16, 40
music, 37, 45, 69n.

Najara, Battle of, 97
Nevill family, 147
Neville, Sir William, 202-203, 216, 217
New Forest, 223
New Poetry, 67
New Troy, 220
Newgate, 221
Newgate prison, 198
Norfolk, 256
North Petherton, 229-231
Northampton, John of, *see* John of
    Northampton
Northwell, Agnes de, *see* Chaucer, Agnes
Norwich, Bishop of, 201
Novelle, 242, 242n.
Nun's Priest, the, 269, 300-303

Orleans, Duke of, 202, 232n.
Orleans, university of, *see* universities
Ovid, influence on Chaucer, 36, 62, 114,
    128, 192, 262n., 278; *Art of Love,* 72-
    73, 75, 79, 151; *Metamorphoses,* 36,
    90, 192
Oxford, 241, 268
Oxford, Countess of, 210n.
Oxford, Earl of, *see* Vere, Robert de
Oxford, university of, *see* universities

Oxfordshire, 146

Paddington, 20
Padua, 280
Palamon, 259-263
Pamela, 271n.
Pandarus, *see Troilus and Criseyde*
Paradise Lost, 240
Pardoner, the, 200, 245, *256-257*, 258, 291-
    293, 294, 305
Paris, 47, 126, 149
Paris, university of, *see* universities
Parliament, 24, 31, 95, 98, 118, 119, 141,
    143n., 196, 202n., 318; House of
    Commons, 97, 142, 147-148, 207, 210,
    318n.; Parliament of *1386,* 211-216,
    217; Merciless Parliament, 219-220,
    222, 223, 224n., 317; in Chaucer's
    poetry, 133, 182, 252
Parliament of Birds, The, see Chaucer, works
    of
Parma, 55
Parson, the, 66, 203n., *254-255*, 272, 308-
    309
Paternoster Row, 149
patronage, 60n., 63-64
Paul's Head Tavern, 237
Pavia, 124, 125
Pearl, The, 66
Peasants' Revolt, 196-200, 205, 213, 282,
    304
Pedro, King of Castile, 97
Pembroke Castle, 203n.
Pembroke, Earl of, 227
Pennell, Lady Isabel, 191n.
Perkin Reveller, 269
Perrers, Alice, 95, 98, 118, 119-120, 121,
    121n.
Pertelote, 301-303
Petrarch, Francis, 42, 49, 55, 63, 126, 149,
    150; as a writer, 103n., 151-152, 281;
    as a humanist, 88n., 253n., 261-262;
    relation to Boccaccio, 103, 103n., 127,
    281n.; relation to Chaucer, 126, 128,
    280-282
Philip of Dartmouth, the, 44
Philippa of Hainault, 22, 40, 43, 51, 52,
    54, 59, 63, 95, 96, 97, 185, 227n.

343

347

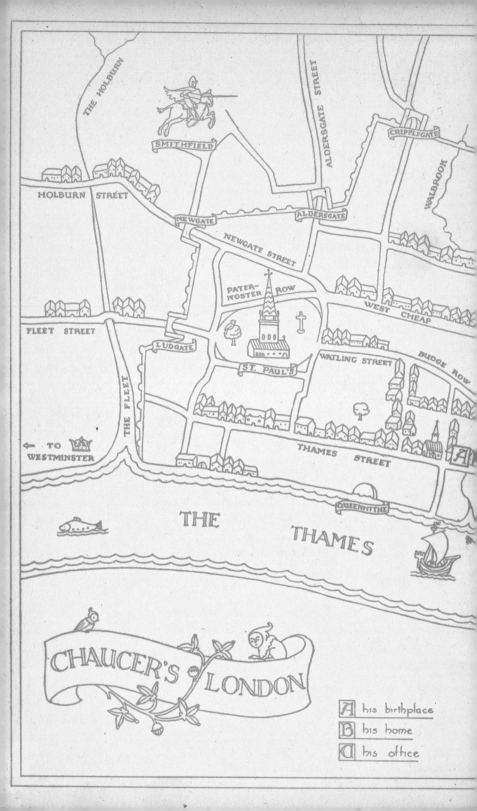

THE HOLBURN

SMITHFIELD

ALDERSGATE STREET

CRIPPLEGATE

WALBROOK

HOLBURN STREET

NEWGATE

ALDERSGATE

NEWGATE STREET

PATER-NOSTER ROW

WEST CHEAP

FLEET STREET

LUDGATE

ST. PAUL'S

WATLING STREET

BUDGE ROW

THE FLEET

←— TO WESTMINSTER

THAMES STREET

A

THE   THAMES

QUEENHITHE

CHAUCER'S LONDON

A his birthplace
B his home
D his office